D1205081

Messages from the Wild

An Almanac of Suburban
Natural and Unnatural
History

Frederick R. Gehlbach

UNIVERSITY OF TEXAS PRESS, AUSTIN

Publication of this book was made possible by the generous support of Emily S. Young

First edition, 2002

Requests for permission to reproduce material from this work should be sent to Permissions, University of Texas Press, Box 7819, Austin, TX 78713-7819.

⊗ The paper used in this book meets the minimum requirements of ANSI/NISO Z39.48-1992 (R1997) (Permanence of Paper).

LIBRARY OF CONGRESS CATALOGING-IN-PUBLICATION DATA

Gehlbach, Frederick R., 1935–
    Messages from the wild : an almanac of suburban natural and unnatural history /
Frederick R. Gehlbach. — 1st ed.
        p.   cm.
    Includes bibliographical references and index (p.   ).
    ISBN 0-292-72837-9 (cloth : alk. paper) — ISBN 0-292-72838-7 (pbk. : alk. paper)
    1. Natural history—Texas—Anecdotes.   2. Gehlbach, Frederick R., 1935–
I. Title.
    QH105.T4 G45 2002
    508.764—dc21   2001027584

For Gretchen and Mark, who understand the spirit of the ravine

CONTENTS

A Wild Place to Live In

I am one who cannot live apart from the wild. Natural values are important to me, particularly the reassuring cycles of wild lives. I am fascinated and instructed by nature's repeated patterns, because they are so ancient and work so well. I want to know how and why, and why humans respond the way they do. Nature's messages in the seasonal events of a forested ravine in suburban central Texas are the themes of this book. Time is the last thirty-five years of the twentieth century, when eighty percent of Texans live in cities that sprawl over 670 acres of countryside every day.

Growing up on the edge of the wild in Ohio, I roamed freely. Then, for a decade, I lived in the southwestern outdoors in summer but studied in tamer northeastern places in winter, dreaming of open-window connections and a walk out the front door into nature. One day, Nancy, my wife, and I found a seminatural landscape to call home at the edge of a forested ravine in suburban central Texas. We built a house and moved in November 1964. Our children, Gretchen and Mark, were born and grew up in that ravine community.

Because of its outburst of mourning cloak butterflies at the time of our discovery, Butterfly Hollow is the name we gave that first home. Soon, however, suburbia began to engulf the naturalness, which shrunk to half its former size in fifteen years. This hastened our decision to build again beside the promise of a wild sanctuary a half-mile away in the same ravine. Eastern screech owls nested next to our new house under construction, so we called the place Owl Hollow and moved in April 1980.

Our wooded property borders a ten-acre nature preserve shared in a homeowners association and adjoins additional private acres, mostly wooded backyards, that comprise the ravine. The land is in various stages of recovery after human impact, so there are overgrown remnants of pasture and cropland, old cattle tanks, a small public park, and some steep rocky slopes immune to commercial land gobblers. For me, this place is a small part of prehistory and a much larger exhibit of how humans change living landscapes.

The ravine is my living classroom, theater, art gallery, and concert hall. As an academic ecologist but a naturalist at heart, I've tried to blend a rational sense of data-keeping and analysis with intuition and emotional appreciation of this heritage. As Thoreau did in Walden, I try to learn *from* while learning about and being delighted by natural history, so I keep notes on almost daily sojourns in the ravine. These notes, both experiences and ruminations, are the basis of this book.

Among the natural and unnatural lives that intersect mine, I'm particularly drawn to the eastern screech owl's. This native resident is a special mentor. Its annual cycle involves many other species and furnishes seasonal anchor points about which I share experiences, including drawings. I'm partial to flying and crawling creatures, but the natural world always provides interesting and important messengers, if the object of one's search doesn't appear. My operating perspective is the whole Earth, in which the ravine is but a microcosm.

The following pages present daily and longer events introduced by monthly prologues. All were sketched as I experienced life's lessons, although I may assemble several years of the same message in recognition of naturally repeated patterns. My color photos are but a small personal selection of that nature. I want to relate what I've been taught about belonging. Like the biblical Job and modern prophets, I've found that humans would do well to listen to their wild elders.

Of course, this almanac recounts lives and events that are unique for one place and time, but the basic patterns—the messages—are universal as revealed by my experiences and those of other naturalists worldwide and throughout human history. The almanac format is important, because messages are repeated daily, seasonally, and in lifetime events. Besides, a wild dooryard is a delight to be cherished every day for its wonderment and refuge from cultural stress.

In the first chapter I briefly describe the ravine's space and time, and in the last chapter I reconnect its messages. Also at the end are selected references with brief identifying comments and a calendar of seasonal events with graphics of exemplary cycles and linear trends. The calendar recounts biotic and physical happenings, both natural and unnatural, that most commonly remind me of how and why I live here.

Species common names are the ones most familiar and descriptive to me, and in some places I give alternatives. Scientific equivalents, the most recent I know of, are in the appendix and index, although in a very few cases my experience with identity differs from others. I do not name human neighbors, who were very kind in talking with me and showing me things but had no idea I was writing about them. I also omit place names or keep them general to protect privacy.

Temperatures are in degrees Fahrenheit. Times are central standard (November–March) or central daylight savings (April–October). Weather is from my home forest which averages four degrees warmer and ten inches more precipitation annually than the official reporting station. That's because the ravine is part of a heat island created by suburban structures and activity and, at 650 feet maximum elevation, is 200 feet higher on an escarpment that lifts moisture-laden winds into the city's face, triggering additional rain.

Biosphere is the term for life's realm and is capitalized, because it is Earth's one inclusive community (ecosystem). I use Biosphere in the functional sense of our planet's interlocking biological and physical processes—its uncounted systems of relaying energy and recycling nutrients that I like to think of as the play of life. Although this play is unique in the universe as far as we know, its planetary theater, local stages, seasonal scenes, and actors are made of star dust like everything else.

About natural and unnatural (cultural) history, I distinguish nature's use of direct sunlight for energy transfers from modern humanity's reliance on fossilized sunlight (coal, oil, gas), because we are the only species that employs fossil fuels in ways that disrupt Biosphere function. Humanity began to separate itself from nature long before the industrial age, certainly, but its impact took an unprecedented major step with the widespread burning of fossil fuels.

Acknowledgments

My debt to Nancy is immeasurable. As a trained biologist, retired science teacher, co-author of scientific reports, and everyday naturalist, she too is immersed in the ravine. She has helped in all I've done here and in our many studies elsewhere, recording messages, discussing their meaning, and critiquing my writing.

Baylor University and my academic chair, Keith Hartberg, were most supportive. Many colleagues, students, and friends, especially my late companions, Jochem and Chris Burckhardt, discussed universal messages. Neighbor, friend, and ecologist Darrell Vodopich helped with ideas and a rascally computer. Cynthia Stickney drew the screech owls from my photos, and Cherie McCollough recorded their messages in my absence.

Of course, this book would have been impossible without the ravine's own teachers. Not only the wild animals and plants, people, pets, fossils, rocks, rain, and sun of everyday experience, but the bacteria, fungi, human artifacts, creeks, comets, wind, ice, moon, stars, and others that have acted in the great drama of life over its four-billion-year run.

Owl Hollow
December 31, 1999

I went to the woods because I wished . . . to front only the essential facts of life and see if I could learn what it had to teach and not, when I came to die, discover that I had not lived. *Henry David Thoreau*

Messages from the Wild

CHAPTER I

NATURE AND CULTURE

One hundred million years ago a shallow sea housed a myriad of tiny organisms eaten by larger creatures, including ammonites whose extinction was a message set in stone. The smallest life was important, not only because it fed others, but because it became the ravine's bedrock. Eventually the sea drained away, and the earth cracked, shifted, and eroded, leaving a ravine-cut, tree-covered escarpment overlooking a river basin. In the last second of Earth's history, humans sheltered here and changed the landscape more quickly than ever before.

The Landscape

Central Texas is a biological crossroads, the meeting ground of humid eastern forest and tallgrass prairie with dry western woodland and shortgrass prairie, all lightly touched by the tropics. This transition zone is demarked by the two-hundred-foot-high Balcones Escarpment that runs south from Dallas through Waco, Austin, San Antonio, and westward. About two-thirds of the living landscape is southeastern in geographic and ecological character, but the mix varies naturally year to year, directed largely by the weather.

My particular ravine is the work of water cutting through Austin chalk limestone that caps the Balcones Escarpment. The cleft is about twenty-five to seventy-five feet deep and two hundred to six hundred feet wide. Upstream portions are two semi-wild cul-de-sacs truncated by a four-lane highway and industrial park. Downstream hills, dales, and tributaries coalesce into a single biotic pathway sliced by a four-lane street but connected beneath it to parkland around a reservoir. The whole—all remaining seminaturalness—is encased in suburbia.

Both cul-de-sacs have creeks that join to form a larger stream that empties into the reservoir. One fork that I call Arrowhead Hollow, because of its human artifacts, is fifty-five acres of forest and perennial stream plus two dammed ponds at its spring-fed headwaters. The other fork is Butterfly Hollow, thirty-two wooded acres with an old livestock tank and summer-dry creek. Eighty-three additional wooded acres comprise land below the junction and include a forested tributary draining the seventeen acres of Owl Hollow.

Forest was the pre-settlement vegetation but has regrown after being cut to supply firewood, building materials, and crop and construction sites since the mid-1800s. From growth rings in logs, I estimate that mature canopy trees average seventy years old, although a few originals are two hundred years and more, particularly some of the largest scalybark oaks that grow anywhere. Trees along creeks are diverse, tall, and mostly deciduous, while those of the warmer, dryer slopes represent fewer, shorter, more frequent evergreen species.

Creekside trees include American and cedar elms, sugarberry, eastern cottonwood, pecan, black walnut, bur oak, red mulberry, and eastern red cedar. Plateau live, scalybark, and Shumard oaks, white ash, and Ashe juniper increase on the slopes and once grew in island-like groves called motts amidst prairie that became ranchland and then suburbia on the ridgetops. If natives survive among the exotic plants of suburbia, they are usually oaks, elms, pecans, and ashes and, if planted, are mostly cultured varieties of oaks and pecan.

Our house in Butterfly Hollow sat in juniper-oak woods above a small draw. We'd saved the trees but planted exotic shrubs and San Augustine grass around the house, because in those days of young adulthood we felt constrained by suburban yard culture. Across the street behind a row of houses was farmland that became the park. I often followed white-tailed deer paths through the woods into the ravine's main forks and downstream across ranchland to what eventually would be named Owl Hollow. Those paths and later sewerline scars became my trails.

After moving, we were alone in Owl Hollow's regenerating forest as our planned-unit development took shape. We knew we'd have close neighbors and designed our house to merge more with the wild than with cul-de-sac culture. We dwell beneath a complete canopy of forty-five foot, deciduous oaks on a sunrise hillside seventy-five feet above the creek. Most windows look to the morning sun, which heats us in winter. A transition from unnatural to natural history replaces a lawn, and a walk of flat stones gathered on our walks around the world reminds us of planetary connections.

Short paths take me to a trail through the nature preserve. Southward I stop near the head of Owl Hollow cut off by a city street. Northward I curve east and intersect the main trail across Owl Hollow's junction with the main watercourse. Continuing north, I wind a quarter-mile to the four-lane city boulevard. Southward again, I walk to the ravine's forks. One branch crosses a tributary and a city street in Butterfly Hollow; the other traverses two creeks but no streets in Arrowhead Hollow. Each long route is a round-trip of about two miles from my door.

These are my learning ways, some traversed daily, all every few weeks when I'm home. As with Charles Darwin's sandwalk, they are also thinking paths. I amble along, cogitating, taking notes, just looking or poking into this and that, maybe counting, tape recording, marking animals and plants for reacquaintance, or photographing. Or I may simply sit to learn with less intrusion. There are many secluded, off-trail confessionals for conversation with wild lives.

Seasons and Longer Time

In its annual circle around the sun, the ravine averages sixty-six degrees Fahrenheit, forty-two inches of precipitation, and has four seasons, each different from the four seasons so widely chronicled in the northern United States. That's because it lies at only thirty-one degrees north latitude. The result is an average twenty-one degrees warmer and forty more freeze-free days annually than, for example, central Wisconsin, which is nine hundred miles farther north. Consequently, summer is longer, autumn is later, winter is shorter, and spring earlier.

Spring in the ravine is as rainy and life-promoting as in the north but begins a month earlier than in central Wisconsin. Northern cardinals sing thirty-two days earlier in the ravine, migratory geese, American robins, and house wrens arrive twenty-five days earlier on average, and anemones and spiderlilies (spiderworts) begin to bloom here in February but not until April in Wisconsin. March is the ravine's most eventful month, with novelties such as the first tree leaves and blooms and migratory birds traveling on the winds (see Appendix).

Although it warms up slowly, about one degree Fahrenheit per week, spring initiates the year's greatest burst of seasonal activity. Between Valentine's Day and Mother's Day, frequent but increasingly mild cold fronts bring increasing rain, which stimulates plant growth and reproduction with the consequent rush of insects and larger animals of the green food web. March peaks with seventeen new events weekly, followed by April with thirteen, but then comes a real slowdown to seven weekly events in May and two in June.

June, in fact, is mostly summer despite its rainfall. By Memorial Day weekend we often feel the first string of ninety-degree days, and our air conditioner is on to stay by mid-June. The heat continues with increasingly fewer breaks through at least Labor Day weekend. Life events decline to an average of one per week from July to September. The air dries out and changes less in temperature, day to night, than in other seasons. Summer often features at least a month without rain and two and a half weeks of hundred-degree weather.

September can be summery, or it may cool down with renewed rainfall and become fall—or switch back and forth. Often we welcome earliest autumn indoors about mid-month and stay joyfully reconnected with open windows until the furnace goes on with the first freeze around Thanksgiving. Even after the first frost in early November, autumn adds another month and a half of multiple Indian summers with foliage color, falling leaves, and arriving winter birds. Novel life events remain at one per week from October through December.

The pace of nature's surprises really slows down around Christmastime. Winter is signaled by novelties only every two weeks in January and February. There are periodic awakenings on mild days, but much of the living landscape sleeps, dominated by cold until about Valentine's Day, when we turn the furnace heat off on a full-time basis. Unlike the northern winter, however, some plants grow and bloom, frogs sing, and hibernating butterflies resurface momentarily.

Late in November the forest canopy of deciduous leaves disappears. This climate-control system has furnished seven and a half months of shade and insulation since mid-April, a month after the last spring freeze, although creekside trees are bare for several days longer than those on hillsides, because the creek bottom averages four degrees colder. Overall, the ravine averages 249 consecutive freeze-free (growing) days annually, but it is warming up at the rate of about two more growing days each year.

Not all changes are linked to climatic warming, though. Summer resident birds are disappearing at the rate of one species every four years and a breeding pair yearly due to suburban sprawl and natural reforestation. Migrant birds that travel through are also declining but not the species, indicating the ravine's continued suitability as a re-fueling stop. Instead, fewer individuals denote lower reproduction or survival elsewhere, because the Biosphere's most important principle is connection.

Long-term changes are natural, such as the forest's self-restoration following damage from severe storms. But changes due to human activity fueled by fossil energy appear to be directional, at least for the time being—the gradual displacement of nature by culture according to our linear concept of time and progress. Over the past thirty-five years my suburb has doubled in population and tripled in area at the expense of wild and agricultural land, although the sprawl may be only a passing stage for a species that learns to hear messages from the wild.

For still there are so many things that I have never seen. In every wood in every spring there is a different green. J. R. R. *Tolkien*

CHAPTER 2

Winter IS SURVIVAL

January's Active Forest

Now is the peak of cold, a time of cold rain or cold sun—ice or snow rarely—and lots of gray skies and foggy mornings, as Arctic air clashes with warm moist air from the Gulf of Mexico. January lacks deciduous leaves, but green cedars and live oaks are cheery enough; and early wildflowers, particularly trout lilies, poke up, grow a bit, and bloom on the warm afternoons near month's end. Resident birds begin to sing, woodpeckers drum, and armadillos dig grubs in sunshine instead of the night.

1st. Three- to five-degree temperature drops in an hour are typical, when strong cold fronts or blue northers follow mild weather; so I am leery, as New Year's day begins with fog and a relatively warm fifty degrees. An eastern screech owl in a nest box at my house puts off its daytime nap and looks out in the dim light. It's been a week since the six-year-old male who owned this box was killed by a passing car, and I'm curious about this new arrival. At dusk the owl sings once before leaving to hunt. Sure enough, he's another deep-voiced male, for females are higher pitched.

Male screech owls won't start to advertise their tree-cavity or nest-box homes to lifelong mates until late this month, when they'll sing continuous, mellow, single-pitch trills. Descending trills that sound like horse-whinnies are territorial defense and more frequent in autumn. Hoots proclaim annoyance, barks are predator warnings, and screeches declare real disturbance; and there are rattles and bill-claps plus juvenile peeps, chuckles, and rasps in my mentor's repertoire. Some people disclaim the screech, saying the owl is misnamed, but they haven't listened to its messages.

2nd. American robins and cedar waxwings by the hundreds are feeding on wild fruits. Flocks of American goldfinches eat sycamore seeds, shredding the seedballs so the fragments blow in the wind, reminding me of cottonwood cotton in May. Goldfinches winter here, but the big robin flocks usually don't arrive until later. Mass entry now tells me that severe weather is coming. Today's hoards are such a contrast to the few individuals that stay all winter, singing lyrically on mild mornings. The crowd strips berry bushes clean in a day, drinks my birdbath dry in an hour, and churns the forest's leaf litter like a herd of armadillos.

Robin and cedar waxwing flocks may stay around for several days, joined or replaced by others over the next month or two. Mortality is terrific on streets, at windows, and in the ravine by house cats and boys with BB guns and air rifles. I've just asked two junior-high hunters to vacate our nature preserve, a conservation concept they don't appear to understand because parents and schools teach little or nothing about nature's values. Moreover, human males may have genes for hunting as females do for gathering, now called shopping—both behaviors derived from our prehistoric heritage.

Robins like chinaberries that have been frozen, thawed, and fermented, and they may get tipsy eating them. A clowning event is a flock of robins flapping to stay upright, falling to the ground, flying into trees, hanging upside down from twigs, all the time noisily quarreling over feeding space. Other berry choices, not so entertaining but colorful, are red possumhaws, blue junipers, orange sugarberries, black gum bumelias and Indian cherries, white western soapberries and Chinese tallows, and brown flameleaf and smooth sumacs. Chinaberries are largest, which may be the robin's cue to nutritional value, unless the birds are natural barflies.

3rd. Mildness, cirrus clouds, and a south wind signal change. The screech owl from nest box one looks out in early afternoon, soaking up the sunshine. His eyes are closed, his head and breast feathers fluffed up. Despite their nocturnal habit, screech owls do like the sun, just like the rest of us, and especially in winter when there is less of it. I wonder if he has any food stored away for the coming norther. It wouldn't be unusual to find a robin or cedar waxwing stashed inside. Small birds are feeding furiously. We are due for a blast of winter, but how soon? I promise myself to see what food if any the owl has stored after he leaves at dark.

4th. It is such a beautiful day that I suggest a plant hunt to neighbors, who want some native wildflowers to grow around their deck at the edge of our nature preserve. Several species are peeking aboveground. The air is eighty-two degrees, a record, and it stimulates a golden rain of cedar pollen. It's a January thaw with nothing to thaw. We sneeze and talk about how we miss cold weather, something we'll regret later when winter returns. As we dig Missouri violets, white avens, plateau spiderlilies, and roughstem sunflowers, a hibernating water scavenger beetle is unearthed fifty feet up the hill from the creek—a novelty that so often happens on a day in the woods.

5th. Fox squirrels race around frantically, the males busily following one another, led by a female, up and down, across the ground, and through the tree canopy—a seemingly endless mating chase. Late December, about the time of the shortest day, is usual for the start of this behavior, which I've recorded because I want to learn the repertoire of this competitor with the eastern screech owl for tree cavities and nest boxes. I find sleeping squirrels in some boxes and screech owls in others, but normally no squirrel babies until late this month and no owl eggs until early March.

Especially during cold stormy weather, screech owls use tree cavities and nest boxes as day roosts, so there is a tussle for housing. The first owl egg is usually laid in the first week of March, though the long-term average is March 14, several days after the last time I've noticed new-born squirrel pups in nest boxes. About April Fool's Day the weather is sufficiently warm and fleas are bad enough that fox squirrels forsake cavities for airier tree canopy nests built of leaves and twigs, and these are used exclusively for their second brood in mid-summer.

Even so, from winter into April if the weather is foul, fox squirrels temporarily take over cavities from roosting or incubating screech owls that are only half their size. I've often wondered what happens, when a predatory ringtail—the raccoon's weasel-like cousin—finds them, because I know what happens to screech owl eggs and chicks. The owls' survival strategy is to re-nest elsewhere, which is why each pair owns two or three tree cavities or nest boxes, although they never produce two broods a year.

Ringtails shop for cavity roosts and supper, apparently remembering where they've found them before. On tree branches adjacent to the cavities and on nest-box lids they deposit scat (fecal) piles as territorial markers. These heaps are easy to see from a distance, so I know when a barking ringtail will greet me as I open a nest-box. I really like these lithe, tan, big-eyed, big-eared, band-tailed creatures, but if I am to hear certain screech owl messages, I must dissuade ringtails by spraying pet repellent on the lid and nearby branches.

6th. A ground trap for catching and banding white-throated sparrows and dark-eyed juncos holds a fox squirrel who is displaced to an oak grove two miles away across a four-lane divided highway. I do this each winter—seventy-one squirrels is my seasonal record—because the cheeky critters are so destructive. In attics they destroy wiring, insulation, and make holes in the roof. To mark natural territories they chew a section of tree bark and urinate on the scar, but when they adopt my attic because of the warmth, protection, and plentiful nearby food and water, those rascally critters chew and mark my house, "begging" for deportation.

7th. Today a cold front blows in, dropping the temperature to freezing in twenty-four hours, bringing rain, then sleet, snow, and finally, over two days, a mixture that melts, refreezes, and coats the trees with an increasingly thick layer of ice as temperatures bounce back and forth between twenty-five and thirty-two degrees. Loud cracks like shotgun blasts and some cannon booms reverberate through the forest. Branches and trees are falling. Ice storms are nature's way of pruning and, if severe, they are forest-thinners. But unlike bulldozers and their dump truck accomplices, ice storms leave wood to nourish the injured forest. The openings they create allow new generations of plants and animals to grow and diversify the landscape.

8th. During stormy weather the gray screech owl is ensconced in his New Year's Day nest box but leaves to hunt a few minutes earlier each evening. He may be hungrier in the cold—I certainly am—and because the sky is cloudy, stimulated to forage in the early darkness. Screech owl activity is triggered by amount of light as well as food demand. Nesting males leave their day roosts to hunt earlier when eggs hatch; and, as owlets grow, the males depart earlier and earlier, sometimes hunting in daytime if the sky is cloudy. They are solely responsible for feeding mates, who alone feed small nestlings.

Being hungrier, I eat more and am about three percent heavier in winter than in summer. I've learned that screech owls are heavier too —an annual average seven to thirteen percent—the amount positively related to food availability. The owls and other birds tell me that their heavyweights survive more often than lightweights during times of food scarcity in harsh winters—that extra fat is adaptive. I suspect that winter-heavy humans inherited the same survival advantage from prehistoric ancestors, who experienced weather more directly and had to work a whole lot harder for their food than I do.

9th. The cold front passes, and the dawn is freezingly clear. Despite the temperature, a few resident birds sing briefly, celebrating the sunshine, reminding me that spring is a little over a month away. I rely on the avian ensemble to let me know that days are getting longer, because I won't notice it directly for another week or two. In just three hours the temperature rises from twenty-eight to forty degrees, and melting ice rains from tree branches and roofs. In the acre around my house, three big oaks are lying on the ground amidst lesser prunings. By early afternoon ice remains on only north-facing exposures, as the thawing landscape drips.

10th. After a beautiful sunrise, the temperature rises to fifty degrees, and the wind begins to blow from the south, stirring life out of nooks and crannies. A red admiral butterfly sports about my patio and spider silks are in the air, even this early in the year. Hatchling spiders are dispersing. They use their silk strands as balloons to carry them away from competition with each other, adult spiders, and other predators attracted to concentrations of prey, such as masses of baby spiders. Dispersal means survival and reproductive opportunity for the young of all species, including humans.

Many offspring show instinctive dispersal tendencies written in their genes. The desire for independence by human teenagers was surely adaptive prehistorically, when they didn't need to know so much to survive—when only the nature at hand provided resources. But today's suburban teenagers are economic infants who cannot make it without education and are afforded at home the resources their parents buy from afar. Unfortunately, teenage genes don't know that cultural evolution requires ever more learning and rushes past biological evolution geared to an earlier, simpler existence.

11th. Last October I planted the eyeball-sized seeds of Ohio buckeyes at marked locations to study mid-winter sprouting near this tree's southern limit of natural range. Today the first seedlings poke up in keeping with the buckeye's unusual jump on spring. I want to see the color of first leaves in wooded versus exposed locations, since some seedlings are dressed in bright green while others are scarlet. Reddish photosynthetic pigments are used in reduced light by plants growing through leaf litter in early spring, when the sun is low in the sky. But today's seedlings don't follow instructions; they sprout green and red in all directions.

First leaves endure until late February. Then the scarlet ones blanch and turn slightly greenish before disappearing at the same time as green ones in the forest's April shade. Especially wondrous is the buckeye's fast-growing, extensive tap root. It makes six-inch spiral coils at the bottom of three-inch deep pots, when the leafy sprouts are only two inches tall. Ohio buckeyes live naturally on lower slopes and stream terraces in relatively deep soil, where their long tap root is an energy storehouse for next year's growth and an anchor for survival against the force of floodwater and soil erosion.

12th. I am at work cleaning up ice-storm debris. An oak, fifteen inches in diameter and forty-five feet tall, lies across a shallow draw by my house. Its downed limbs provide firewood, while its trunk is left in place to become a child care center for tree seedlings and a halfway house for small animals. Like so many older trees it has a rotted hollow core and couldn't stand the added weight of the ice. There is much yard damage in my neighborhood, but the ravine has little harm except along the trail where the forest, lacking a protective canopy, is open to the full force of weather. In uncut areas, trees have neighbors as shields and interlocking branches to lean on.

Chain saws are the noise of the day. Walking about the neighborhood, I see no evidence of chipping to recycle the wood as mulch. There is good firewood too and even wood for carpentry, but people are piling it along the street for the city to pick up. No sense in useable wood being burned and buried in the landfill, dumping more carbon into the sky to thicken the atmosphere's heat-retaining, greenhouse layer. Why not a city-sponsored firewood, mulch, and compost center, supplied by the organic refuse it picks up at curbside and funded by selling the products?

13th. Clear, still, and twenty-two degrees with the rosy hint of sunrise at 6:50 A.M. I'm on my front porch, awaiting the dawn chorus of resident songbirds. Today is Aldo Leopold's birthday, so it is a memorial celebration for me to venture forth for dawnsong, as Leopold did so regularly. Because he listened to messages from the wild, he advocated the inclusive approach to life—a land ethic he called it— which underlies modern conservation practice. But all I hear this morning are crows and someone's stuck car horn—a thief alarm like the crow voices, a congruity of signals about those who would rob nature's bank in the play of life.

14th. Snow falls intermittently all day, and ground-feeding finches come and go from the millet I've thrown out in experimental patches. White-throated sparrows and dark-eyed juncos are research subjects that I'm trapping, measuring, banding, and releasing. There are single eastern and spotted towhees and American goldfinches with pine siskins and purple finches beside the resident northern cardinals and house finches. The screech owl in nest box two looks out his open window at 5:00 P.M., faces a snowy north wind, and retreats. As the snow stops, he reappears and watches for twenty minutes before departing. Does he assess the availability of avian food or the possibility of danger on this night bright with reflective snow?

15th. Suddenly, I awake at 4:30 A.M. Some noise or sixth sense triggers it. I find our water taps frozen on the north side of the house. It is twenty-one degrees outside but windy, and I'll bet wind chill is the problem. The north wind is in control, and we forgot to insulate water pipes when we built the house. Our high today is only twenty-six, which makes nearly forty-eight hours below freezing. One more day and night this way and tropical natives like the nine-banded armadillo could be in trouble. They can't dig for worms and grubs in frozen soil, nor can they hibernate. They simply remain inactive underground until the soil thaws. After more than three consecutive days of frozen ground, they may starve.

Nor can wintering northern flickers dig their favored ants in frozen soil, or vultures eat frozen carcasses, so both fly south, staying ahead of the southward plunge of Arctic air. Give them a strong south wind, though, and back they come. Do they associate the south wind with thawing or simply convenience in returning home? It takes only a day for unprotected soil to freeze or thaw, but snow cover usually prevents freezing and leaf litter is a constant blanket of insulation. Without snow, soil surface temperature below the forest's leafy carpet averages four to five degrees higher than air, even in the creek bottom with its nightly cold-air drainage.

16th. Another gray day at the start, but the wind shifts to the west, and the temperature only rises to the freezing point in late afternoon. No one sings this icy morning, although it's certainly the time for dawn chorusing. I'd be glad to hear any prelude. As the afternoon melting begins, blue jays warn about an owl in a cedar tree, and a gray screech owl flies out as I approach. Perhaps it's one that's been in the two nest boxes at my house, because no one's home in either box. Why would it give up the enclosed protection against weather and pesky jays on a freezing dawn? Does the owl predict a warm-up? Wild creatures seem to know about weather changes before technology does.

17th. The sun breaks through clouds for the first time in three days. Ice continues to melt, as the temperature rises quickly to sixty degrees by afternoon. Again, however, nobody is singing on this bright morning. That's curious, and I soon find out why. Clouds return by afternoon, and another cold front comes through in the night. Next day the high is only forty-two, but the sun shines and permanent-resident birds sing, fed by life's ultimate source of energy. Regulated daily by weather and seasonally by day-length, another year's dawn chorus has begun. It will peak with the homecoming of summer residents in April–May and remain a wake-up call through June.

18th. Looking for last year's white-eyed vireo nest is a winter treasure hunt, since we rarely find one in use. They are too well hidden. But, in this leafless month, someone often spots the teacup of plant fibers that a white-eyed vireo weaves in a twig fork at eye to knee level in a shrub within a few feet of an opening. Then the finder challenges other family members to make the discovery, without giving any clues. Last year's nest nearest our door is only a hundred feet away, three feet high in a Mexican buckeye growing four feet from the path. We walked right by it many times last spring, unaware that it was full of life.

White-eyed vireos are part of forest reconstruction. They nest in shrubland and tree-fall or trailside openings, in contrast to red-eyed vireos that must have mature timber. Another local relative, the black-capped vireo, requires short shrub clumps without trees—an early stage of forest recovery. In the pegboard above my garage workbench I keep a few old white-eye nests, whose plant fibers are plucked by garage-perusing Carolina wrens for their own nests. And I protect a special memento, a black-capped vireo nest, the last local effort of this endangered species, as its habitat was being erased by suburban sprawl in 1970.

19th. Nuttall's death camus, a beautiful poisonous lily, has grown just above the leaf litter, but its short slim leaves are easily passed by. Before the tree canopy closes in mid-April, shading the ground, this striking plant will be three feet tall and sport a spectacular head of white flowers. Death camus is one of several woodland plants that get going early in abundant sunshine before the deciduous trees leaf out, limit light, and safeguard soil moisture. It opts for the light, a trade-off like so many in nature—an important lesson for those of us who want it all and are unwilling to wait.

Wild forest lilies have two strategies for avoiding dense shade and taking advantage of winter rain unused by dormant plants. The Hill

Country (false) dayflower's approach is to sprout after autumn rains but stop at that and wait for spring. Another lifestyle, used by plateau spiderlilies, is to grow slowly on mild fall and winter days after those rains, and the third is to begin with lengthening days in January, like the death camus and southern plains trout lily. This does not require immediate rain but a bulb, a larger device for water and energy storage than the fleshy roots of spiderlilies and thin, diffuse annual roots of the dayflower.

The bulbs and seeds of Nuttall's death camus store toxic alkaloid compounds, giving the plant its name. Animals are sickened if they eat these but apparently not when they eat other parts, though I've watched white-tailed deer totally avoid the species. The big clusters of white flowers certainly stand out, advertising the plant's poisonous nature, protecting it while attracting insect pollinators. That the bulbs and flower heads with seeds are guarded makes good sense, since they are necessary for regrowth and sexual reproduction.

20th. Mobbing birds tip me off to a light gray eastern screech owl roosting in a plateau live oak, exposed to the warm morning sun. The owl is thirty feet from an empty nest box, while a darker gray individual peers from another box a hundred feet away. Perhaps a pair is together in old number 77's territory. Is it his widow with a new mate? I look for a leg band, but it's difficult to tell, because screech-owl legs and feet are completely feathered. Knowing that owl widows and widowers quickly find new mates, most likely the one in the oak is 77's replacement. The pair eventually nests but is displaced by a fox squirrel, leaving cold, deserted eggs as their legacy and my regret.

21st. A cloudy cold day is for working wood, and the great ice storm of 1996 will take weeks to reckon with. First I clear fallen branches and trees on our ravine trail, cutting some into fireplace logs. Chainsaw noise would drown messages, and earplugs or headphones would block awareness, so I resort to hand sawing, which takes a long time. I bring another load from the outside woodpile into the garage and put the newly cut logs on one end of the pile. Cold-clumsy wood roaches, ground beetles, centipedes, carpenter ants, spiders, and termites fall out and are swept up and put back into the woods. These aren't worrisome, because nature's natural checks are on hand. But when neighbors call a pesticide company to treat their house, forcing their termites to search for new food, watch out!

22nd. Ambling about in my mind, I try to imagine the uncountable and mostly unknown bacteria on and inside me and other animals, plants, soil, air, water—pervasively involved and indispensable to the Biosphere. I try to name just a few of their incomparable jobs, such as oil and cellulose digestion and nitrogen and sulfur recovery. So many are more helpful than harmful. I visualize these microscopic, unicellular beings on stage with oaks and owls, rather like the tiny, picture-corner characters some political cartoonists draw to tell the straight story. Bacteria are my oldest relatives; they were the only actors for most of life's play, and they still get major billing.

23rd. Southern plains trout lilies have grown through the leaf litter despite twenty-degree temperatures at night. They'll poke through snow too, if we have it. Their green leaves are darkly blotched with purplish brown, like a trout, and they're hard to see unless accompanied by dainty white blooms with recurved petals that remind me of Easter lilies. Today is sunny, a must for finding trout lilies, because their flowers close in cloudy weather and at night—by about 6:30 P.M. under clear skies at their peak on Valentine's Day. Petals turn pink as they age, and by mid-March solid green leaves accompany green seed pods. By the time of tree-canopy shade in mid-April, trout lilies retreat underground again.

Five inches deep, where temperatures are twenty degrees higher, the lilies have a corm (like a bulb) that produces small offsets that break away and grow into single-leaf plants. That's why the species lives in tight colonies. Annually, leaves come up larger than the year before, as each year's leaves feed corms that store more food energy that produces more leaf machinery. After about five good growing years two leaves emerge and a year or two later the single flower appears. The year after that I find only one or two leaves again, because flowering requires extra energy. My marked plants have lived eighteen years so far, blooming off and on, balancing their flower-cost: leaf-benefit ratio.

Trout lily colonies are patchily distributed, possibly because first

Americans ate the corms and carried them from camp to camp, occasionally dropping some (humans aren't native to the Americas but some arrived about twelve thousand years before the rest of us). Comparing modern human impacts on the patches of lilies, I walk from those grazed by cattle to others overrun by Japanese honeysuckle or cut by mountain bike and foot trails, and find progressively more blooms. Yet even the least disturbed lilies are sparser than elsewhere, probably because they are naturally stressed here near their southern margin of range.

24th. My habit at any time of year is to rise by 5:00 A.M. and think and write in splendid solitude before or after an hour of searching for wild messengers. At the appropriate time, most mornings I'll take a few minutes outside to greet the rising sun. Later, when it is warm enough to open windows, I combine writing with listening and, still later, when the dawn is nearer, I'll almost always walk in the ravine before writing. At 7:35 this morning, as the sun peeks over the treetops, daily "moving" eastward, a downy woodpecker drums on wood for the first time in several months—its message about the coming of spring.

25th. Black vultures have begun courtship flying and aerial inspection of potential nest sites. A pair criss-crosses the ravine, flaps in tandem, separates, sails, and begins again. Eggs are laid in early February, about a week earlier in suburbia than in rural areas, always on the ground under such shelter as leaning tree trunks, piles of limbs and dead foliage, rocky overhangs, elevated wooden decks, or backyard sheds. Black vultures are readily accustomed to human activity and nest regularly in the ravine, sometimes roosting on rooftops and patio railings and drinking from bird baths. Despite their aerial beauty, intelligence, comical nature, and role as recyclers in the play of life, my human neighbors think them ugly and a nuisance, and treat them accordingly, much to my dismay.

26th. An invariable aspect of living with wild beings that readily habituate to human ways is that one may acquire rambunctious house guests in the attic, chimney, or the house itself. Mammals especially like warm, soft, attic insulation during winter. Raccoons and fox squirrels are the most frequent and destructive tenants, and the coons do a lot of thumping about at night. Opossums and ringtails are native guests, too, and there are exotic black and brown rats. Honeybees, red paper wasps, and wintering northern flickers that drill through wood siding complete the usual group of natural cavity users that suburbanize by substituting attics for tree holes.

Neighbors have a particularly tough time with raccoons that chew holes in ceilings and roofs and tear up insulation and wiring. One person left his attic folding ladder out for a coon to use to exit through the garage but forgot to leave the garage door open and had a new coon-sized hole in it the next morning. Unknowing folks feed raccoons, squirrels, and ringtails because they're cute, prepping them for winter invasions. My Labrador retrievers have seen to it that wild mammals stay out of our house, but now and then a raccoon, knowing when the dog sleeps, climbs a front porch column and peers in windows at us, who put a little culture in its life.

27th. Every winter I am the creek's trashman. Cans, broken glass bottles, plastic bottles, paper and plastic cups, plastic grocery and trash bags, broken plastic and clay flower pots, bricks, boards with nails, t-shirts, underpants, socks, "bubba" hats, plastic marking tape, ribbons, broken plastic sewer pipe—I could go on and on about human refuse that washes into storm drains or is tossed in the ravine. The operative word is plastic. Today I spend four hours along a quarter-mile of creekbed. I pass a castoff swimming pool pump and two concrete house piers—much too heavy for me to pick up—and carry three full thirty-gallon trash bags and some sheep fencing to our city's landfill.

An aluminum beer can partly encased in travertine reveals nature-culture schizophrenia. The creek cements itself with travertine, a natural deposit of lime percolated from our limestone bedrock. Travertine opposes the natural erosion that created it—a compensating mechanism so typical of the Biosphere—and by partly damming the creek, provides bathing, drinking, and reproducing pools for animals. But floods destroy this natural cement and grow in number and size as humanity warms the climate, increasing the frequency and intensity of rainfall, while pavement focuses runoff and accelerates erosion. Once the ravine tried to bury refuse but now uncovers unnatural trash.

28th. Eastern screech owls will begin singing regularly any night, but not so much now, when the moon is new. In fact, singing is quite cyclic within and among seasons. The male owl's melodious spring trill is sung twice as frequently during a gibbous to full moon as during this new-moon time. In bright moonlight, screech owls are not so inclined to expose themselves visually and thus are more stimulated to advertise vocally. During the full moon I can't approach them as closely as I do now. Nor can I trap small rodents as readily, and I suppose owls can't either. I've noticed that all nocturnal animals are more furtive in bright moonlight.

Moonlight also influences people, who don't sleep as soundly and have more babies, accidents, and criminal violence in the full moon. I've verified our lunacy with emergency room physicians, dentists, and police. Since the moon's gravity pulls water, affecting ocean tides, it may do the same to our bodies, which are seventy percent water, making us jittery or aggressive. So I adjust hunting for the ravine's nocturnal secrets to exploit the new moon's darkness. I concentrate on shapes and sizes with vision directed slightly above or below what I'm looking at, employing light detectors (rods) on the inside periphery of my eyeballs, because I can't rely on color vision.

29th. Behavior that increases body size displays potential power and is protective when an animal is confronted or startled. In winter a fearsome countenance is accentuated by the seasonally long hair more easily seen in the leafless forest. Wild mammals show the most body size by arching their backs and erecting hair and appendages, especially the tail. Eastern spotted skunks stand on their front feet, raising their whole body. We human animals have too little hair to make a difference, so we raise our arms, flex our muscles, and stand face-to-face. Eye-to-eye contact is a natural threat that we use instinctively, since we're taught not to stare in public but maintain eye contact in personal encounters.

30th. Early flowers add to my impression that spring is on its way. It's still winter for sure, cold and blustery, although I've seen the first trout lilies and American elm blooms. Among majestic canopy trees, American elms always bloom first, including a favorite individual two and a half feet in diameter and seventy feet tall. Once the species characterized the eastern deciduous forest, but it is long gone from most places, killed off by Dutch elm disease imported by accident from Europe. Our trees comprise one of the few remaining original populations. Thank goodness the disease didn't get here, probably because our American elms are semi-isolated along rivers and were not planted as ornamentals, a practice that facilitates the spread of disease by increasing tree density.

31st. This blue moon of 1999 inspires dreams of a time when the climate was more like January year-round. Fifteen thousand years ago: I stroll in a moist forest of basswood, sugar maple, alder, birch, and spruce munched on by elephants called mastodons. There are no other people. I watch while five thousand years pass, and most cool-wet adapted trees disappear as prairie develops. Farther north a stupendous ice blanket a mile thick melts back toward the Arctic. Now, mammoths are hunted by newly arrived predators who kill at a distance with spears and fire, exterminating them and most other large animals within a few millennia.

Remaining bison are half the bulk of their Ice Age predecessors, and camels, horses, and lions are gone. Sugar maple takes refuge in other ravines, as oaks and junipers invade, invited by the hotter, dryer climate. Human hunters give up on the dwindling herds and settle into farming villages, some cleared from the ravine's forest. Nine more millennia pass, and the rate of change accelerates as newer, paler, human invaders displace the first ones and extirpate bison, black bears, and red wolves in only a century. Then, they use fossil fuels to pave the land, warm the climate, punch holes in the ozone layer, and increase their own cancer and storm damage.

He who sees things grow from the beginning
will have the best view of them.

Aristotle

February Hints of Spring

February begins with at least two weeks of winter, but Valentine's Day usually brings hints of spring. The change comes a full month before the vernal equinox, the official beginning of spring. Major contrasts mark the transition—the last snows and sustained below-freezing weather followed by the first tree blooms, tiny leaves, and nest building by birds. Sunny afternoons are numerous enough that hibernating butterflies and lizards are active temporarily. Wild plum perfume and chortling martins, just back from South America, are spring signatures by month's end.

⋆

1st. I am greeted by five degrees and eight inches of snow at dawn in 1985. While walking in this rare white world I hear a horrible din and see a snowmobiler—obviously a displaced person. There is nothing so quiet as a morning's snow-covered landscape before the unnatural history of motorized noise. This is our second biggest snowfall—ten inches is the record. Schools and businesses are canceled, allowing full appreciation of nature's gift, because there is no snow removal equipment in this normally snowless land. But most snows are in full retreat the next day. Two and a half days is the longest they ever put the relative quietus on suburbia, permitting me to hear what winter sounded like before the industrial revolution.

2nd. Mexican buckeyes, with their dangling empty seed pods, and chubby-twigged Ohio buckeyes reminded me that the ravine is a meeting place for west and east with some tropical and transcontinental species in attendance. Two-thirds of our biota is eastern or southeastern in geographic affiliation—Ohio buckeye and green anole, for instance. A quarter is western or southwestern-Mexican, such as Mexican buckeye and ringtail. Eastern ruby-throated and western black-chinned hummingbirds nest among eastern red cedars and western Ashe junipers. Transcontinental species include fragrant sumac and common garter snake, while Turk's cap and Inca dove represent the tropical element.

Eastern deciduous forest meets western evergreen woodland along the north-south trending and rapidly urbanizing Balcones Escarpment. These large-scale, structurally distinct communities (biomes), are mostly separated by a forty-mile-wide tongue of tallgrass prairie, now mostly cropland. Before cultivation, prairie life from the Great Plains ranged southward to the Gulf of Mexico. Most forest and woodland creatures can't cross prairie or cropland, although they traversed the land in a trans-regional forest fifteen thousand years ago. Today, such species as Shumard oak and tufted titmouse travel in wooded riverside corridors through the central Texas meltdown.

3rd. Henbit is blooming bright bluish-purple in less-manicured yards and other culturally disturbed areas. It is a European import that especially likes the curbside, where mechanical trimmers chew things up. Our Old World heritage also adds common dandelions to winter lawns and grassy patches in the woods. Their yellow flowers and celestial-white seed heads are a welcome sign of renewal, when there are few blooming natives. I pick seeding dandelions, blow their parachutes afloat, and think about the cottonwood cotton to come. But henbit and dandelion will disappear from any lawn destined for the yard-of-the-month award.

Both plants have been in North America since colonial days and don't bother native plants, only non-native people. Many such aliens are a worry though. A recent study of threatened or endangered natives of all kinds indicates that forty-nine percent are confronted with extinction wholly or partly because of competition with introduced species. That investigation also discloses that eighty-five percent are threatened by habitat loss, seventeen percent by human overuse, and three percent by alien and native pathogens. These values add up to more than one hundred percent because native plants and animals are often hammered by more than a single negative impact.

4th. On this bright sunny day northern cardinals begin fighting their reflected images in our windows, and they will continue to do so regularly. An occasional northern mockingbird or American robin perhaps, but why cardinals so invariably? Are they the most undiscriminating? This behavior lasts with decreasing intensity into summer, for cardinals produce their third and fourth broods as late as August. Why with such vigor now? Is it the spring rush of hormones? Are they anxious yearling breeders? It's not the lack of a tree canopy that causes image reflection, because cardinals are still at it well after the trees leaf out.

A neighbor calls to say that a large owl has been banging on her window for the last several days. I go to the house with a book in which she identifies a barred owl. It fights one particular pane in a large array of windows and does so with and without lights turned on inside or out, day or night. I've never heard of regular window fighting by an owl and can't figure out why it concentrates on just the one window pane and why in daylight. So I walk outside to get an owl's-eye view. Inside, directly across the room from me, is a large mirror in which I see a puzzled naturalist. My neighbor moves the mirror, and that's the last of it.

5th. Well-meaning folks add no end of comic relief to owl studies, but others express greed and control, two human characteristics that cause life so much grief. One person had a screech-owl nest box that attracted a nesting pair. It didn't open, so we could monitor events, but he allowed us to substitute our box. The owls accepted it. Then he thought if one pair of owls was nice, more would be better, so he put eight more boxes in his one hundred by one hundred-foot backyard. But one pair of screech owls defends several cavities, as we'd told him earlier, so, of course, he never had more than a single nesting pair.

Saddest of all is separation from nature so complete that the separatists are oblivious. They don't or perhaps can't acknowledge a natural situation. Another family had a large dead oak that they decided to cut down in May in the midst of the nesting season. As the chain saw started, an onlooker saw a bird fly out of a hole in the tree (later believed to be a screech owl). The downed oak was loaded onto a pickup truck, taken to the city dump, and when tossed out, some "small, white, fuzzy, baby birds" rolled out with it, according to my informant. She didn't know if anyone did anything with the owlets or just left them—dumped!

6th. In the hour before dawn I try to census singing screech owls along a mile of trail, but I hear nothing. It's cloudy, hiding the gibbous moon that should stimulate them to sing. Aside from an angry striped skunk, who smells badly because he's encountered someone besides the female he's looking for, nothing much is stirring. The north wind pushes clouds southward, and by dawn the sky is clear. Venus shines down from the southeast. The air temperature drops from forty-two to thirty-five degrees, reaffirming that cloud cover insulates the Earth. I sit for awhile until a Carolina wren sings a few times, but that's all. Like me, the songbirds are more interested in eating.

7th. At 4:00 A.M. thunder, lightning, and tapping rain on skylights and deck awaken me. The pyrotechnics pass, but drumming rain sounds like I'm in a tent and lulls me back to sleep. Curious about the seeming recurrence of early morning rains, I recorded the starting times of all precipitation over a three-year period. I found that rain associated with fast-moving cold fronts usually begins between three and nine in the morning, whereas rain instigated by northward-moving or stalled warm fronts starts in early afternoon, and the rain of convectional thunderstorms is mostly from mid-afternoon to early evening.

Closeted in dry, heated, and air-conditioned comfort, suburban folks pay little attention to such regularity, but behavior in the wild is keyed tightly to it. Wild creatures are busiest feeding during the build-up of thunderhead clouds. Traveling snakes and digging armadillos are most likely before storms. Songbirds scramble at my feeders the afternoon and evening before a cold front, and ants invade the kitchen that night. Screech owls seek cavities at these times but normally choose foliage roosts. I expect that these creatures detect and respond to the falling air pressure before stormy weather.

8th. Rain continues with three inches in two days, and the creek roars with water drained from asphalt and concrete, channeled into gutters and storm sewers. Three-fourths of my neighborhood is impervious, although in the ravine, buffered by a tree canopy and leaf litter, rain soaks into soil, is retained by the spongy organic layer, and drips slowly through limestone cracks, surfacing in seeps and springs. Those drips used to deposit travertine that held water in shallow pools, but now the water simply races, washing out everything in its path.

For stream-breeding insects, crayfish, and amphibians, flooding is disastrous. Eggs, nymphs, and tadpoles are smashed if not washed out —a waste of breeding effort. Amphibian reproduction is generally unsuccessful except in summer, when only Gulf Coast toads lay eggs. Woodhouse toads, Strecker's chorus frogs, southern and Rio Grande leopard frogs, and smallmouth salamanders have been eliminated from the creek and its ponds or severely reduced in numbers, but a few long-lived adults keep trying. Even a creekbottom stocktank, a breeding pond in ranching days, has been destroyed by the floods.

They can come at any time, but the really big floods like today's, when inches-deep water rises several feet, are usually in our spring and fall rainy seasons. The sound from my front porch, 150 feet away, is like river rapids. Since I live about 200 yards from Owl Hollow's head, now buried by construction of a through street, I hear only the beginning of "gully washers" and "toad stranglers," as ranchers call them with good meaning. I can imagine what it sounds like downstream, as tributaries swell the main creek's flow and contribute to erosional destruction.

9th. Like most animals that don't make their own nest holes but use naturally rotted or woodpecker-drilled cavities, eastern screech owls start early. The males try to tie down predator- and weather-proof sites ahead of competitors and usually patrol alternatives in case their first nests are disturbed or predated. Females lay eggs earlier in warmer weather, because they can afford to divert food energy from self-maintenance into egg-making; and I'll know about when, because average annual or winter temperatures are good predictors. This year I expect the first egg on March 9 and am checking all nest boxes to be certain they are ready.

Three with whitewash on the outside and cleaned of leaves are sure signs of European starlings, and five with fresh cedar-bark nests, including one with the fox squirrel in it, are additional competition. Some owls will wait for the squirrels to vacate boxes in April, but they have a tougher time with starlings, who don't lay eggs until then.

Which bird winds up nesting successfully is an even proposition, for the much smaller starlings are feisty, persistent, and cooperative, despite the threat of being eaten by the owls. Starlings are new actors in new scenes called suburbia, and the owls don't understand all their lines.

10th. When a small forest preserve is surrounded by culture it becomes weedy, because the Biosphere requires that energy flow from simple, disturbed, and productive communities such as shrublands, yards, and gardens, into complex, energy-storing depots like forests. Escapees from cultivation and weedy natives such as greenbriar and poison ivy proliferate in disturbed spots, because they are long-distance invaders and rapid reproducers. Weedseep is accentuated in a narrow ravine, with a considerable porous edge relative to its interior, and trails that are invasion pathways for seeds inadvertently carried by people, pets, and wildlife. Chunks are better nature preserves.

Today is my annual census of woody invaders along the preserve trail, and I try to eliminate as many exotics and trailside hazards as possible. The most insidious contaminant is Japanese honeysuckle along one-fifth of the trail, having doubled its coverage in the nine years since a sewer line was built creating bare earth receptive to invasion. Other exotic invaders are two loquats, twelve Chinese tallows, fourteen ligustrums, seventy-one nandinas, and over one hundred chinaberries. I yank seedlings and cut saplings, which will resprout but won't reseed for awhile, and I spray poison ivy and honeysuckle, because a corollary of the weedseep principle is that management is mandatory in island-like suburban wildlands.

11th. This winter of 1997–1998 is the warmest in thirty-five years, because we're experiencing one of the biggest El Niños ever recorded. Also, winter rainfall is heavier than average. We've had only one hard freeze. Spring will be buggier than ever, says local folklore, and I add that the growing season has started earlier for natives who've played in this scene for a long, long time. I sit on my patio at sixty degrees in the twilight, listen to chirping crickets, and watch the new moon rise behind winter moths flitting about bare treetops laying eggs. Yes, this growing season may be longer, but we've had long ones before.

The important question is whether they are increasing and what that means.

12th. Today is Charles Darwin's birthday (1809). He's an inspiration for his broad perspective and exposition of evolution, the core of biological thinking. Once I visited his home and strolled slowly on his sandwalk, his thinking path, my head down to avert distraction, hands clasped behind my back, hoping to connect. I thought about present-day arguments of gradual versus sporadic evolution and concluded that both occur. Fossil and modern observational and experimental evidence indicate convincingly that change usually is slow but tends to spurt across abrupt physical boundaries and especially when catastrophes redirect the play.

Furthermore, whether physical or biological factors are major operators between catastrophes is no either/or proposition in the inclusive Biosphere. Yet some argue about that too, and I don't understand why. Do we seek authority in exclusive explanations? It's clear to me that physical factors are more influential in climatically stressful situations such as species-poor desert and polar regions and early successional stages. Conversely, biodiversity's regulation through competition, predation, and other interactions prevails in the relatively benign tropics and older, species-rich, highly structured communities.

13th. This afternoon a neighbor who enjoys the ravine's wild offerings uncoiled her garden hose to wash winter debris off her deck and found the hose plugged up. Despite turning the water on full force, she only got a dribble. So she unscrewed the nozzle and out gushed a green anole (chameleon), frothing at the mouth and nostrils but otherwise none the worse for the attempted drowning. Since it was cold and limp, she held it several minutes and called me over to look. Soon, like any hand-heated anole, it warmed up, turned from brown to green, bit its benefactor, and jumped into the bushes. My puzzlement is how and when it got into the hose, because it obviously couldn't escape with the nozzle in place.

14th. A bright sunny Valentine's Day is perfect for windflowers (ten-petal anemones), whose blooms are closed in cloudy weather. The white and occasionally blue or pink flowers decorate open grassy patches and lawns in shallow soil. Windflowers won't grow inside forest, so they're not easily found in the ravine. But I know some places to look. I wonder why the colors are patchy, only white flowers here but mixed with blue ones there? Some of the ravine's other early-blooming plants such as trout lilies, spiderlilies, and violets are either white or blue, or both. Are they "experimenting" with the best color for attracting early-spring insects?

Two weeks hence blooming windflowers will peak. When folks start to cut grass, the seeds are already dispersing—fortunately. Windflowers join spring beauties and Missouri violets but follow southern plains trout lilies as harbingers of earliest spring. Spring beauties are an eastern plant near their western edge of range in the ravine. I know of only one population and one other in a cemetery, both gradually being extirpated by mowing. Why can't folks leave these beautiful natives alone until they finish reproducing? In cemeteries they are an especially fitting reminder of life's cycles.

15th. In late winter I transplant seedling plants from the ravine's trails to more protected spots to help restore this semiwild, seminatural landscape. Right now seedling Ohio buckeyes are moved from germination experiments that yielded a forty-five percent success rate but no insight concerning scarlet versus green first leaves. Overwintering butterflies greet me, and little brown (ground) skinks rustle through the leaves as the mid-day temperature reaches sixty-two degrees. I can't find a Missouri violet in bloom, although it's the right time to look.

Violets, plateau spiderlilies, roughstem sunflowers, baby blue eyes, and hill country dayflowers are replanted in east-facing draws. A few degrees warmer and sulphurs and goatweeds join the anglewing butterflies in sunny spots. Green anoles put in a brief appearance. All are especially wily because the air is quite cool though the sun is warm. Cold-blooded creatures like insects and lizards don't allow a close approach now, because they are relatively cool and thus slow to escape predators. They are genetically programmed to need more space and time to compensate.

Finally—one violet is blooming on the creekbank in a patch of afternoon light as if, like a butterfly or lizard, it picked that spot for sunning. Around my house and the surrounding woods above the creek, I can't find any others. That's curious, because over the twenty-nine years that I've made the comparison, violets on the sunny ridgetop bloom an average of six days before those in the cooler ravine, and others near my house, aided by its escaping heat, bloom earliest of all. But there are always modifications of repeated patterns as environments change, and that keeps me looking.

Some years Missouri violets bloom in late January but don't peak until mid-March. Then they enliven woods walks until the tree canopy closes. Their sky-blue freshness is so much more appealing than the dark blue garden violet imported from Europe. Missouri violets die back and may disappear in mid-summer, as the air turns hot and dry, but reappear with the first autumn rains, when they produce freeze-resistant leaves and a capsule that explodes seeds in profusion, too often onto trails. This time next year violets will again grow on the footpath and I'll continue transplanting.

16th. Since 1974 I've recorded breeding birds from now to mid-June. I'm dismayed by the fifty percent decline of summer residents that migrate to the tropics, but intrigued by the sixty-seven percent rise of permanent residents, coincident with suburban sprawl, and their apparent stability in the 1990s when my suburban census area ceased growing. Downy and red-bellied woodpeckers, Carolina chickadee, tufted titmouse, blue jay, northern cardinal, eastern screech owl, northern mockingbird, mourning dove, Carolina wren, house finch, and American crow are common residents. None declined or disappeared, qualifying all as reliable neighbors, by contrast to the forty-three percent of human families who moved over the same twenty-five years.

17th. Traffic and industrial park noises are louder in winter, because the colder, denser air carries sound better and there are no deciduous leaves to help block it. I must wait two months until the forest grows its full complement of sound-, sight-, odor-, and dust-buffering vegetation. How I wish eastern red cedars and Ashe junipers (cedars) were saved more often, since these evergreens are good winter screeners. But people dislike them. Aside from allergic reactions to cedar pollen, caused only by male trees with yellow, pollen-producing cones, I don't understand. Despite my own sneezing, juniper's many positives, such as wildlife food, water recycling, gas exchange, erosion control, and screening, far outweigh its negatives.

18th. Tonight, with Tchaikovsky's "Winter Dreams" playing, I sit down to read an editorial about the impending extinction of naturalists, since specialization is the mode in our culture. Folks can hardly talk to each other, let alone other people, because their languages are so different. No wonder the public has difficulty understanding that all life in the Biosphere must work together. Outside, in the drizzle of dusk, a male eastern screech owl sings. With the rhythmic beat of rain on the deck and the sweet trill of the owl, I need no other music and turn off the recording, put the reading down, and remember a night four decades ago—the first night Nancy and I spent in Butterfly Hollow, welcomed by the owl's universal language.

19th. With few exceptions plantings around my house are local natives, including the coralberries along the front walk sporting tiny new leaves today. Their magenta berries remain from last year, so this small shrub is decorative for several months. Most everything else is bare and brown, although trout lilies bloom, little brown skinks wriggle, and green anoles clamber into the bushes. Turning leaves under the coralberries, I may find torpid DeKay's (brown) and rough earth snakes. Leaf litter blankets these small creatures, protecting them against cold in winter, dryness in summer, and aerial predators all the time.

20th. Today is Mark's birthday. His love of hiking, skiing, and mountain climbing, and his general regard for the environment, must be traced in part to growing up in the ravine. Perhaps also to his childhood years of sleeping-bag living with us for months at a time in remote places, playing with the sticks and stones at hand because we had no way to bring other toys. Mark's appearance in Butterfly Hollow coincided with the annual reappearance of mourning cloak butterflies. Living practically worldwide, mourning cloaks remind me of the global community that my family has had the good fortune to experience.

Two months from now a new brood of adult mourning cloaks

will emerge, fly awhile, and become inactive in hollow logs or under leaf litter with the onset of hot, dry, summer weather. Like other overwintering butterflies, this species' irregular wing edges and color-pattern on lower surfaces make it a dead-leaf mimic, easily overlooked. Beginning in autumn and during sporadic warm spells all winter, mourning cloaks that have slept through the summer will fly about. Each one can live a full year without participating in summer, a natural lifestyle mimicked by certain humans who leave in summer for cooler climes in other spaces.

21st. Spring is often launched this last week of February. Its earliest nesting birds are secondary cavity users, who've begun looking at old woodpecker and natural holes. Added to these permanent residents are purple martins, the first returning neotropical migrants. Today is the average arrival date for males, locally called scouts, though we may occasionally see a few in late January. Martins fly about in small groups on mild days, feeding on aerial insects and checking nest boxes, but move southward on north winds ahead of freezing weather, only to return on south winds in a few days. They won't nest until April.

Do any local martins still use tree holes? All those I know of in suburbia use the apartment-type nest boxes that are so popular. Martins are colonial like most other swallows and require more than one woodpecker hole or other cavity per tree or several nearby trees with cavities. Similarly, all our chimney swifts appear to use house chimneys, although their natural nesting place is a hollow tree with an open top. While people erect nest boxes for martins, they cut down hollow trees and put screens over chimneys to keep swifts and other wild animals out. Consequently, chimney swifts are declining as purple martins are increasing.

22nd. Thanks to increasingly mild weather my furnace goes off today, although I may have to turn it on for short periods in the early morning after strong cold fronts. Running it all day after late February is a rare event. I prefer open windows, for then I can hear and smell the ravine's messages. My desk in Owl Hollow sits by a six-foot square window that admits a stimulating share of the natural world. Looking up from paper toils, as I do every so often, my biggest surprise was a young bobcat sitting twenty feet away, watching me intently, listening, and perhaps wondering with me what sense to make of its shrinking habitat.

After once looking at shy and secretive animals, like bobcats, and successfully photographing them, I began to realize that I usually averted my face when we crossed paths again. Even really big mammals were "disregarded," such as black bears that foraged around me, as I sat monitoring nature in remote places. It seemed to be a subconscious reaction that overcame curiosity. But why? I recognize that just being there changes naturalness, because I am novel and unnatural, but I don't respond that way to dooryard beasts, only to those that have a hard time with humanity. It must be a subconscious desire to interfere as little as possible.

23rd. Adding green to the brown landscape is a daily occurrence. At ground level, leaves are growing on trout lilies, spiderlilies, death camus, sunflowers, white avens, baby blue eyes, violets, and hill country dayflowers. Elbowbush, coralberry, possumhaw, and Ohio buckeye leaves are expanding above the wildflowers. Possumhaws' tiny lime-green leaves complement the darker green of shorter coralberry bushes and sapling buckeyes and the reddish hue of so much new growth at this low-light time of year. The springtime of native plants starts with those protected by the forest's leaf-litter carpet and moves up into the warming air.

For many mornings lately, the sun seems to swing ever farther north across the front of my house. I have a wooden bench a hundred feet away, where I often sit and meditate or think about such things. No need to worship the sun as ancient people did, hoping to control it, for its cycles are no longer mysterious. Religion as a means to placate or control might have been understandable once, but not now. Mystery, however, is a certainty, for I am awestruck by the coincidence of Earth's watery nature and its correct distance from our sun of correct age and energy and hence its ability to underwrite the play of life.

24th. The annual fashion show of deciduous trees—the beauty of lifestyle diversity—continues with falling American elm seeds, although cedar elm won't even bloom until late summer. Shumard, scalybark, and bur oaks will flower in succession soon but will eventually lose leaves in the reverse order. Pecan and western soapberry are always last with spring flowers and leaves. Since most trees are deciduous, folks expect the brown look to replace green in autumn, but Ohio buckeye surprises everyone with the fashion change in midsummer. More than appearance, though, trees parade single file along time's runway as a means of reducing stress that includes competition with each other.

25th. My favorite tree of the early spring is Mexican plum, but most people prefer redbud, because its profuse pink to magenta flowers are unmatched, whereas the plum's white is a common color. Perhaps folks don't like the plum's spines, but its astringent fruits are edible, if one is really hungry, and in autumn its leaves are beautifully orange. Most of all, Mexican plum adds an outstanding fragrance to early spring, a uniquely pervasive aerial perfume. Redbuds start to flower now, complementing arboreal Mexican and shrubby creek (hog) plums that began to decorate forest-edge galleries a few days ago.

26th. Carolina chickadees are conspicuous dooryard birds, very vocal in pairs or family groups, and amusing as well as instructive to watch as they store seeds behind loose bark or the siding on my house. They are cooperative, scrappy, and persistent. If they want a nest box, they get it, even though a tufted titmouse twice their size started to build there. And if they want a small tree hole, they get it, despite ownership by a downy woodpecker twice their size. Long ago, Nancy and I adopted the chickadee's whistled, four-note family call ("fee bee, fee bay") to use in assembling our own family in noisy public places.

Unlike titmice, chickadees like to re-excavate appropriated cavities. If my bird boxes don't have wood chips or other debris to throw out, chickadees may not use them. Titmice like hard-bottomed natural cavities, while chickadees prefer old rotted woodpecker holes, which usually keeps the two out of each other's feathers. Also, chickadees start to excavate and build several days before titmice and a month before downy woodpeckers lay their first eggs. In fact, wood-pecker holes usurped by chickadees are usually test holes or those drilled for winter roosts that are lower than holes drilled for nests. I've never seen downies contest the loss of their winter holes.

Chickadees fuss and fidget over the holes they remake to personal specifications. They'll work furiously for a few days starting about now, rest a few days, construct a nest, rest again, and lay eggs by mid-March. Nests are mostly grass, moss, and hair—no cedar bark, snakeskin, or bits of paper as used by tufted titmice. Four to eight fledglings appear in early April and feed themselves by late that month. Also, like titmice, they remain with parents through much of the summer, the last one usually leaving in September to join other adults and young in autumn-winter flocks that often include titmice and migrant or winter-resident species this time of year.

27th. A half-century ago the ravine's headwaters extended farther south, but construction of perpendicular four-lane divided highways cut that area off, and it became industrial and commercial. Among re-maining original trees is a giant eastern cottonwood sheltering a red-tailed hawk nest the size of a washtub, because redtails reuse their nests, which bulk up from sticks added each year. This nest is sixty feet high but only two hundred feet from a shopping center at the highway junction. When the cottonwood blooms, the female redtail incubates her first egg and watches humans who rush about, noisy and congested. Eventually, the cottonwood is cut down to make way for more construction.

28th. Eastern cottonwood is the second large tree to flower in the ra-vine, and today is its day. This majestic species, sometimes three to four feet in diameter, is neighborly with American elm, which bloomed a month ago. Both thrive along the creek, where the air is cooler than on hillsides, so it would seem that they should bloom later than upland trees. But they don't, even though at least eight streamside companions do, including bur oak, pecan, and black wal-nut. Cottonwood may flower early, because its floating seeds require spring winds for dispersal to bare creekbanks, where the young trees stabilize soil, permitting companions to join them in community. But why the earliness of American elm?

What a natural wellspring, cooling and refreshing the years, is the gift of wonder! It . . . keeps our days fresh and expanding. *Edwin Way Teale*

CHAPTER 3

Spring IS RENEWAL

March's Pace Quickens

Trees are busily leafing, but the forest is mostly bare, as light freezes slow growth until St. Patrick's Day. Even so, greening rains offset the early cold. The year's first broods of butterflies emerge, while others return from migration and add moving color to the stationary patriotism of rose, white, or blue windflowers. Blooming Ohio and Mexican buckeyes ratify our continental character. Earliest migratory birds augment the greatest explosion of biotic events all year. March is a burst of sensory enjoyment and learning with more daily firsts than any other month.

1st. Warm drizzly rain laden with Mexican plum perfume is irresistible for wandering, so I poke slowly along the creek looking for any remaining Rio Grande leopard frog or narrowmouth salamander tadpoles. Purple martins warble overhead, and redbuds have joined the blooming, but this morning's treasure is the first flowering baby blue eyes. Soon the drizzle stops, and the peeping sun heats the air to eighty degrees, the warmest so far this year. A rusty (Texas spiny) lizard scampers but does not climb, as a cold front seeps in through the bare trees.

While getting another plum fix at dusk, a pair of eastern screech owls gives sweet monotonic trills. Typical of mates, the two sing antiphonally, the high-pitched female in the entrance of my nest box, the low-pitched male in a nearby red cedar tree. Then the plum perfume gradually turns into essence of skunk. Someone's dog may have been reminded that this is skunk mating season. The males are wandering about, too often on the roads, as I note every year, when they become common highway casualties. I go inside again, as the front blows cold rain.

2nd. At dawn it is forty degrees. Enough damp and cold that I click the furnace back on and wish for sun. The temperature drop was thirty-five degrees last night. This time of year even fifty-degree changes in less than twenty-four hours aren't that unusual. Ten to fifteen degrees per hour is typical, often to freezing, followed by rises of five degrees per hour if the day is sunny. Today, though, no sun—the right condition for soaked fox squirrels to evict screech owls from snug roosting cavities, and that's exactly what happens, as my attention is drawn to an afternoon scramble. Yesterday's singing female is routed, while her mate sits impassively in his red cedar roost.

3rd. Spring may be sensed in a greening rain, followed by sunshine. I smell ozone and warm organic dampness, see tiny, lime-green leaves, and hear birdsong—the ambience of the season. As a child, Gretchen loved to dance in the rain and still likes to run in it. I purposely walk woods paths in the rain to feel the musty leaf litter and soil enriched by the nitrogen I can smell and use indirectly, deposited by raindrops and nitrogen-fixing bacteria in soil and plant roots. Greening rains arrive anytime from late January through March, once a year, more often, or not at all some years. They bring the landscape to life, but we will know it only if we walk in the woods on a day like today.

4th. The guttural chorus below my house belongs to southern leopard frogs. They croak and growl, not just at the water surface but completely under the relatively warmer water when air temperatures dip into the forties. They select ponded spots in the creek as did Rio Grande leopard frogs and smallmouth salamanders last fall. Sometimes tadpoles of those species swim freely among the breeding southern leopard frogs. I wonder what competitive or predatory effect the older tads have. Anything must be temporary, because transformed Rio Grande froglets and salamanders exit these creek pools in the first weeks of May, leaving the tads of southern leopard frogs alone for a month.

Shumard (Texas) oak is another reproducing southerner. Its reddish blooms dangle among tiny reddish green leaves. Locally called Buckley, Spanish, pin, or red oak, this much-confused relative of the southern and northern red oaks is a local favorite. One grand old tree is two and a half feet in diameter but only thirty-five feet tall, since it was topped in a storm. Most were cut in pioneer days and sprouted around stump edges, forming circles of multiple-trunked trees. Now they may die and fall, because a fungus plugs their circulation systems, and supporting heartwood rots. Their scarlet to burgundy leaves in November will remind me when Rio Grande leopard frogs and narrowmouth salamanders return to the creek.

5th. Oak acorns are sprouting in the leaf litter. Bright red seed leaves of the Shumards call me to survey seedling establishment and restock native plants. Because the ravine was abused ranchland, livestock gobbled everything edible, including small oaks. So I study forest regeneration and dig plants for restoring our nature preserve. Here and there in open patches amidst the oak seedlings, false garlic blooms and will flower again in autumn like the few other species, such as Texas aster, that connect our two rainy seasons. Greenish to reddish white (Texas) ash flowers make a first appearance too, and tonight I hear the first spring song of snowy tree crickets.

6th. Tufted titmice have begun nest building. I'll find their complete clutches of five to nine eggs in a week or two. After laying one egg each day, the songbird mode, females cover the clutch with nest material, which may include snakeskin, moss, cedar bark, mammal hair, and paper, effectively hiding the eggs from view. Carolina chickadees do the same thing. As I throw out combed hair from our dog and cat, titmice and chickadees pick it up for nesting. When I open nest boxes to examine their contents, incubating females of both birds hiss like snakes, an excellent ruse to foil predators, except snakes.

Titmice babies hatch in early April, fledge two weeks later, accompany their parents to my feeders, and feed themselves by late April, about the same time as fledgling Carolina chickadees. Conflicts are not apparent, because the families avoid one another. Scrappiness that so characterized chickadees during nest site selection has disappeared. I guess it's because the nesting effort is successful, so why spend unnecessary energy at an abundant food supply—a matter of food's cost: benefit. The youngsters will stay home through the summer, apparently because a familiar area with food, family alarm system, and other learning opportunities outweigh early dispersal.

Our titmice are intermediate between eastern tufteds and southwestern black-cresteds. Most adults have moderately dark crests with rusty foreheads. In the west, they sport longer black crests with tan foreheads, and to the east they have undistinguished gray crests with blackish foreheads. Our hybrid zone is around four miles wide along the north-south trending Balcones Escarpment and has been stable over the four decades that I've watched it. Black-crested and tufted titmice maintain their separate identities except in the ravine and vicinity—this meeting place of eastern deciduous forest and western evergreen woodland.

7th. Years ago, we might rush to open windows to see and hear returning geese or sandhill cranes, traditional signs of spring. Today, windows are too often closed—permanently. Folks sometimes confuse geese and cranes, but the cranes' long trailing legs and rollicking musical notes give them away. Many wheeling, swirling, lyrical flocks of dozens to hundreds of sandhills pass over in a day—untold thousands in late February through March. Crane music is as instructive to me as goose music was to Aldo Leopold, because sandhills also need wetlands to feed and nest in, and much of that habitat has been drained and plowed for crops. Both cranes and geese speak of our separation from the wild orchestra.

8th. Slowly ambling through my fifteen-acre bird census plot, I note early migrants but am pleasantly distracted. Looking and listening, I see that tiny leaves and flowers have appeared, especially on shrubs and small trees, allowing them to get a start on light gathering before taller trees clothe everything in shade. Mexican and creek plums, redbuds, and scalybark and Shumard oaks are well into bloom, and Ohio buckeyes are starting. Plateau spiderlily dots the warmer, upper slopes and ridgetops with blue and will color the cooler lower slopes and stream terraces a week from now. It lives only in central Texas—an endemic.

I discover a newly excavated red-bellied woodpecker hole twelve feet up in a dead white ash. An eastern phoebe catches honey bees on plum blooms but leaves a feeding monarch alone, apparently recognizing its toxicity. Phoebe and monarch are spring firsts this day, the *bienvenida* (welcome) monarch two weeks ahead of schedule. A flock of common grackles turns leaf litter on the forest floor, replacing migrated American robins and joining nine-banded armadillos in aerating the natural compost. I follow the leaf sorting, designed to uncover insects and last year's fruits, and see tiny spiderlily seedlings.

Carolina wrens are merry troubadours that sing with mouthfuls of nesting material, reminding me of Mark's comments about these "cheat-a-ba, cheat-a-ba" birds that disturbed his teenage sleep. Incubation begins in another week or two, eggs hatch in early April, and wrenlets fledge two weeks later, as second nests are already underway. Last year's nest that I remove from our old wicker fishing creel has animal hair and fine cedar bark inside coarse strips of cedar bark and leaf skeletons. No oaks but softer sugarberry, elm, and ash leaves with grass and small twigs are present with someone's grocery list, a sign of suburban living.

Older, more experienced eastern screech owls nest earliest, and I guess correctly that the gray male I've known for six years has a new gray mate with eggs. Screech owls make no nest but lay two to six eggs on whatever debris is in the bottom of tree cavities or nest boxes. Two other boxes have gray owls that fly out as I climb the ladder, and two more have familiar gray females, one eight years old and the other five, a bird that I banded as a nestling in another ravine a half-mile away. It is reassuring to see all the wild neighbors and know that we still share the same home.

9th. A dime-sized spot of "reflected sky" moves among grass clumps, and I follow. Its blue becomes gray as the butterfly rests with closed wings, hairstreak style. I peer closely, because I don't net butterflies anymore and want to see if this tiny creature has orange among the many dark spots on the back edge of its hind wing. If so, it is an eastern tailed blue, but if there's no orange it's a spring azure, and both should be tasting spring by now. If, instead, it is more gray than blue above with a white-bordered dark band and orange spots below, it is a gray hairstreak, another tiny early species, and if brown above it may be a female. Blues and hairstreaks are always a challenge to identify.

Their domain is the last patch of prairie in our preserve, now invaded by escaped yard grasses that replace the natives. Downhill, the butterflies and I fade into the woods. We reappear together in an old

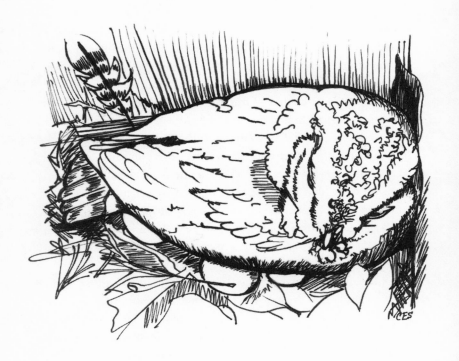

floodplain farming area overgrown with greenbriar, poison ivy, and thickets of roughleaf dogwood, smooth sumac, and eastern red cedar. A managed fire would help to restore the grassy habitat but is not permitted in suburbia. We fade again under a huge scalybark oak, a possible resting place for a pioneer farmer, since it escaped the saw that felled its neighbors. Here I pause to be reminded of forest grandeur that used to be.

10th. Green dragons are an early spring greeting, though it will be a month before they bloom. Expanding greenery at ground level hides these perennials, but I relocate them in places I've known from other years. This unusual wildflower with its single compound leaf and pulpit-like flower, enclosing a tapered yellowish "dragon tongue," is a cousin of the familiar jack-in-the-pulpit, a more easterly species that doesn't grow here. Green dragon is eastern too and reaches its western limit in central Texas. About the time autumn rains begin, dragons are easier to find because they advertise for seed dispersal agents with bright red berries.

11th. Blue jays are carrying sticks, building nests as high as they can get in canopy trees. While nesting, they are especially pugnacious around screech-owl cavities remembered from years past. They'll even fuss at new owl boxes in new spots, but they never mob chickadee or titmouse-sized boxes. Obviously, they've learned or instinctively know the potential for danger associated with larger cavities. By mobbing, I believe older individuals warn and instruct younger ones and inadvertently teach avian compatriots. Blue jays rank fourth on the screech owl's grocery list of birds but first in frequency of mobbing.

Jays themselves are predators on the eggs and young of the same songbirds that may join them in mobbing screech owls. And predator-prey relations may extend to two hawks, which the jays mimic in the right season. By mid-February they quit sounding like redtails who wintered here but left to nest in the open countryside, and they don't begin to sound like broadwings until they arrive from the tropics in about two weeks. Broad-winged hawks will nest and leave in mid-August to mid-September, after which the jays mostly forego hawk calls until redtails arrive again in December.

Blue jays must achieve something by mimicking the correct hawk, but I have no good evidence of what it is. Our nesting broadwings do catch a few birds, but I haven't seen them with a jay, and I don't know about redtails eating local birds, only rodents and snakes. Does the vocal mimicry deter predation, because hawks believe that another hawk already has that territory? Does the mimicry disperse other predators or potential competitors? Blue jays avoid the area of last year's broadwing nest, and, since they begin nesting before broadwings return, memory must serve them as well as it does with screech-owl nest cavities.

Predator-prey relations include American crows that are also building nests high in plateau live oaks and eastern red cedars with evergreen foliage to hide them. Both crows and jays are very secretive around their nests. One neighbor had a crow nest ten feet above her front door and never knew it. Crows may have learned to be that way for successful suburban nesting, because they are quite bold otherwise, casually feeding in open lawns and prospecting for bird nests. Crows eat bird eggs, nestlings, and fledglings, including those of blue jays, so they're greatly mobbed by the jays who are, after all, just small brightly colored crows.

12th. Both eastern tiger and pipevine swallowtails appear for the first time today, which is no surprise, since the tiger may depend partly on the pipevine. Both are certain spring heralds, but the mostly yellow tiger is more colorful than the blackish pipevine and thus more noticeable. A week ago I found fresh new tiger swallowtails on the Texas coast, and I might find the first ones in central Wisconsin in another month. This butterfly tells me that spring in eastern North America moves northward about two hundred miles per week in the warmer south but slows down north of the Mason-Dixon line.

Instead of being lemon yellow with black bars like males, early female tiger swallowtails are black with black-bar "shadows." They emerge a few days after the males but before yellow females and mimic the distasteful pipevine swallowtails for protection. Male tigers seem to prefer yellow females as mates; but black ones survive better, because predators leave them alone, so both color morphs persist in the population. In directing the play of life, natural selection puts black female tigers in the same scene with pipevines, thus gaining protective resemblance and the chance to mate with choosy males.

13th. Lucky day! Spring coralroot orchids are blooming for the first time in five years—spike-like singles or clusters of yellowish, reddish, or purplish stems up to ten inches tall, arrayed with dainty white, magenta-spotted flowers. They can't make oxygen from carbon dioxide and water, for they lack chlorophyll, but they are saprophytic. They absorb organic matter below ground, aided by micotrophic fungi, a habit shared with the crested coralroot orchid that blooms here in May and June. Both saprophytes live in areas of deep leaf litter and rotting wood, where they obtain nourishment from decay via their fungus partners.

The spring coralroot's infrequent flowering is no cycle that I've discovered. Six of my nine records of first appearances are between February 12 and March 13, so I look closely at winter temperature and precipitation and find that flowering is associated chiefly with rains totaling at least six inches between New Year's Day and first bloom. That's exceptional rainfall, since the January-February average is five inches. I'll bet that soggy soil enhances fungal activity, which promotes the nutrition needed for reproduction.

Reproductive interdependency is a common message. Plants bloom or not, produce seeds or not, or propagate vegetatively depending on the weather. Barred owls may not breed in food-poor years, and butterflies are unsuccessful seasonally if plant foods are scarce. Eastern screech owls lay more or fewer eggs depending on more or less animal food which depends on plants which depend on rainfall and soil nutrients dependent on soil bacteria and fungi. Relations are complex, but if I look and listen carefully, I see and hear all life dancing together.

14th. It has been a few days since I've walked in nature's busiest month of the year, so new exhibits are expected, and there are always surprises. As I approach a fallen oak, still holding last year's brown leaves, out jumps a black vulture. Only fifteen feet from the trail, it has two eggs on the ground under the leafy cover. Hatchlings will be black-faced, fuzzy, cinnamon-colored creatures, but I'll have to wait the forty days required for incubation. By June they will be adult-sized, have black feathers, and run about in a hunch-backed crouch, apparently trying to be inconspicuous. By August they'll fly. Black vultures habituate well to suburbia, an attribute I appreciate but my neighbors disdain, since vultures rank with snakes and bugs as undesirables.

15th. The Ides of March are portentous for Ohio buckeyes. The smallest mature plants are blooming today, but tree-sized individuals will require more time to transfer nutrients out of taproot storage. Following the gradient of increasing temperature from suburbia into the city, a tree at my house blooms a week after one inadvertently saved by a school in the city center. However, Ohio buckeye leaves turn yellow and begin to drop in July or August before any other trees, so they appear to be dying and are often cut down—the eventual fate of the downtown individual.

Do we lack curiosity about this unusual native? Is it lack of patience to wait a year to find out what's going on? Perhaps it's our penchant for control—for manicured landscapes that don't allow trees to lose leaves before we think they should. Ohio buckeye has a very different lifestyle that begins its growing season now, well ahead of most other trees, puts energy for next year into a taproot, and avoids summer heat and drought by becoming dormant early. This tree is nearly leafless by September, adding visual diversity to the forest's gallery of living art.

Local Ohio buckeyes usually have seven narrow leaflets instead of five broad ones and are considered a distinct variety or species. Yet their showy flowers are yellowish white with reddish touches, arrayed on five-inch, upright clusters at the twig tips, as they are in Ohio. Although beautiful alone, when decorated by feeding butterflies and day-flying hummingbird moths, the blooms are extra special. Some flowers develop into round, dark brown seeds, each with a tan spot that looks like a deer eyeball, encased in a golf ball-sized tan pod that dangles like a Christmas tree ornament until it opens and the buckeye falls out in October.

16th. Among March's butterfly flowers is fragrant sumac, the earliest of our four sumacs to bloom. It dwells in sunshine. Its inconspicuous flowers are butterfly magnets, especially for gray, northern, and juniper hairstreaks and Henry's elfins. Although named for its pleasant flower scent, the plant is also called skunkbush due to the skunky odor of its crushed leaves. These resemble poison ivy leaves in shape and autumn orange but have rounded instead of pointed tips. Moreover, fragrant sumac's berries are reddish brown, unlike poison ivy's white berries. I used to enjoy fragrant sumacs outside my study window, but they died in the increasing shade—traded for shade-tolerant American beautyberries and strawberry bushes in the relay of reforestation.

17th. St. Patrick's Day may be wintry with a freezing night, but spring will return promptly. Despite the increase in vernal signs, including longer days, it is easy to be reminded of the seasonal seesaw. Freezes can be as late as April, fittingly on April Fool's Day, although late freezes usually are no lower than about thirty degrees for an hour or two. Native vegetation is unaffected, since it has acted on this stage for several thousand years, but exotic fruit trees can take a hit. Peach trees froze again this year, although their chances may improve, since the average last freeze has "improved" twelve days over the last two decades.

18th. *1960s*: Black-chinned hummingbird, white-eyed vireo, blue-gray gnatcatcher, and black and white warbler are earliest returning summer residents, and they are back. Chuck-wills-widow and ruby-throated hummingbird will appear in another week. Hummers weave turret nests on top of branches at or slightly above head height at the edges of clearings, and the gnatcatcher has a similar nest but higher. The vireo hangs its egg baskets from low twig forks on border shrubs, while the warbler, a strikingly striped inspector of tree bark, nests on the ground deep in the forest. But ground nesting is ill-advised in suburbia because of cats, rats, and fire ants.

1970s: No surprise that black and white warblers have ceased nesting because of predation and shrinking habitat. Black-chinned hummers were slowly evicted too, but naturally. They were common before clearings became shrub- and tree-choked and the forest grew taller, more shaded, and more humid. Natural plant succession substituted ruby-throated hummers for black-chins in one decade. The same thing happened for the same reason at the same time to two resident pairs of birds. Nesting ladder-backed woodpeckers and Bewick's wrens preferred the original grass and tree-clump ranchland and were replaced by forest-loving downy woodpeckers and Carolina wrens.

1980s: Metamorphosis of ranch into suburbia invited more brown-headed cowbirds that began to stay all winter because of suburban food and warmth. Then blue-gray gnatcatcher, painted bunting, orchard oriole, red-eyed vireo, wood thrush, and summer tanager disappeared as nesters. Cowbird parasitism and shrinking habitat were likely extirpating factors. Reduced area of habitat was critical, because restoration and growth of the forest should have promoted the forest-loving thrush, tanager, and vireo while demoting the gnatcatcher, bunting, and oriole that prefer shrubby thickets and tree-grassland mosaics.

1990s: Fragmented and reduced habitat and their suburban side effects are undoubtedly the chief causes of disappearances. Shrinkage and separation into semi-natural patches amidst manicured yards create edge habitat, which fosters edge parasites, like cowbirds, and edge predators, such as blue jays and American crows, not to mention the introduced cultural predators. Of thirteen original summer residents, only yellow-billed cuckoo, great-crested flycatcher, ruby-throated hummingbird, white-eyed vireo, and chuck-wills-widow remain. They employ the creek-bottom corridor for movement to and from a larger refuge of wildland around a public reservoir.

19th. Green darner dragonflies and painted lady butterflies are migrating on the wind's aerial expressway. Adult ladies overwinter at the south end of their range or migratory journey—ours in the U.S.-Mexican borderlands—and return a short distance north to breed and die. Their local offspring, like those of monarchs, take up the relay baton and make another northward flight. These produce a generation of great grandladies further north to make the southward jaunt in autumn, or no ladies if all die, and the migration starts anew from border populations next year.

Nevertheless, most butterflies are homebodies, as are two nickel-sized species I'm seeking—the black and orange pearl crescent of remanent grassy patches, and the juniper (olive) hairstreak of cedar breaks. I search to no avail but am distracted by swishing and swatting flimsy brown mosquitoes, active at cool temperatures when the sky is overcast. They're usually not so bothersome but are super-abundant now because of recent heavy rains. More than the biting, it is their pesky buzzing that bugs me. The green darners are refueling on this abundant food and, happily, I leave the ravine to them.

20th. Winter officially turns into spring on this vernal equinox, but only up north, for spring has been here a month already. On this sunny, seventy-degree afternoon, ripe for rambling, I find a favorite insect. Running, flying ahead, and doubling back to stay on familiar turf are several six-spotted tiger beetles. These perky, half-inch creatures with white spots on shiny green backs and large white jaws always sit facing whatever frightens them. As I approach, they raise up on straightened legs as if to elevate their watchfulness. I engage perhaps a dozen in wooded but sunny hundred-foot sections of the trail, half that or fewer in semi-shade, and none at all in grassy places or the deep woods.

Among other seasonal announcers are at least five species of june bug (beetle), the first of which emerges tonight—a nocturnal herald. June bugs begin life as plump white grubs in the soil, eating plant roots, including yard grasses, and thus are anathema to suburban lawn growers who use poison to get rid of them. The adults swarm to patio lights, making them easy pickings for many nocturnal predators. Spring would simply not be spring without june bugs. I used to joke about people raising them in lawns to feed our wild neighbors, but now that pesticides are so widely used I worry about secondary poisoning of the predators.

21st. Presaged by its white flowers, I can almost taste the wild treats offered by southern dewberry vines. Dewberry is our local version of the eastern blackberry, and its vines have taken over a sunlit area of disturbed soil on the sewer line scar. Traditionally, Gretchen, Mark, and I will harvest the berries for Mother's Day. Today we locate several potential sources—roadsides as well as trailsides—because alternatives are needed when backdoor supplies run out. Like natural predators we've learned where to find concentrations of food and return to them in sequence of the best potential harvest.

Mexican buckeye grows above the spiny vines on an open slope, adding pink above white and mild perfume to the spring air. Its showy blooms replace fading redbuds as it reaches the peak of flowering about April Fool's Day. This shrub with pecan-like leaves is what local folks think of when I mention buckeye, because it has dangling seed pods housing dark brown seeds with light tan "pupils." But unlike the much scarcer and less familiar Ohio buckeye, Mexican buckeye seeds are the size of small marbles and usually number three per pod, which is lumpy looking and remains on the bush for up to a year after dumping seeds.

An empty seed pod may become home for the bold jumping spider, a hairy, black and white, half-inch clown. All jumping spiders are wonderfully instructive, but this striking species is just plain brash as the common name implies. One can fool these comic creatures into investigating a poking finger or twig and watch them jump several inches out of the way when they see it isn't food. Courting males wave their banded forelegs at females, running back and fourth around them. I think bold jumpers are the ravine's smallest comedians, so we search for them in buckeye pods while evaluating the dewberry potential.

22nd. Redroot is blooming, and beneath these small shrubs of forest glades I find the earliest narrowleaf puccoons with their frilly yellow flowers. Redroot has tight, round clusters of white blossoms and a heavenly odor that attracts me and a myriad of insects. I see giant swallowtails, painted ladies, monarchs, and dogface sulfurs from a distance and, close up, the little juniper hairstreaks I couldn't find earlier. Redroot is closely related to New Jersey tea and a cousin of our Indian cherry. It must live in a well-drained sunny site to survive, which I regret, as my yard-woods is too shady for this special native.

Downslope in the wetter creek bottom is a gustatory spring delight, the morel mushroom. Tan in color and only a few inches tall, morels look like small conical brains. It's a good spring for them because we've had so much rain. Some springs our harvest is zero. We'll pick enough for omelets or a lightly buttered and sautéed accompaniment to a salad supper. They must not be overcooked. Sometimes I find that an eastern box turtle beats me to a patch of morels, but I've never noticed that these mushrooms are anyone else's taste treats.

23rd. Along forest paths I brush away the single silken strands of inchworms and owlet-moth caterpillars that descend these "bungee cords" from oaks to the ground to pupate and become small brown moths. At the peak of brush-the-face walking, these tiny but voracious eaters may defoliate trees. Birds love the outbreaks. There will be uncountable fat, dangling caterpillars on a warm sunny morning, and dozens of cedar waxwings and yellow-rumped warblers flycatching them. It is a veritable aerial circus of avian high divers, cannon ballers, and trapeze artists with a wandering ground crew of thrashers, wrens, and perhaps grackles picking up.

Not only do the first migratory waves arrive at the right time, but resident birds reproduce in concert with the caterpillars. Chickadees, wrens, and titmice in particular begin nesting by this date and fledge youngsters as the bungee jumpers peak in April. There is plenty of fresh protein for growing baby birds with extra for hard-working parents. Thus does spring's flush of vegetation feed the herbivores, who may feed insectivores, who feed carnivores such as ringtails, eastern screech owls, and black ratsnakes. This forest chorus harmonizes with seasonally tuned events.

The danglers have a specialist predator at night, an inch-long, metallic, greenish purple, orange-rimmed beetle with a repellent odor. It is the fiery searcher and appears a few days after the first bungee jumpers. On the ground and in trees, it lives to eat caterpillars, mate, and produce flat, black, equally predaceous larvae. Considering the likely toll by so many predators, it's a wonder that any jumpers become moths, but only cold dry springs really depress them, for the predators are regulators that appear in proportion to prey numbers. When caterpillars are few, fiery searchers are scarce, and the avian circus stops in other cities.

24th. If we had an invasion of northern finches during the winter, most of them leave for home in this last week of March. Purple finch, dark-eyed junco, pine siskin, American goldfinch, and white-throated sparrow, plus a few non-finches such as northern flicker and red-breasted nuthatch, comprise the departing group. Through the last week of April, though, the white-throats, flickers, and nuthatches are gradually replaced by brethren from farther south. Having banded the winterers who've left, and their replacements, I've learned the repeated pattern that adults and males are replaced by yearlings and females.

Purple finches and goldfinches are especially colorful, since they began molting into bright breeding plumage a month ago. Older male purple finches stay plum-red, but the yearlings are coloring up and are easily distinguished from brown females and our resident "strawberry-spilled" house finches. Male goldfinches really brighten in white, yellow, and black. But I don't see hordes of northern finches every winter—often none at all. Northern food supplies have to fail coincidentally with harsh weather to force them this far south. We've been heavily invaded just fifteen times at an irregular cyclic interval that averages three years.

However, something new is happening, because big purple finch and pine siskin invasions seem to have ended in 1982–1983, after which goldfinch-only winters began. Could warmer weather be the cause? Are the birds staying north or going somewhere else? Is the increase in northern bird feeders sufficient to tide them over? One of my banded purple finches spent a subsequent winter in Nashville, Tennessee, a much larger town with perhaps more feeders. If the cause for change is at the breeding end of migration, it may be widespread, since colleagues found my winter-banded purple finches nesting in northern Minnesota and western North Carolina.

25th. Glancing outside, I see a freshly minted giant swallowtail, the last emerging and largest of our four common swallowtails. Pipevines, blacks, and eastern tigers appeared two weeks ago. All adults are feeding well, since seven native wildflowers and five native shrubs and trees are near their peak of bloom. These include Missouri violet, plateau spiderlily, Ohio buckeye, and rusty black haw in my yard-woods. Eventually, I'll find giant swallowtail caterpillars eating hoptrees, prickly ashes, and patio-potted lemon trees about the same time as black swallowtail caterpillars eat garden parsley, dill, and carrots.

Giant and black swallowtails and migrating monarchs decorate an Ohio buckeye, inviting me to search for a snowberry clearwing or nessus sphinx moth. Both are small, day-flying, and hover like hummingbirds—really marvelous creatures. Sure enough, a chubby nessus darts between buckeye blossoms. Also about are the last few overwintered mourning cloak, red admiral, and questionmark butterflies, but they're listless and ready to turn the ravine over to this year's first descendants. My break from culture is a reintroduction to the cycles of old masters, new art, and the interlocked diversity of flower and pollinator color.

26th. Leaves appeared on upland oaks, elms, and ashes ten days ago. Today, the first creekside trees have tiny leaves, particularly American elm, box elder, eastern cottonwood, black willow, and sugarberry, but it will be several days until bur oak, black walnut, and red mulberry buds burst forth, and weeks before leaves appear on pecan and western soapberry. Pecan is always last in the ravine, as is velvet mesquite in upland drainages and culturally disturbed sites. Folk legend says that danger of freezing weather is past when pecan and mesquite leaves appear, and that's certainly been my experience.

27th. As a card-carrying member of the Biosphere I dislike any verbal expression implying that humans aren't animals—for example, veterinarians who say that animals get arthritis just like people do. We too are animals by comparison with plants, fungi, and bacteria; and we are mammals like raccoons, mice, and skunks, all distinguished from other animals such as birds, snakes, insects, snails, and worms by our insulating hair and homemade milk for feeding infants. The major difference between us and other mammals is our huge brain, which invents a culture that puts the Biosphere in harm's way. People could learn to say "humans and *other* animals," recognizing kinship as well as our unique unnatural history.

28th. For twenty years Louisiana waterthrushes were among the ravine's earliest and most regular pass-through migrants, merrily singing their wild ringing notes as they teetered along the creek. But they began to arrive less and less frequently through the 1980s and disappeared altogether for several years after 1990. In winter I continued to find them in Central American tropical forests, prospecting at ponds, along creeks, and on wet road surfaces after rains, but I very much missed them here. Now, in 1997, one intrepid individual arrives during the night, adding its much needed voice to the March music of home.

29th. Northern cardinals, often called redbirds, are among our best known and loved resident birds and are usually the first species European friends want to see when they visit, for there is no really red bird in Europe. The bright red males and their more somber brown mates make themselves well known by singing loudly and fighting windows or anything else that reflects their image. Moreover, cardinals come readily to bird feeders and are invariably the first and last birds to do so, especially at dark in winter when the demand for food is high and daylight is limited.

Can that be why eastern screech owls catch them so often? Cardinals are third among birds on the owl's local shopping list. More males than females are caught, although I find both sexes feeding equally early and late. I think it's because of the boldness and dominance of male cardinals, who displace shyer females at feeders. I can readily retrap banded males but not females, who seem to learn caution more quickly. Regardless of species or sex, however, it is the inexperienced fledglings that screech owls catch most often in the nesting season, and afterward they catch more of the domineering males.

The male cardinal's red plumage is no factor, because red is the weakest wavelength of visible light and is rapidly filtered out, especially at night when the eyes of diurnal animals become more sensitive to blue. Furthermore, red isn't seen by nocturnal, mostly color-blind predators. In trying to figure out why rufous screech owls predominate at mid-latitudes in North America, I discovered that those areas have the most humidity and cloudy weather. Water vapor in the air readily scatters weak red light and, together with overcast conditions, tends to hide reddish organisms.

Of course, male cardinals don't suffer excessive predation, or we wouldn't have cardinals. I banded one that lived eleven years, another one lived eight. Those that survive their first winter average three more, although I did find a small difference in longevity favoring females. Despite their predilection to catch permanent-resident birds in cold weather when cold-blooded prey are unavailable, eastern screech owls have made no dent in any of the ravine's breeding bird populations. Actually, as suburbia sprawled, cardinals and most other permanent residents increased in numbers. None declined!

Today, northern cardinals are building nests about head high in dense young cedars. Brown-headed cowbirds are least abundant now, so these first nests are scarcely parasitized. First fledglings will appear in late April. Second nests are started within a few days at the peak of cowbird parasitism and screech-owl predation on young cardinals in behalf of young owls. But any hard-hit cardinal pair will raise one or two more broods. Cowbirds are finished egg-laying and screech owls are through nesting when the last cardinal nest is started in late July, and the redbird's success increases accordingly.

30th. A few shrinking grassy areas are the only homes remaining to four small butterflies. Two orange and black species have caterpillars that eat asters in these prairie patches. The pearl crescent, an inch between wingtips, and the two-inch silvery checkerspot are flying now but are increasingly scarce in proportion to decreasing grassy habitat. Like most early spring butterflies, both will have at least three more broods in a normal year, but, during one hot-dry summer followed by excessive autumn rain and rejuvenated plant life, they surprised me with fifth broods in October.

The other two are brown, and their caterpillars eat—not overeat—their environment's superstructure. The little wood satyr is an eastern species with two white-ringed eye-spots on all-brown forewings, the red satyr is a westerner with one eye-spot and a burnt-orange patch. Wood nymph caterpillars also eat grass, but this larger butterfly has vanished because it demands more habitat area. The original ravine, a grassland-forest chessboard maintained by fire, plow, and livestock, is now a forested suburban "island," though I try to maintain a one-tenth-acre, grassy remnant in our ten-acre nature preserve.

31st. Each day I scan the sky for migrating broad-winged hawks. They return from a tropical winter in swirling flocks called kettles containing dozens to thousands of individuals. A really big kettle of a thousand or two flyers is one of nature's most awesome sights, and it's not seen every year. Each year, though, a pair of broadwings nests in the ravine, using only scalybark or bur oaks for its tree-canopy nests. Fledging is in late June. Before that the two or three chicks climb branches and make short hop-flights for a week or two, returning to the nest to be fed. They begin serious flying by mid-July and are mostly independent by late August.

When broadwing chicks hatch in May, their parents put red mulberry twigs with leaves in the nest. Such greenery characterizes the nestling stage of many hawks and eagles, but its function is uncertain. Sanitation, air freshener, camouflage, and sun or wind screen have been suggested. All local broadwing nests I've looked into have red mulberry leaves, which are among our largest. Bur oak leaves are large too, but the twigs are stout and perhaps harder to snap. Because the leaves are concentrated on the nest's west side, which is only partly shaded by the nest tree's growing leaves, I guess that they shade chicks when an adult can't.

Local broadwings represent a small, disjunct, western population of this eastern species. They were newcomers to the ravine in 1975, about a hundred miles removed from brethren in east Texas. Blue jays immediately began to imitate them, as they'd always done with red-tailed hawks. Perhaps they learned the un-hawklike call, a plaintive "peer-ee," through cultural contact with east Texas cousins, who'd known broadwings for millennia. This hawk is the only local colonist among neotropical migrants, since the ravine forest grew vertically while shrinking horizontally. I'm not sure why they're here but I'm happy that we've gained one summer resident, because we've lost eight.

If future generations are to remember us more with gratitude than with sorrow, we must achieve more than the miracles of technology. We must also leave them a glimpse of the world as it was created, not just as it looked when we got through with it. *Lyndon B. Johnson*

April's Bustling Woods

Warm days, cool nights, everything greener—that's April. The tree canopy closes, not to open again for seven months. Blooms of all descriptions scent the air, enticing insect and avian pollinators. Joyful song greets every dawn, and once the sun is up tiger beetles and lizards join me on trails. Name-calling nightjars and sweet-trilling toads announce nights illuminated by firefly lanterns. Fledglings of some cavity-nesting birds enter the proliferating world, mingling with newly arrived summer residents and accompanied by the year's major push of northward-heading passage migrants.

><

1st. Black-chinned hummingbirds return from the tropics nearly a week before ruby-throated hummers, although they live in more exposed habitats. I'd think the cold winds of early spring would be stressful in their open, ridgetop woods compared to the rubythroat's ravine forest. Somehow, though, they are adapted to temperature extremes in a habitat without a buffering tree canopy. The two hummers are equal in size and otherwise similar enough that I wonder how blackchins tolerate the earlier exposure. They've been here a few days, while rubythroats just arrived.

Immediately, a courting male rubythroat does his lateral buzz display before a perched female. I linger but don't see the slower, aerial, arc-like whistle-dive that usually comes first. This behavior is like the blackchin's and requires aerial space. Today's rubythroats are in a shrubby clearing on the mend from bulldozing, a spot where the sewer line turns across the creek. They hawk tiny insects in such openings and, similar to blackchins, place their nests close to head high in the outer foliage of trees at or near natural or cultural edges.

2nd. Another edge species, an occupant of leaf-mulched, rocky slopes and draws, is blooming. The ravine is its northeastern limit of range. This pretty little annual plant, the hill country or false dayflower, lives only in central Texas—an endemic like plateau spiderlily and twist-leaf yucca. Unlike widow's tears, a perennial dayflower that grows as scattered individuals and blooms later, the hill country dayflower forms dense colonies, apparently because its tiny seeds can't move far. The flower's light blue petals frame yellow stamens with a white petal below and suggest a smiley face—a good message as I stroll by.

Natural edges are rarely abrupt but are gradients of grasses into shrubs into trees, or rivulets into creeks into rivers. Suburbia, however, produces sharp edges as between lawns, gardens, walkways, and streets and then barricades them with fences and "no trespassing" signs. Gradual natural borders are living space for distinctive natives like hill country dayflower and hummingbirds, whereas suburban edges are uninhabitable estrangements between "mine" and "yours," nature and culture. Why aren't we comfortable with transitions? Ownership is involved, of course; but fear, condescension, and condemnation are pertinent human views.

3rd. If I don't walk before dawn, I step outside in the dark and sit to listen. At night I may read outside and watch the insects attracted to patio lights, in turn attracting toads and geckos. How long I stay depends on how cold, wet, or mosquito-bitten I get. I can hear migratory birds now—the first upland sandpipers (plovers) chortling in the sky—inviting me to tomorrow's pastures to hear their wolf whistles. No pass-through whip-poor-wills yet. They precede nesting chuck-wills-widows by about a week, and mimicking northern mockingbirds will tell me when they arrive.

Yesterday's chimney swifts and a flock of green darner dragonflies rode the south wind. The swifts are punctual, always arriving within a few days of this date, whereas other species such as ruby-throated hummingbirds are affected by inclement weather and have a two-week leeway in arrival time. Chimney swifts roost and nest in more protected places, such as hollow trees and suburban chimneys, while hummers shelter in foliage. Moreover, swifts reduce their metabolic demand for food and become inactive (torpid) for days in weather too cold and rainy for catching insects, whereas hummers are torpid only overnight.

Most new houses in the ravine have wire over their chimney tops, so the swifts can't enter. My house does. Without the barriers we could be bed and breakfast for such guests as fox squirrels, raccoons, opossums, and ringtails. I do worry about the fate of swifts, though. Suburban chimneys are necessary substitutes for naturally hollow nesting trees, as the woods are cut and old trees fall down and are removed from yards because they are unsightly. I'm thinking of building a chimney tower just for swifts, whose happy clicking overhead is such a welcome sound.

4th. Halfway down the Owl Hollow trail is a rocky gully where I pause to hear the discourse of fossil ammonites. They are shelled creatures, almost a cross between a squid and a snail, that grew to six feet in diameter in seas that produced the ravine's bedrock. They vanished when a giant asteroid or meteor hit the Earth and severely changed its climate sixty-five million years ago. Yet their extinction, together with other prehistoric life, averaged only about one species per year. That's miniscule compared to today's unnatural cataclysm of an estimated one hundred species per day. Asteroids and meteors are brainless, but humans are not and might listen to fossil messages in this age of missing information.

5th. Flying just ahead of me along the path, a white-lined sphinx moth zips a few inches aboveground, pausing on small plants to drink dew. It ignores the first possumhaw flowers. It too is an annual first, a dawn and dusk flyer that sandwiches its role in the play of life—its ecological niche—between the day and night niches of other nectar feeders. It is an edge inhabitant in both time and space from boreal Canada to tropical Central America; and, like other natives that live life on the edge, it is quite tolerant of change compared to the many species extirpated by suburban sprawl.

Once we had a group of property owners interested in conserving the ravine but couldn't agree on methods, because we'd have to give up a few personal rights and resale value—or so some of us thought. And our city refused to create an ordinance to protect the forest that brought us all here. Fortunately, my planned-unit development had already agreed to protect its ten wild acres, two other owners expressly saved twelve adjacent acres, and the city has about three disjunct forested acres in a park, but the total is a paltry fifteen percent of the wild landscape.

My suburb has only two-hundredths of a wild acre per human resident to supply necessary natural goods and services such as oxygen,

climate moderation, and water renewal. We can't do these things ourselves, certainly not without great expense; and, behind closed doors
and windows, equipped only with electronic messengers, we forget or
never learn about our need for wildland. We require about five wild
acres per person in my town, based on a calculated wildland to human ratio that depends on regional climate (more land per person if
cooler and/or dryer, less if hotter and/or wetter), and this morning's
white-lined sphinx reminds me of that need.

6th. Hawthorns have an identity crisis, because they hybridize and
blur the absolutism so dear to some people. New study is needed, including molecular analysis, the kind of laboratory work that I'm not
interested in doing but is important to my understanding. Maybe
hawthorns aren't crossing locally, for I think I can tell three species
apart in time, space, and by appearance. Hybridization might not
happen here, or not often, since green hawthorn is flowering today,
two weeks after downy hawthorn reached its peak, and a week before
I will see flowers on cockspur hawthorn.

Downy hawthorn blooms first, perhaps because it lives in creek
bottoms beneath taller trees and displays flowers to insect pollinators
much better before the leafy tree canopy clouds them over. Green
hawthorn lives on forest-grassland edges, an intermediate habitat,
while cockspur grows under a clear sky on rocky slopes in the shal-
lowest soil. It is exposed to browsers such as white-tailed deer that
could knock it over or pull it out, which may be why it has the longest, stoutest thorns of all. Cockspur thorns are well named—they're
really fierce!

7th. All this first week of April, white ash and Shumard oak frass
is blown into windrows, then washed into spongy rainrows. I sweep
every few days to get it out of the garage and off our walks, because it
sticks to my wet feet, gets tracked inside, and, if I let things go long
enough, fills a sweeper bag in no time at all. The oaks around my
house drop frass in the same sequence as they bloom: Shumards first,
then scalybarks, and finally plateau live oaks, although there is considerable overlap. I like to think of frass as spent oak blossoms, although
traditionally it is arboreal insect droppings.

I use it as mulch around repositioned native plants or throw it back in my yard-woods. People use their electric blowers to blow it away from private concern, meaning into the trash. Spent blossoms, acorns, cottonwood cotton, soapberries—practically all reproductive efforts by native trees—are scorned because they are "messy," and the offending trees may be cut down. We can't have it both ways, though. The beauty and shade that drew us into wooded suburbia must reproduce, or there would be no such natural amenities. Why then are we more protective of the things we build than those that built us?

8th. Most resident birds begin singing about twenty-five minutes before sunrise. Migrants sing twenty minutes later. Each clear morning since the vernal equinox, birds start about one minute earlier. Northern cardinals and Carolina wrens are first, followed by Carolina chickadees and tufted titmice. A male screech owl hunts well into the morning twilight. He's active at least fifteen minutes after the songbirds begin or about fifteen minutes before sunrise. No wonder I find bird bodies cached in his nest, especially when the first owlets hatch and his responsibility to feed his family increases. Fifty degrees at dawn is too cold for him to find enough insects.

This male's mate is ten years old, so she's been handled a lot and only snaps her beak as I count six eggs, none hatched. The next pair I check on is a total surprise, because the female had two eggs a week ago but none now. Yet her larder contains a green anole from yesterday and a Nashville warbler from this morning. Either a predator got her first eggs or she removed infertile ones (females may carry unhatched eggs in their mouths and dump them in the woods). If predation, why is she back? Screech owls renest but normally not where they've experienced disaster, since predators revisit good restaurants just as humans do.

She's unmarked, so I band her and check her age based on flight feathers, which in yearlings are broader and more easily worn at the tips and have breaks in the color pattern called fault bars. She's a first-timer alright. Perhaps her mate has nowhere else to take her, or his hunting prowess, revealed by the stored food, is too strong an argument against moving. I have a hunch that something's happening at another nest box by my house, because a screech owl flew over

my patio yesterday morning, bill-snapping at foraging fox squirrels. Thus cued, I look and am thrilled to find an unbanded female with four eggs.

9th. With the bedroom windows open at night, a newly arrived chuck-wills-widow lulls me to sleep. Nesting "chucks," our wintering poor-wills, and pass-through whip-poor-wills sing their names explosively at night, so they're called nightjars. To me, however, they are night crooners. Why do I sleep through a chuck-wills-widow but not a neighbor's patio party or barking dog? Maybe I'm just happy to have a bird back from migration this spring of 1989, since they are declining. After 1990 they no longer nested in Owl Hollow, probably due to disturbed ground of the new sewer line and consequent explosion of introduced fire ants, the scourge of all ground nesters like chucks.

Tonight they begin singing about 7:15 P.M., knock off for a few hours around midnight, and resume about 5:30 in the morning—a great beginning to any day. In about a week, they'll sing off and on all night, beginning at 7:25 P.M. A month from now they will get the evening started about twenty minutes later and be back to their initial bimodal schedule, because they'll be settled and nesting. Eastern screech owls don't like them and give defensive descending trills or screech and snap their beaks at flyby chucks. If competition for food is involved, the owls have an edge, for they begin hunting about half an hour earlier.

Chuck-wills-widows move their eggs if disturbed, although maybe not in response to fire ants that swarm too quickly. Like screech owls, they transport the eggs in their mouths, but will tolerate a couple of flushes, flying around in circles "growling" before moving. Yes, indeed, they make a sound like a growl! I just wish they weren't so difficult to know personally, for I'll bet they have other strange messages. Nests are very hard to find, since the birds sit tight and are the cryptic equivalent of a screech owl but with feathers colored like leaf litter instead of tree bark. I've only chanced onto two clutches and one flightless youngster.

10th. Folks are driving about the countryside enjoying bluebonnets; and I can smell them, although the nearest patches are a half-mile away on a highway embankment. Chinaberry, an escaped exotic from Asia, blooms just as sweet and blue, and I enjoy its odor on the night air despite its weediness. Black willow and Eve's necklace join the burst of mid-April's flowering trees. Eve's necklace in fragrant shades of pink and white lives mostly along the Balcones Escarpment. Usually it is a small tree that grows vine-like beneath the forest canopy, but a large local individual is fourteen inches in diameter and thirty-five feet tall. Folks want to know why it's named Eve's necklace, and I tell them to look for its strings of black-bead seeds this fall.

11th. Once upon a time a favorite butterfly, the California sister, expanded eastward and included the ravine in its new digs. Perhaps the invasion was caused by a population explosion to the west. The sister characterizes southwestern woodlands with a summer monsoon and evergreen oaks, junipers, and pines, although our summer is dry and pineless. I first noticed adults on plateau live oaks this day in 1971. They were common for awhile but began to decline in 1975 and vanished by 1980 as mysteriously as they arrived. In April 1998 a few reappeared but disappeared quickly. Such colonizations and extirpations typify species at their range margins, where environmental restrictions are so severe for them personally that the pioneers are in constant jeopardy.

12th. This is late in the season for tree-pruning wind, but it's a hard wind we've had the past few days. At twenty-five miles an hour, wind strips tender new leaves and green twigs and breaks dead twigs. At fifty miles an hour it breaks branches and fells damaged and dead trees. I've wondered why our woodpeckers don't get started nesting until now, although they drill holes in February. Are they waiting for the spring wind to test a new nest site's durability? They may take time to assess new holes, since they drill several but raise only one brood annually. Chickadees, titmice, and great-crested flycatchers also raise a single brood but mostly use old woodpecker holes tested in the high winds of previous years.

13th. Nesting is over already for some successful cavity users. Carolina chickadees and tufted titmice just fledged, and the male ladder-backed woodpecker who used the titmouse nest box as a winter roost returned at 8:00 P.M. to spend the night—a seasonal exchange of tenants that has occurred on schedule for the past three years. The vanguard of migrants is finished too, because house wrens are here to lead the main parade. Carolina wrens and northern cardinals are among multiple-brooded songbirds that have begun second nests, summer residents arrive, and every few days new passage migrants freshen up the forest.

Wood ducks are back and inspect my owl boxes. They are too big to enter but attempt to squeeze inside. The male sits on a nearby tree branch, while the female pushes but can't get in the two-and-three-quarter-inch opening. Sometimes she gets stuck temporarily. Woodies nest in natural cavities, and we see the females leading fuzzy, bobbing, ducklings down the creek. Black-bellied whistling duck is another tree-cavity nester, a new arrival from subtropical south Texas in the early 1990s, perhaps invited by climatic warming. I hope a pair will nest eventually, for any native addition is welcome as the ravine loses biodiversity and corresponding functional integrity.

14th. Mid-April is a time of major change in the living landscape, because deciduous leaves have grown sufficiently to close the tree canopy and shade everything below. Only streamside pecans and western soapberries are still mostly bare. Canopy closure is determined by the date of the last freeze, coming about one month afterward. Over the years we've had a few April freezes, mostly non-damaging, but twenty-eight degrees last year killed new leaves and delayed the canopy for three weeks. Only freezing weather tells me why and when the canopy closes and gives new direction to so many lives.

In the shade, trout lily and death camus are dying or dormant underground until next year, but the forest-floor fauna of cryptic critters is more active. Now the understory stays cooler, its temperature less variable. Mid-April's maximum temperatures average three degrees lower in the daytime, and the minimum is four degrees higher at night than in the open, whereas the difference was only a half-degree one month ago. Because the ground is cooler and the leaf-litter carpet is buffered against strong winds and the physical pounding of rain and hail, moisture is retained longer in the soil.

Mature forest is a space-stabilizing, impact-resistant influence, not only in terms of moisture and temperature, but in its support of multiple energy transfers and nutrient cycles. The vertical layers of ground-level plants, shrubs, small trees, and tall canopy trees offer a wealth of living space and food that cycle predictably among seasons. Wood, leaf litter, and organic soil are cyclic nutrient banks guarded by tree roots, especially on slopes and creekbanks. While the forest's arboreal set varies seasonally, its flooring is more stable stage space.

15th. A strong south wind brings calling, northward-heading Franklin's gulls by the hundreds. High wispy clouds, additional forebears of a weather change, come into view during the hour or so I sit beneath the gulls. A yellow-bellied racer crawls by. These several cues trigger thoughts of first Americans, whose survival depended on reading the wild—the south wind, migratory birds, cirrus clouds, and foraging animals. What a contrast to culture's indoor weather reporters, who are called meteorologists because they read the output of satellite data on computer screens and don't need to get it right to survive.

16th. Spice pervades the morning woods. The fragrance belongs to hoptree in the small-tree layer of vegetation—a singular community member because of its pleasant odor. A giant swallowtail lays eggs on its leaves that will be eaten by the butterfly's brown and white caterpillars in a few days. Although conspicuous against the bright green foliage, these caterpillars resemble bird droppings so well that they are ignored by hungry birds. But if physically disturbed, the caterpillars rear up and protrude a bright red, forked "snake's tongue" from their head. Now, that's a real shocker!

From blooming hoptrees shaded by blooming plateau live oaks comes the "buzz-buzz" of clay-colored sparrows, whose percussion-like music accompanies the swallowtail's egg-laying dance. The migrating sparrows seem to eat the blooms but hunt for pollinating insects. Their song is a guttural version of the high-pitched grasshopper sparrow's song, both easily mistaken for singing insects but real giveaways after one learns them. More importantly, their buzzing signals the interdependency of lives in the oak-mott community of springtime.

17th. On sunny mornings I may overturn flat limestone slabs in grassy openings and mark, record, and release small snakes that warm themselves beneath the sun-heated rocks. These heating pads are re-placed to protect habitat and the snakes are released back under them after jotting down body sizes, temperatures, and associates. I am curious about the usually unseen leaf-litter and earth-burrowing guild of five species, each less than a foot long. Particularly interesting is the Texas blind snake, whose togetherness under limestone, like humans in saunas, is special behavior. This species' moist-heat parties can number up to twelve per rock in late April.

Also astonishing is an estimate of 150 small serpents of all species per acre. Can that be right? No wonder a fifth of the eastern screech owl's vertebrate prey is snakes! The rough earth snake comprises sixty-seven percent of my catch and sixty-nine percent of the owl's serpen-tine food based on my observations of stored prey. Now, when owlets are hatching, I can count on finding a dead, rough earth snake in at least one of a dozen nests. Texas blind snake is the second most common species found by me and the screech owls (twenty-five percent). DeKay's, flatheaded, and lined snakes are much less numerous, according to both of us.

Rock turning and owl-nest inspections underscore the Biosphere's principle that predators take the most abundant prey. They also select vulnerable individuals such as inexperienced youngsters and old or infirm adults by contrast to prey that readily defends or easily escapes. Large individuals are chosen if possible, although two of predation's rules may cancel a third. If fledgling birds are abundant, for example, they are more likely to be eaten than larger, fiercer adults. Humans, by contrast, kill all with impunity. Scarce, large, defensive — it doesn't matter, because we employ weapons and strategies that separate us from natural constraints.

18th. Summer tanagers should be home from the tropics by now, but the ravine is no longer home. Their scratchy-robin song is seldom heard. The last pair nested in 1986, high in a big sugarberry tree by the creek within hearing distance of my open window. I miss the bright red males, yellow females, and their distinctive chattering. The summer tanager is another declining neotropical migrant, although its ravine habitat has improved in structure if not area. Reduced amount of habitat together with increased edge, leading to increased parasitism by brown-headed cowbirds and predation by jays and crows, are probable negative factors.

Returning summer tanagers were accompanied by thrushes, whose lyrics are mainstays of my spring fever. Before 1970 I could hear passing wood thrushes and our single nesting pair. Now there are no nesters and fewer passersby! A veery, gray-cheeked, or overwintered hermit thrush may sing special joy, but the first two pass-through thrushes are increasingly scarce. Nevertheless, every April I can count on Swainson's thrushes, and I try not to think of a spring without them. Certainly my grandchildren's experiences in the ravine are not like those of their parents, let alone grandparents, who are among the architects of unnatural history.

19th. Nancy and I take our dog and leave the ravine for a five-mile walk in ridgetop pastures along the Balcones Escarpment. We are seduced by the heavenly odor of Texas bluebonnet, blooming with Indian paintbrush and Texas star. Amidst motts of plateau live oak and Ashe juniper, the bluebonnets provide a classic hill country scene, often photographed or painted and proudly displayed by Texans near and far. Scissortail flycatchers scold our passage. Eastern meadowlarks and grasshopper sparrows sing in the grass, and a red-tailed hawk totes its snake lunch overhead. All are messages from a prairie springtime.

20th. Japanese honeysuckle blooms beautifully and smells wonderful but covers large patches of the ravine, twisting and strangling small trees and shading out native wildflowers. It doesn't shelter vine-loving green anoles and rough green snakes because of its immunity to the leaf-eating insects these reptiles require, but its small black fruits feed winter birds that disperse the plant from cultivation. This vine belongs to Flora Texana Diabolica, as one botanist puts it, so I try to destroy trailside honeysuckle but honor a neighbor's request to transplant some to hide an ugly electrical transformer. No doubt that this exotic's bad qualities outweigh the good ones, and the mixture confounds sound management by me—so far.

21st. As reliable mid-spring messengers, hackberry butterflies have just appeared. They also certify the end of autumn as the last large butterfly to disappear. Hackberries are conspicuous and dramatic—

eventful, to say the least—because they chase people, pets, and native animals besides other butterflies. Their caterpillars feed on netleaf hackberry leaves but primarily on sugarberries in the ravine. Locally, sugarberries are called hackberries and, indeed, netleaf hackberry and sugarberry may be respective dry-upland and moist-lowland varieties of the same adaptable species.

Tawny emperor and empress leilia are similar orange butterflies in this guild of hackberry leaf eaters. But emperors are darker in hue, lack white-ringed, black eye spots in their forewings—hackberries have one—and won't appear for another week. Empress leilias have two eye-spots in each forewing, are paler, and emerge the week after emperors. The threesome's staggered appearance is surely scripted by natural selection to minimize competition. As the play's director, natural selection's job is to arrange stage space and timing among actors to allow the largest, most harmonious cast of characters permitted by local resources.

22nd. Each July fourth for two centuries Americans have celebrated their political home but only thirty years ago did we designate Earth Day to pay true homage. All days are celebrations of life, but today is formally assigned to remind humanity of the inviolate alliance it has with the Biosphere. While ambling along the ravine's paths or just sitting at home, I am powered by sunlight with energy that rises through tender new sprouts of greenbriars I may nibble or the wheat, corn, or meat I eat. One day in time's circle, I'll return nature's favors, but today I sit in the forest and contemplate my role as land steward and leg in the relay of natural to cultural messengers.

23rd. Usually I don't band yearling female screech owls until they have hatchlings, because flighty ones may desert eggs. The longer I let them incubate without disruption, the less likely they are to abandon a clutch. Older owls have learned who I am and sit tight. Some snap their bills or hoot or screech, their way of grumbling, but let me pick them up for sure identification. Then I can set them back down on eggs or hatchlings without more fuss. Attending males, roosting in front of the nest hole, are unmoved. Later, when females roost outside and nestlings protest handling, I'll have to keep a close eye on both parents. Males with owlets may wake up to the defense of family, though their wives are usually the feistiest.

My oldest female parent is fourteen. She has four large chicks ready for banding and two cold unhatched eggs that I freeze for later chemical analysis of possible pesticides. Of course the eggs could be infertile, or she just couldn't get all six warm enough to incubate successfully. But she's always hatched five- and six-egg clutches before. Lately it seems that I've found increasing numbers of unhatched eggs. Surely she wasn't too hungry to incubate properly, because her mate is an expert hunter. Four headless black rats and a rough earth snake are stored in the nest box. Five days ago it was a male cardinal, cedar waxwing, and Mediterranean gecko. What's happening?

I exit from today's nest inspections quickly, because a cold front drops the air temperature ten degrees in thirty minutes, and I don't want to cause eggs or hatchlings to chill and die. As I climb one tree the yearling female flies out, leaving a hatchling and two eggs uncovered. True to form, her mate remains impassive. But she only goes about thirty feet and, as I carry my ladder away, flies right back into the nest box. It is a good thing, because time is increasingly short for this species that requires half the year to produce independent offspring. Walking back, I notice that the first white avens flowers announce spring's finale only about a month away.

24th. For daylight mammals like me, nighttime orientation is still mostly by sight, but I employ odors and sounds to fill in. Sometimes I walk trails to evaluate eastern screech owl densities based on their songs. Five males in a lineal mile of streamside forest is about average. Other times I take a clue from the owls' hunting strategy and just sit and wait at various intervals to hear or see what comes along. Last night a chuck-wills-widow sang taps for several minutes, then flew near me and "growled," disturbed by my presence. Every once in a while—probably more often than I detect—a gray fox trots down the path and detours around me, for it has learned about the cost of humanity.

25th. Purple martins are out and about in the pre-dawn darkness before we're chased indoors by thunder, lightning, and a downpour. It rains off and on all day, three inches total, as a norther blows cold air against warm clouds from the Gulf of Mexico. Between the "gully washers" a fledged family of Carolina chickadees forages, forming a nucleus for passage migrants of seven species. Cold fronts cause migrants to pause and feed temporarily—the "drop out" phenomenon —and their tour usually "employs" permanent residents who act as guides. Migrants will stay as long as necessary to refuel and catch the next south wind express to northern lands.

Stimulated by the rain, Gulf Coast toads travel to my pond and downslope to breeding pools in the creek to begin the first of several songfests. A month from now transformed toadlets will leave the water, and some will find suburban residences. If they're lucky enough to make it to a yard, garden, or potted patio plant and not be unduly disturbed by squeamish folks, they'll find insect food concentrated at lights during the hot-dry summer and won't have to dig in and become inactive. They'll grow into fist-sized, pop-eyed, comic creatures who window shop for survival, balancing their foraging time and distance against food availability—sending messages about cost: benefit analysis.

26th. Luminary naturalists have come and gone, so many before my time of course. I'd like to have known more of them. I'm thinking of John James Audubon, the great explorer and painter of birds, because he was born on this day in 1785. He explored more naturalness on foot and horseback than I will ever know, finding new birds and shooting them for art subjects, scientific specimens, and dinner. He didn't have a car, binoculars, or camera. I marvel at his accomplishments and can only try to comprehend his pioneering.

There is no wilderness left, in fact no unimpacted nature of the kind Audubon knew. I cannot venture anywhere on this planet without finding direct or indirect evidence of industrial technology. Humans have been everywhere, leaving chains of disruption or destruction, such as a thickening atmospheric greenhouse layer and warmer climate, even in the heart of vast preserves. Moreover, I rely on binoculars, cameras, and cars, whose manufacture and use bring more repercussions for the Biosphere than Audubon's spyglass, shotgun, and horse. And there are many more like me compared to Audubon's day. I am part of the concern!

Yet nature is only injured, not dead as some declare. All life changes nature, but modern humans have a destructive heritage, aided by the power of fossil fuels. Even my prehistoric ancestors were such devastating predators by dint of brains and tools that they caused or contributed to extinctions—a unique role for any actor. And now technology disrupts the Biosphere with extinction rates unheard of in ancient times. But nature is not dead, fortunately, or we would be too, for we are irrevocably bound to it. Nature remains the only model against which we measure humanity's increasingly lonely trail out of the wilderness.

27th. Painted buntings are flying rainbows. Each spring my first sightings are this week or in the first week of May. I'm prompted to keep close track, because bird-hungry visitors always want to see one, and Nancy or I will surely get a neighborly phone call that may sound something like, "Now I don't want you to think I've been drinking, but I have a bird in my yard that's blue, green, yellow, and red all over." Painted buntings are declining but still migrate by, stopping occasionally at our birdbath. They no longer nest, but I think that's partly because their shrubland habitat has been replaced by forest.

28th. When our homeowners association formally declared its ten acres of jointly owned ravine slopes and creek as a nature preserve in 1985, it was recognized by the National Wildlife Federation as the first such use of the common property of a homeowners association. I agreed to keep the trail clear for walking, since my neighbors knew I didn't mind "wooly boogers." So I cut gaps through fallen trees, clear branches, pull out poison ivy and cut greenbriar, poison exotic fire ant mounds, and mow a path through exotic hedge parsley before its tick-like seeds can hitch free rides. My human neighbors must enjoy semiwild walks or they won't support semiwild lands.

Nancy and I take interested folks on a guided stroll along our preserve trail—four-tenths of a mile—each spring and fall. At the entrance we descend a natural draw made shallow by our subdivision's developers, who dumped wood, concrete, plastic, and other scraps and covered it all with exotic soil. We point that out and show neighbors how our native plantings help to restore naturalness. We note how rapidly Japanese honeysuckle, poison ivy, greenbriar, cedar, and sugarberry invade, because their fruits are selected and the seeds distributed by animals. These plants are weedy—adapted for the fast growth necessary to hold the land together in early stages of reforestation.

"Wooly booger," by the way, is local country parlance for a really varminty-looking creature. One usually learns to fear a wooly booger and, because people live mostly indoors, hardly anyone has an impartial experience anymore. We tell our group about the new and strange life European pioneers found here, how their fears developed, how they attempted and in many cases did extirpate species considered fearsome or inimical to civilization as defined by their believed dominion over all life. On our walks we see people's reactions to organisms new to them and try to understand what they were taught to fear.

29th. Mississippi kites have just arrived from the tropics. They are the hawks that look and act like giant swallows. They nest only fifty miles northwest of the ravine, but I wish it was here, for they are the most graceful of local raptors. And what fierce nest defenders they are. Where they nest in golf course trees, these small hawks see a lot of club waving in their behalf. Although human caddies have been replaced by mechanical golf carts, some still have jobs as body guards against the diving attacks of Mississippi kites. Their reputation is notorious in certain west Texas towns.

Through early May I'll see a dozen or more in a migrating flock heading north on a stiff south wind or slowly circling in a morning thermal. I always hope they'll spend the night at my house. If so, they settle down by 8:00 P.M., a few per tree but not necessarily close together, the entire flock within an acre. They'll wake up, preen, look and jump about for perhaps thirty minutes, and begin flying around 7:30–8:45 A.M., or later when the weather is rainy or the wind from the north. If a really strong cold front moves in, they may stay, hunt locally, and return to the same roost, awaiting the next south wind.

30th. The spring parade of neotropical migrants is nearly half past my viewing stand, but this spring has been stormy, either delaying or diverting some floats. We've been two degrees warmer than usual but have had three times the normal precipitation thanks to *El Niño*. Yellow-billed cuckoos are due back to nest, but only ruby-throated hummingbirds, white-eyed vireos, and great-crested flycatchers have returned. Nesting chuck-wills-widows aren't back either, though I heard one passing through with orchard orioles and red-eyed vireos that once called this home. Late appearances are worrisome now that migratory birds are ravine dropouts.

Flower- and insect-decorated floats are easier to keep an eye on in the seasonal parade. They're built mostly of residents, appear earliest in the city, a few days later in the suburbs, and finally in the countryside, according to our warm-urban to cool-rural parade directors. Roughleaf dogwood and Texas marbleseed are blooming, and hoptree is at its peak. Fireflies (lightning bugs) are scheduled to emerge tonight. I can't wait, for I've loved these beetles ever since I kept a jar of them beside my bed as a child. Their blinking light in the darkness is a friendly message of reassurance—of belonging to their world.

This world, after all our science, is still a miracle; wonderful, inscrutable, magical and more, to whosoever will think of it. *Thomas Carlyle*

May Is Almost Summer

The bird migration is mostly over by mid-month, indicative of spring's fading. Countryside wildflowers have appeared and are disappearing. Cold fronts become infrequent and mild, sometimes stall, and often lack the punch to bring rain, although thunderstorms become more frequent. Towering cumulus clouds and lightning can be the year's best. This is a time of crawling snakes, cottonwood cotton in the wind, white-blooming yuccas, yellow cacti, and baton passing in the second stage of the monarch butterfly relay. Mother's Day is a dewberry feast and Memorial Day a chorus of green summer cicadas.

>̧€

1st. The overture starts at about 6:15 A.M. Singers are permanent residents and passage migrants such as orange-crowned and black-and-white warblers, blue-headed vireos, and Swainson's thrushes. Directed by the rising sun, the oratorio begins a few minutes later. An increasingly rare soloist, a wood thrush, has the lead, followed by black-throated green, blackburnian, yellow, Tennessee, magnolia, and chestnut-sided warblers plus red-eyed and warbling vireos with ovenbirds, least flycatchers, gray catbirds, Baltimore orioles, and rose-breasted grosbeaks in bit parts. I love Beethoven's Ninth Symphony but am just as awestruck by biodiversity's billionth.

2nd. A Great Dane runs to a fence across the creek and barks maniacally, a lesson in cultural stress, as Nancy and I return to our concert gallery of migratory birds. Farther down the path, through a grassy patch studded with flower color to match the birds, a gray fox sits quietly and attentively looking at us. How often such people-watching has happened over the years, I can't really say, but it's always a thrill to know that our interest is reciprocated. As I reach for binoculars, the fox walks nonchalantly into the woods, a study in the perceptive unobtrusiveness of nature.

Low petunia is flowering on the trailside and in similarly disturbed places, even in a few seminatural-looking lawns. It's an early sign of summer, mostly blue-flowered but also white in a few patches. Now we see the first strawberry bush (purple wahoo) flowers. Where did the name wahoo come from and what does it mean? I'll bet it's first American. This four- to six-foot shrub is pretty bland right now, the beautiful but tiny magenta flower clusters almost unseen, but it will become spectacular at year's end with scarlet fruits and leaves after most other woody species are bare.

Bumblebees bumble on blooming Texas marbleseed, and sitting quietly among them is a robber fly eating a honey bee. It's a mimic with black and yellow coloration that matches its bumbling companions. It fools larger predators into avoidance and unsuspecting prey into acceptance. Nancy finds an eastern box turtle with an olive shell, bright yellow eyes, and red polka-dotted skin. Confronted by such imposing predators as us, it closes up. I sit down to reduce the size of the threat, and the turtle reopens to the glories of our spring day.

3rd. White wisps float and eddy overhead, swirling in the breeze. They are cottonwood "cotton," white parachutes carrying the seeds of eastern cottonwood trees to disturbed spots, where they will sprout, protect the soil from erosion, and provide nest sites for orchard orioles in about ten years and red-tailed hawks in a century. Some folks don't like cottonwoods, whose roots can crack pavement and parachutes clog window screens. Neighbors felled a big one on my cul-de-sac, cutting off conversation with its wind-tossed, talking leaves, although a year after the sewer line was built in Owl Hollow, cottonwood seedlings appeared on the scar and discussed suburbia's changing stage in the play of life.

4th. Because birds select its black berries to eat and distribute its seeds, and its seedlings are hardy, Indian cherry (Carolina buckthorn) can be invasive. But it is a beautiful understory tree, growing to five inches in diameter and twenty-five feet tall in the ravine. Its lustrous lance-shaped leaves appear in March, turn all shades of bronze, orange, and red in autumn, and persist into the new year, so the foliage is decorative almost year-round. No other native woody species is easier to transplant or grows so readily in sun and shade. Yet its white blooms are so tiny that I often forget to look for them these days, unless the bees remind me.

5th. Hill country dayflowers are dying now, although a few plants may persist into June before becoming slug and snail food and scattered seeds among last year's moldy tree leaves. Their replacements, the year's first widow's tears (erect dayflowers), have begun to bloom. This darker blue species, a perennial more tolerant of shade, is scattered singly throughout the woods. When I gently squeeze the leaf that encloses the flower spike, a small drop of sap, or "widow's tear," appears at the tip, and I speculate about the sad circumstance when someone first noticed it.

6th. Curious how the air temperature always drops fastest in the hour before sunrise. Cloud cover moderates the drop, and today's clouds dissipate gradually, as the air heats from an early morning sixty degrees to a mid-afternoon high of eighty. Then a breeze stirs, and great cumulus clouds begin to form. They billow in the late afternoon. The breeze turns into a slight south wind, and I hear thunder. The wind stops—ominously still. The sky darkens and an east wind blows in the ozone smell of a greening rain, a favorite feature of spring.

May provides five to six inches of rain—our rainiest month—but its thunderstorms can be quite local. Owl Hollow gets nothing today, which is okay because I am still attending to the damage at my house from the last winter ice storm. I have new mulch, a many-winter wood pile, and new pubs for sap-sipping butterflies. Climbing, cutting, hauling, mulching, stacking, and sweeping wipes out four of us, who sit and sip sweet liquids, as the butterflies do. Several hackberry and leafwing types cue up on dripping tree sap, because we don't seal the cuts with tar. Native drinkers prefer them that way.

7th. I'm on banding duty, for eastern screech owlets grow quickly and are big enough to band at one week of age, just as their eyes open and dark feathers begin to show beneath white down. Earlier I painted their toenails to distinguish siblings. At one box I invite folks to see what I'm doing and learn why. The brooding female, used to my handling, is moved aside so the fubsy owlets can be extracted, weighed, banded, and replaced one by one. A freshly killed orange, white, and black Baltimore oriole is stored food, which I hold up first for all to see, and one person remarks, "My goodness, I didn't know baby screech owls were so brightly colored!"

8th. Polyphemus moths are impressively beautiful tan and reddish brown giants, whose forewings span six inches. Their hindwings are even more interesting because each has a round, translucent eyespot bordered by dark blue "eye shadow" in a brownish "face," semi-ringed with a dark wing band. A resting adult polyphemus hides its hindwings beneath its forewings. If disturbed, it suddenly raises the forewings, exposing the eyespots in an anti-predator display that I call owl blinking because the false eyes, accentuated by dark bands, resemble an owl's facial disks.

The display is no protection against owls, though, for I find severed polyphemus wings in eastern screech owl nests. Owl blinking may be effective only in daylight against mammalian predators and perhaps the songbirds that are startled when a screech owl suddenly opens its eyes, signaling threat. Several times I've watched birds harassing a slit-eyed, roosting screech owl until its eyes snapped opened, whereupon the mobbers squawked and "stepped back." When I climb to a screech-owl nest near fledging time, and nearby roosting parents give me the big eyes, I must take care. I may be attacked!

9th. The ravine's tree cavities house eight different mammals, including white-footed mice, bats and ringtails, six species of birds, two lizards, a snake, and untold insects and other arthropods, especially wasps, bees, and ants. These are secondary cavity users because none makes its own home in wood, although squirrels, mice, and carpenter ants, aided by termites and fungi, are hole-home remodelers. To this guild of forest dependents, add three species of woodpeckers (five in winter) who are primary cavity nesters, because they do original house construction. Their older homes are in great demand, as are natural cavities made by weather and rotting.

Cavity trees usually are members of the forest canopy—large, old, and thus more likely to have heart rot and be drilled or damaged. Many have been injured by wind, lightning, ice, and falling neighbors with sufficient time afterward for the animals and fungi to hollow out breaks and splits. Once formed, cavities are used by eastern screech owls for at least eight average owl lifetimes (thirty-two years). But suburban yard owners don't like the damaged look so fashionable in nature. They cut the trees, remove limbs with holes or fill them with concrete, leaving fifty percent fewer natural homes in wooded yards than in the adjacent forest.

10th. This sunny morning neighbors call to say that a big, brown, rough-looking lizard is digging in their flower bed. "Can it be an iguana?" I suggest not, because the brown species usually aren't sold as pets. I propose that it's an outsized rusty (Texas spiny) lizard, a large but often unseen tree cavity user, and walk over to their house to look. It is a rusty, indeed, a ten-inch female. She is laying eggs in a hole dug

beneath bedding plants only three feet from a mound of exotic fire ants. She fills the hole and leaves in an hour. Expecting to learn about hatchling rusty lizards, I return in two weeks to find that fire ants eat buried lizard eggs.

11th. Bright orange and black monarch butterflies have just emerged from gold-spotted, lime-green chrysalises that are my favorite living jewels. The adults are clearly labeled poisonous glycoside containers, because their caterpillars ate antelope-horn milkweed. They're a real contrast to the tattered, faded individuals of last March, newly returned from wintering in Mexico. I'm inspired to see fresh vigorous monarchs heading northward to find more milkweeds and begin the annual breeding relay that will take three or four generations of travelers into Canada and back to Mexico by November.

Monarchs are Texas' state butterfly and should be North America's symbol of internationalism, since their migration signifies the natural unity of our continent. They are teachers of a lifestyle befitting varied cultures—of the mind-opening messages of travel and temporary residence in places away from home. As Mark Twain once said, "travel is fatal to prejudice, bigotry, and narrow-mindedness." Monarchs are easily raised from eggs or caterpillars in small terraria. Nancy does it every year, and frees the adults as seasonal reminders that fenced political borders are the unnatural history of ancient human tribalism.

12th. Grassland plants such as milkweed are patchy in the ravine —just hanging on as this habitat shrinks under the successional onslaught of pioneering sumacs and disappears under cedars that thicken in the absence of fire. Cactus and yucca also live in the grass. Engelmann prickly pear, a low-growing cactus with red-centered yellow flowers, is the first to bloom, often surrounded by narrowleaf snake herb, as interesting for its name as for its demure blue beauty. I wish it was safe to burn the grassy patches and rid them of woody invaders, since fires caused by lightning, and those set by first Americans, have always been so important to prairie maintenance.

A reminder of those historic fires, some covering hundreds of miles, is in the air this May of 1998. All of Texas is enveloped by haze from cropland and forest fires burning out of control in Mexico and northern Central America. The smoky "flavor" has been here for several days, blowing straight north, and will remain for two months. By diffusing sunlight, it drops our normal high temperatures about five degrees, and by shielding us from nightly re-radiation, it increases the lows by seven degrees. Plant growth is slowed. What about winter habitat for migratory birds in the burned-out tropics? Because fires are natural, the Biosphere simply reverberates and readjusts, if human hands aren't too heavy.

13th. I am sitting quietly on a log watching a yellow-bellied racer climb into shrubs, prospecting for lizards, grasshoppers, and crickets. It is about three feet long, uniform olive-green on the back, yellowish below. This snake sees the world with binocular vision, as I do, and requires open country like that my prehistoric ancestors lived in. Those earliest humans inherited binocular vision and hence good spatial perception from even earlier days in three-dimensional forest. Occasionally, yellow-bellied racers rear up from ground cover and look me squarely in the eye, but, however cautious I am, they always "down-periscope" so quickly that I don't have the eye-to-eye photo I really want.

Driving down my street one afternoon, the car in front of me stopped abruptly, all the doors flew open, and two women with baseball bats and four uniformed children ran to the front and began pounding on the pavement. I pulled over in time to see the last pieces of a harmless yellow-bellied racer smashed into the asphalt by batting coaches of a different kind. I've seen other drivers run their cars back and forth across hapless serpents on roads. There is no greater human fear or hatred of a wild creature. Where did the biblical prejudice come from? Is it primitive instinct related to poisonous species or the serpent's utterly different shape and locomotion? Whatever its roots, the fear is definitely reinforced by teaching.

14th. The spring migration of birds gears up and winds down rapidly—just a matter of a few weeks. I really enjoy this time-traveling exhibit of modern art and know-how. Ambling in the cool dawn, enjoying a thrush serenade and feathered "rainbows," I recount the passing parade. Species richness triples abruptly from thirteen to forty-two between mid and late April, increasing to a peak of forty-seven in the first week of May, and declining to thirty-nine species this week. I can expect fifty-three species altogether, but I'll be lucky to find seven by late this month and in early June.

Seasonal migration is nature's cycle but not the decades-long decline of migrants that winter in the tropics. I first noticed this ominous pattern in the mid-1980s. Thankfully, the common trio of Swainson's thrush, least flycatcher, and Nashville warbler remains, but in declining numbers, and in the 1990s I rarely see baybreasted, cerulean, or golden-winged warblers. Yet winter residents, also migrants, cycle up and down in numbers—white-throated sparrows, dark-eyed juncos, and American goldfinches, for instance—while permanent residents increase. Is my counting correct, or have I succumbed to the doomsday fever that infects many naturalists these days?

Unhappily, the trends are real according to my teachers. Screech owls cache birds in tree cavities for later eating and are unbiased census takers, because they follow the rules of natural predation and capture what is easiest and most abundant. Since the mid-1980s neotropical migrants in owl larders have declined steadily, while owl numbers have cycled. The concomitant cycling of stored winter residents and the increase in stashed permanent residents also parallel my visual census. Causes for the neotropical decline remain to be sorted out but include damage and destruction of all habitats—tropical winter, temperate breeding, and stopover.

15th. Mid-May brings the second big prairie and pasture flower spectacular, although most species no longer grow in the ravine. They are missing because they need full sun. Some are disturbance indicators of places such as overgrazed pastures and mowed roadsides. The first big bloom in mid-April, dominated by bluebonnet, paintbrush, and Texas star, has been succeeded by a firewheel and Mexican hat show with dozens of other beautiful species. It's true—there's nothing like Texas prairie wildflowers anywhere that I've ever been.

Larger ravine species are twistleaf yucca and standing cypress, the latter named for foliage that resembles cypress tree leaves. The yucca's tall stalk of creamy white flowers and the standing cypress's tubular red flowers are very showy against the dark of forest edge. Both grow along trails, forming corridor displays with star violet, mountain pink, and plains pincushion cactus. But their flower stalks may be decapitated by hungry eastern cottontails and itinerant white-tailed deer, who follow human trails to these gardens of our visual and their gustatory delight.

16th. Smooth sumac and purple clematis (leather flower) are also blooming on the woods border. This sumac and the narrower-leaved, more drought-resistant flameleaf sumac are pioneer shrubs on disturbed ground. Both appeared in numbers as if by magic after sewer lines were dug, smooth sumac primarily toward the ravine bottom and flameleaf nearer the more exposed top. Owl Hollow was abundant with sumacs only a year after scarring. In five years the largest were six feet tall, but they began to die as shade increased and were succeeded by the sapling sugarberries and cedar elms of forest reconstruction.

Meanwhile, vines grew among the woody plants, holding them together against the winds of open spaces. Greenbriar and poison ivy were first, then heart-leaf pepper vine, mustang grape, Carolina snailseed, and Virginia creeper. Last in the developing shade came supplejack, yellow passion flower, and purple clematis. Earliest appearing grape and pepper vines rambled laterally, since they invaded sunny spots before tree growth. Species arrival time, whether vines, shrubs, or trees, depends partly on seed dispersability, a function of size and favor of the fruit as food among animal travel agents.

17th. "Weeep, weep—burrr-eeep," is the great-crested flycatcher's message of forest suitability. Even in tropical winter retreats, I find cresties mostly in mature forest. Their "police-whistle" song tells of natural-cavity trees and vacant woodpecker holes or suburban nest boxes. They'll use almost any cavity of sufficient size if no screech owl recently used it for a nest, roost, or food storage locker. How do they know? Is it odor, owl pellets, or prey remains? Since cresties and eastern screech owls have performed together for millennia in spring and summer scenes on the same forest stages, they certainly know the cues.

I'm watching a pair of the flycatchers contend with European starlings for a nest box. They take natural material in and the starlings take it out, substituting suburban lawn cuttings, paper, and plastic for the cresty's native plants and snake skins. If the flycatchers outlast these starlings, they'll have a four- or five-egg clutch this week or next. But the starlings are *äuslanders* and do not respect native actors. Fortunately, cresties prefer tree cavities in the forest, while starlings choose open, park-like habitat where the two overlap in wooded suburbia.

18th. About this time of spring some huge beetle buzzes by, its hard wing covers held up in a V—a flying apparition. It may be a fierce-looking, big-jawed, three-inch longhorn or a burly, two-inch ox beetle. My favorite is the eyed elator, a two-inch click beetle with large, white-ringed eye spots and white speckles on its black wing covers. Putting click beetles on their backs to marvel at their clicking, jumping, escape behavior is something I've always done. What an adaptation to startle predators, especially when accompanied by two sudden, staring "eyes!" This afternoon, as I band young screech owls, an errant eyed elator flies onto the chest of a female onlooker who is not as bemused as I am by the living brooch.

I'm totally fascinated by the variety of animals with false eyes. Insects, both adult and larval forms, fish, amphibians, reptiles, birds, and mammals have them. They must be very effective deterrents, and maybe social signals as well. Some owls have feather-pattern "eyes" on the backs of their heads and can "look" in two directions at once. No one has investigated whether this arrangement deflects pesky mobbing birds, predators, or has another function entirely. A direct look is a certain dominance signal in nature and culture, and I suspect that wide-eyed looks were part of hierarchical structuring in our prehistoric family groups.

19th. Stepping outside to pick up the newspaper, I find my neighbor plowing again. She's a nine-banded armadillo who aerates soil, distributes nutrients, and controls grubs, all of which enhance the growth of native plants. My yard-woods needs regular plowing to mix the rich but thin organic surface into the more sterile rocky layer underneath. Once my neighbor fell unhurt into an empty swimming pool, where she gave birth to four females (armadillos have identical quadruplets, since their one fertilized egg divides four ways for development). After I rescued them, the big bulldozer and her four little front-end loaders plowed together for several weeks.

Armadillos survive well despite being hit by cars and shot by suburbanites who dislike their digging in lawns and flower beds. One will dig several burrows, using them in rotation, apparently depending on the providence of local foods. Foxes, skunks, opossums, snakes, and other animals shelter in the temporarily vacant housing. Bedding material is dry leaf litter pushed and pulled inside, which blocks the entrance, insulating the burrow against freezing weather. "Dillos" don't hibernate and can't dig for food in hard-frozen soil, but they can withstand freezes for up to at least three days by staying indoors. They are nocturnal in hot weather but cycle the forest's nutrients in sunshine on a mild winter day.

20th. Outside my study window roughleaf dogwood has peaked in white, and roughstem sunflower (rosenweed) begins to bloom in yellow. It is hot at eighty-five degrees because of sky-high humidity, despite the south wind signal of an approaching cold front. A pair of Carolina wrens has completed their second nest in the old wicker fishing creel that has hung on our front porches for thirty-five years. Their first nest in a corner cranny under the upstairs deck fledged five youngsters three weeks ago. A yellow-billed cuckoo sings its rain song —a weather forecast that sounds like my tongue clicking in the roof of my mouth. It's a sultry signal on a muggy afternoon.

21st. Nancy runs while I ramble or write in the pre-dawn darkness, then we take a two mile walk on neighborhood streets, rain or shine, freezing or not, almost every day we're home. Our Labrador retriever leads Nancy, while I pick up trash and field questions about a dog who's happiest carrying a discarded drink cup or bottle. We observe and discuss cultural scenes in life's play. Since we've walked the same several routes for decades, we're often greeted and sometimes thanked for retrieving trash, though we can't always tell who's waving behind tinted closed car windows. We knew a lot more people before air conditioning, automated lawn sprinklers, and cell phones and this morning talk about the increasing isolation of modern suburbia.

22nd. Rechecking eastern screech owl nests on the verge of fledging young, I find that the youngest chick in one brood of four has a dislocated leg. Its three siblings have left. It is the original runt, now large enough and sufficiently well-feathered to fledge, but it cannot climb to the hole. Father watches the nest from his customary roost. How long will he attend? Mom stays with the three fledglings, all together about a hundred feet away. It is rare to be debilitated in a manner that prevents leaving—more common for a runt to starve, suffocate by being sat upon, or be killed and eaten by older siblings if food is scarce. I do not rescue this chick because I try to minimize interference in natural events in order to learn.

23rd. A blue haze covers the Balcones Escarpment's rolling fields and wooded waterways. At dawn the haze is punctured by an orange sunball. It is 1981, and the atmosphere is clouded by ash from the Mount Saint Helens eruption in Washington, the haziness reminding me of a hot, humid July day. Yet the morning is chilly because the sun is partly blocked. I walk down the hill and whistle our horses in from a pasture along a river west of the escarpment a few miles from our suburb. They are in no hurry to come, for the grass is lush with springtime. I take their cue and poke around.

Surprise, surprise! I find a coral snake, a secretive, poisonous species that hunts small snakes and lizards under ground cover. Poked gently with a stick, it strikes down and sideways with its tail, which is coiled, raised, and has yellow and black bands like the head. The effect, a tail that becomes a "head," is called self- or auto-mimicry. The real head is hidden under body coils. Never does this individual try to bite but soon crawls into trailside vegetation, and I remember being asked to confirm the identity of a coral snake that was badly mangled by a medical patient who showed only psychosomatic symptoms of snake-bite.

24th. Mare's tail clouds are the sky's giant parachutes. They may forecast rain, triggered by an approaching cold front. Or they could tell of a weakened cold front stalled over us as a warm front. Late May is midway into the spring rainy season. Together, May and June bring a quarter of our annual rainfall. September and October are a secondary monsoon, dependent on tropical storms and hurricanes as well as cold and warm fronts. Record rains in Owl Hollow were 1.6 inches in ten minutes, 8 inches in twenty-four hours, and 16 inches over five days. What do today's mare's tails foretell?

25th. Working inside with open windows, I hear a mix of natural and unnatural history. A Swainson's thrush sings as house painters play honky-tonk music across the ravine. Does anyone else listen? I decide to survey the eight houses in my cul-de-sac, all situated so they have or could have windows facing the woods or other common green-space. Four have no such windows. Two have them, but only one has windows that open, and they're closed. Of course, it is mid-morning and most owners are away turning fossil fuel energy into money, while the thrush translates solar energy into music that soothes my spirit.

26th. Egg-leaf skullcap's first blue flowers appear at the bottom of stalks, a nice strategy for assuring reproduction if the succulent grow-ing tip is eaten—and it often is. Young eastern cottontails are the cul-prits—just four or five inches long but able to stretch like rubber bands. I'm amazed at how they stand on hind legs, reach up, pull, and nip. I know they're about because of the clippings and the calls I get from neighbors for the "animal doctor." Folks retrieve them from pets and children and want me to raise them, or tell them how. I advise them that it is illegal to keep wildlife without special permits and to put the wild babies back after cultural threats are averted, for they are either independent or well cared for by parents who've been fright-ened away temporarily.

27th. During the pesticide controversy of the early 1960s, I corre-sponded with the late Rachel Carson, who's book, *Silent Spring*, about pesticide abuse, stimulated society's thinking. I greatly admired but never met her. Today is her birthday, and, serendipitously, my phone rings with the excited call of a neighbor, who says our city is spraying herbicide in a curbside swath along her street, including on a colony of hill country dayflowers. Because U.S. society now employs twice the amount of poisons as in Rachel Carson's day, my concern grows, so I call my city council representative to suggest why my suburb should have an environmental advisory committee.

Other scattergun approaches are equally misguided, such as drop-ping pesticides from airplanes to eradicate exotic fire ants that refuse to be killed. But Texas horned lizards soon succumbed—a mysteri-ous circumstance. Another harmful approach is dispersing poison bait over the countryside to kill coyotes, resulting in the deaths of farm animals and wildlife including coyotes, which are, however, more abundant and widespread than ever. Of course it takes more effort to sort out and eliminate particular offending individuals, but the cost: benefit ratio favors targeting culprits, as we can easily learn from the selectivity of prey by natural predators.

28th. The wings of large, brightly colored moths, peeled off by eastern screech owls, are nature's candy wrappers. These days I may find wrappings from a beloved underwing moth—three-inch bark-colored forewings and contrasting black-banded, crimson-red hind-wings—or a polyphemus moth, the largest local "candy bar." Smaller and generally duller colored moths are eaten whole. I watch screech owls flying about tree foliage hawking insects, sometimes catching them in their bills but mostly with their feet, and doubt that they find quietly resting moths, whose forewings are excellent camouflage. I'll bet they get their candy in flight.

29th. Freshly excavated turtle nests and broken eggshells on the trail-side tell me about population resilience. They are from red-eared slid-ers mostly, but also a few Texas cooters and snapping turtles. Raccoons and skunks cruised this trailside cafeteria, while egg-laying females wandered across neighborhood roads, to and from choice nesting spots, and were smashed by cars. How suburban turtle populations survive is a mystery, because the carnage appears to be considerable. But I do find hatchlings in our creek and its headwaters ponds, indi-cating that perhaps the killing paths aren't as serious as I think.

30th. Inch-long, brown insect skins cling tightly to tree trunks and my house. They are signs that fledgling eastern screech owls have new hunting practice. The skins clothed green cicada nymphs, newly emerged from the soil and easy prey for inexperienced owlets. At dusk I watch four of them on a tree limb making repeated trips to the ground, one at a time, returning to the same perch with a juicy nymph held up in one foot for nibbling. They remind me of a child-hood soda fountain, each of us served ice cream cones in succession. When the morning air heats into the mid-seventies, the former own-ers of brown skins that escaped the predators begin to rasp—"dog-day harvest flies" filled with the song of summer.

31st. Sometimes I sit near the creekbank at dusk or dawn. A screech owl family may fly there or to the edge of my little pond and take turns drinking and jumping into shallow water to catch fish or transforming leopard frogs. Parents go first and owlets follow, reminding me of a family at the beach or lakeshore. The youngsters instinctively know some things to do but now seem to learn by example. They must prepare to fend for themselves in another two months, for I find an adult's shed wing feather, a sign of annual molt and perhaps impaired flying and hunting ability—another sign of summer.

. . . with an eye made quiet by the power of harmony, and the deep power of joy, we see into the life of things. *William Wordsworth*

CHAPTER 4

Summer IS MELODY

June's Cycles Slowing

Summer rolls along for several weeks before the summer solstice. Ohio buckeye leaves begin to turn yellow and fireflies disappear, seconding the message that the year is half over. But cicadas are as boisterous as ever. Besides days that will get shorter, unnoticed because the high sun and rain ensure verdure, there are other hints of slower cycles. Migratory birds are finished nesting by month's end. June's mid-year messengers include rasping katydids, blooming Turk's caps, the billowing clouds of afternoon thunderstorms, and cedar needle rain.

1st. From a front-row seat on my porch I'm watching, listening to, and smelling a thunderstorm with mothball-sized hail. Rarely do we get hail that defoliates trees and knocks out car and building windows, but my roof has been damaged. Heavy hail seconds the high winds of spring, or winter's ice storms, as nature's way of pruning vegetation. The forest's light-catching, photosynthetic machinery, damaged by serious spring weather and burgeoning leaf-eaters, will be restored. Hail is house cleaning, followed by replaced equipment, generated by the release of nutrients from the leaf debris of former years.

Tornadoes may accompany these storms. A small one came through the ravine this day in 1969 and cut a sinuous swath about one hundred feet wide and a thousand feet long. There was major damage to be sure, a forest makeover followed by a garage sale for small animals that shelter in and under logs, and for me, who picked up deadwood for marking trails and stocking my fireplace. But that was nothing compared to the fifty-foot-wide, four-tenths of a mile long path the bulldozers blazed through here in July 1990, clearing more land than needed for a six-inch diameter sewer line and removing all the wood. The comparison of natural and unnatural history is like that.

2nd. As born swimmers with webbed toes, Labrador retrievers love to fetch sticks thrown into the water, so I take ours to the reservoir for a half-hour weekly workout. We go to a city park, which means refuse, some of it thrown into the lake by boaters—out of sight and, therefore, out of mind. Broken glass and jagged cans are treacherous to a dog's feet, so I take plastic grocery bags to pick up and dispose of the trash along a five-hundred-foot section of shoreline. Large items such as broken lawn chairs and car tires I carry out separately. Bags are filled and weighed often enough to estimate that three pounds of litter accumulates on each foot of shoreline each year.

3rd. Among the ravine's most specialized predators is the cicada killer wasp, so finely tuned to its singular food supply that its numbers each June track the number of singing cicadas. This two-inch creature with bright yellow and black warning coloration has a larval stage that only eats cicadas and emerges from its underground burrow as an adult wasp about three days after the first cicadas appear. The correspondence of cicada and wasp population sizes must be food and reproduction—cause and effect—but what about the timing of emergence? While underground, wasps must detect cicada nymphs digging toward the surface, and I'd like to know how.

4th. By now most screech owlets have fledged, and I remove debris at the bottom of their nest cavities to assess prey remains and the food web of associated animals. These include acrobat ants that eat stored owl food and Texas blind snakes that eat the ants and other soft-bodied insects. In the dark, moist, decomposer community of nest debris, blind snakes are top predators as long as the owls bring them in alive and leave food scraps and feces to energize the web. Once owlets fledge, nightly food deposits cease, decomposer insect larvae transform into adults and fly away, and blind snakes climb out and down the tree trunk, burrow in soil, and go back to eating subterranean ants and termites.

When they come to the ground surface, blind snakes up to ten inches long are caught by the owls. These snakes are smooth-scaled, cylindrical, and they smear themselves with a slick repellent fluid to ward off ant and termite attacks, so they can live in the insects' colonies. This makes them so hard to kill that screech owls deliver most of them alive to their nestlings, whereupon the snakes escape and burrow into cavity-bottom debris. Blind snake predation on the debris-dwelling insects, including the ants' immature stages, apparently reduces competition between the insects and owlets for food, because nests with live-in blind snakes fledge more faster-growing owlets than nests without them.

But that's only part of a potentially more complex association called a symbiosis. Cavity-dwelling ants don't bother screech owls directly, only indirectly by eating stored food intended for the owlets, and, of course, they don't bother blind snakes, who are crawling "bug-bombs." They do, however, swarm, bite, and spray their own repellent fluid on cavity intruders like me, so by protecting their colony from would-be predators, they also protect the owls. Yet by eating ants, blind snakes reduce the size of or eliminate their colonies which reduces or negates the ant's defensive effort. Is there a tradeoff? Apparently not, since owls' nesting success increases with live-in blind snakes, not with ants alone, in my experimental nest boxes.

The energy relay system must work quite well, or owl nests wouldn't house these associates (symbionts). Any actor ignoring cues would be removed from the cast by natural selection. Of course I could be missing some scene or actor, since the food web is complex in seasonal time, sunlight, and dark-cavity space. But think of it! Owls and ants, both grazers, eating stored animal bodies produced by sunshine via plants and linked by insect-eating blind snakes to decomposers like fly maggots that eat food scraps, feces, and occasional dead owlets in the dark. What a fascinating diversity of interacting roles in this very unusual scene from the play of life!

5th. The rasp of round-winged katydids in the trees at dusk is an early summer lullaby. As the sounds of sweet-trilling screech owls and night-jarring chuck-wills-widows fade with the season, katydids lull me to sleep. They sound like begging owlets. Katydids start singing about fifteen minutes before sunset, just as owlets and their parents become active, and quiet down around 11:00 P.M., about the time owlets cease begging because they're satiated. Does the katydid chorus disguise the owlets' loud calls, so predators have a hard time finding them? Interesting, too, that the katydid season ends in late July, when owlets are hunting on their own, no longer begging, and dispersing from parental home ranges. Is the seasonal synchrony of katydid and owl cued acting or serendipity?

6th. Why would someone build a house in the woods with windows that don't open? Why be shielded from the delightful sounds and scents of breezes, birds, rustling leaves, insects, and flowing creek— the wild orchestra—unless, of course, one's allergies don't permit the outdoors. But then, why move here? I've discovered that some neighbors are hearing- and odor-impaired, because none of their house windows open. Their houses must be cooled, heated, and the air circulated by fans all the time. The inhabitants must use extra energy, which causes extra air pollution, since our electricity is generated by burning coal. They're incommunicado except by sight, unusual for a social animal heavily dependent on vocal communication.

7th. Since late March, june bugs have staged their seasonal relay. Timed like new generations of butterflies, different species appear almost monthly from March into June and at longer intervals afterward. The spotted goldbug emerges now, to be followed in two months by the last and only daytime flyer, the green june bug. Most species are a half-inch to an inch long and clumsy on the ground—large, abundant, easy food for small predators. A fledgling screech owl I once hatched and raised in order to learn more ran, hopped, fluttered, and pounced on 128 june bugs in an hour on my lighted patio but caught and ate only 52, a lesson in juvenile inexperience and practice for survival.

Because june-bug grubs eat grass roots, suburbanites raise great numbers of them by continually fertilizing and watering lawns, and then poison them when they find dead spots in the grass. A while back I watched a pair of screech owls use the same nest for eight consecutive years. The female always laid five or six eggs and fledged all nestlings until the year after her human neighbors contracted with a pesticide company to spray their yards. That spring she laid five infertile eggs, which she incubated seventy-eight days—two and a half times longer than needed. Then she left the five dead messages and disappeared.

8th. Contemplating the reciprocal dynamics of extinction and colonization of wildlife in the ravine, a seminatural "island" in a suburban "sea," I think about thirty years of controversy about one large versus several small preserves as the best way to protect local biodiversity. Because big animals are important community regulators, carnivores especially, and they require big areas, as does a diverse biota and populations big enough to withstand natural and human impact, big is the operative word. Nevertheless, the natural world is now so fragmented that we have to make do with whatever islands we can save.

Practically speaking, money to buy and protect wildland is limited, so the best strategy is to survey prospects and conserve the largest, most diverse, least impacted, best interconnected properties. Then preservation management is feasible, even if one isn't convinced about carnivore regulation of natural energy exchanges and keystone species that, if extinguished, topple the community. Not only do large landscapes allow large numbers of natives, they also permit them to stay farthest away from humans, which is usually the healthiest thing to do. Large linked parcels is the best strategy, but smaller areas are more realistic in and around suburbia.

Most of the summer of 1978, Nancy and I lived in the former West Germany, a smaller, more crowded, less natural place than Texas. Weeks in and about huge West Berlin and small Heidelberg taught us that clustered housing with limited private space but more and larger public areas among the clusters, including connected natural remnants and parks, preserved natural history and cultural opportunity. That's why we chose to live in a planned unit development, designed with our input to integrate natural and unnatural history. Inside sprawling suburbs, particularly, such development may be the only way to save nature's daily marvels and support systems.

9th. American beautyberry's flowers are pinkish white but so tiny that I must look closely to be certain they are really open. This isn't the shrub's best season, but I'm glad it lives in the moist shelter of the ravine, lending foliage diversity to the lush forest of summer. In fruit, however, beautyberry is one of our prettiest shrubs. Its silver dollar-sized clusters of purple berries, evenly spaced every inch or two along stems bearing large yellow-green leaves, are a notable decoration of the autumn trailside. Berry-eating birds relish the bush, quickly stripping its ripe fruit in late August through October, when I too may plunder it by cutting twigs for a bouquet.

10th. One screech-owl nest has chicks that must be replacements for a nest lost earlier, since it is very late in the season. An average of only thirty-six percent of nests fail each year due to predation or desertion, compared to ninety-one percent of northern cardinal nests, a typical songbird figure. I'm looking for late nestlings, because I have an orphan owlet that needs a home. It was on the ground of a once-wooded lot that was cleared to build a house; and there's no sense hand raising it, when natural parents can do better. If they're in good condition and placed in families with step-siblings of a similar age, orphans thrive, as I've discovered by seeing banded adoptees grow up to become successful breeding adults.

Saving this owlet accords with my ethics, because an unnatural bulldozer killed its nature. All the owlets that I've placed for adoption come from similar destructive family backgrounds. I've not saved nests from natural predators or rescued owlets that fell by themselves from nests, although I have deflected squirrels, starlings, and ringtails from certain nest boxes in field experiments that required it. If technology is the primary negative impact, I counter it if I can, but I don't otherwise choose species or individuals to protect. That's because humanity's script in the play of life reads stewardship, not dictatorship.

11th. Despite our attic fan, the air conditioning goes on to stay today, unless a cold front teases us momentarily. This means closing windows and temporarily isolating myself from natural neighbors. Now I can't write, listen, or sniff the wild but only look, although I'll spend many early mornings outside, and evenings too. My constant temperature chamber will remain until mid-September, when I'll welcome nature inside once again. Air conditioning at my house is correlated with humid stillness and daily temperatures above ninety degrees, although a recent survey says that most people select seventy-eight degrees. They must not have my forest luxury.

12th. Great-crested flycatchers that decided to nest in one of my owl boxes draped a piece of plastic grocery bag out of the hole instead of

the usual snakeskin, which supposedly deters predators. Either the plastic works or there are no predators, for three fledglings appear today. Last year cresties successfully used my neighbor's newspaper delivery tube under the street-side mailbox beside his driveway. Thinking he would give them a safer spot, he took the tube down and built a tube-like wooden nest box, which he placed away from the street. Cresties looked it over but chose my owl nest box—a humbling experience for those of us who think we're in control.

13th. When I mow the trail in our nature preserve, northern mockingbirds, blue jays, and screech owls occasionally fly down behind me to pick up exposed insects and skinks—the owls always at dusk. They are like farmland gulls and hawks that have learned to follow "the plow." This afternoon I see the adaptive advantage of a quick behavioral change and an easily broken-off tail, as a mockingbird swoops on a scrambling little brown skink and gets only its tail. Upon exposure, the skink switches from crawl to exaggerated sinuous wiggle, which misdirects the bird's attack. Silent-flying eastern screech owls must catch skinks and other lizards by the head or body, for I've never found just their tails or tailless individuals stored in nests.

14th. Pecan is Texas' state tree, widely cultivated commercially and domestically; and Texas bluebonnet is the state's official wildflower, widely planted, painted, and photographed. But sideoats grama—the state grass? Whoever heard of it, much less planted it purposely for ground cover or livestock food because of its superior nutrient quality? No ranchers that I know of. Before suburban sprawl, sideoats grama grew with little bluestem, tall dropseed, and Texas needlegrass in prairie openings amidst motts of oak and juniper (cedar). Needlegrass needles stuck in my pants each June before suburbia checkmated the wild players, eventually clearing the mott and prairie chessboard.

Mott, or motte, is a clump of trees in grassland or pasture, a term for a distinctive landscape in central and south Texas. The word was apparently imported by Irish settlers who used the Gaelic, *mote* (grove of trees) in naming towns on the Gulf Coast prairie over a century ago. The Spanish *mata* has much the same meaning; but the Irish are a better bet as importers, because they took mott along to name new places, as their generations migrated inland. We have Elm Mott, for instance, a small town north of the ravine. Regardless of which culture is to be credited, I like to use mott, because it reminds me of the importance of cultural as well as natural diversity.

Live oak motts second human messages of integration in a foreign land, for they are hospitable, protective, and self-perpetuating in naturally fiery prairies. Motts begin when an animal-transported acorn germinates in a bare spot amidst grass that doesn't burn for a few years, so the sprouted oak grows tall enough to raise its green foliage above ground fire, which its thick bark resists. Annually, this tree surrounds itself with a blanket of shed leathery leaves that is both fire- and moisture-retardant. Offspring sprout from its own roots protected by the blanket and form a clump (mott) of genetically identical trees that eventually shelters a diversity of forest life.

15th. One month ago three owlets fledged from a brood of four, leaving the youngest in the nest box. It had a dislocated leg but no other apparent injury and couldn't climb out. Possibly it got caught in a tug-of-war with brood mates, as youngest siblings sometimes do. An animal rehabilitator said there was a fifty-fifty chance the leg could be mended, but I left the situation alone to learn more about wild ways. My observational approach to learning from natural history is neutral as much as possible, although my presence, let alone hands-on checking, certainly is not. I may affect a situation inadvertently but try not to take sides.

Through mid-May the male parent roosted in his customary position near the nest box and continued to feed the crippled nestling, while his mate stayed with the fledglings farther away (males typically attend remaining nestlings, and females accompany fledglings). By late May, Dad was no longer present in the daytime, as the rest of his dependents ranged ever farther afield; but the nestling was still fed, for its weight remained steady. Then, a week ago, the owlet began to decline. It died of starvation today, and I learned that triage is no snap decision but is sometimes necessary, as support of the living demands all one's time and energy.

The reason is simple according to the play's directors—that environmental group called natural selection. Surviving offspring carry parental genes, which permit their parents' acting ability in concert with the plot. For the screech owls' part to continue, some youngsters must survive to become parents, which requires parental care that includes making choices. If roles aren't perpetuated by offspring, who may also exercise unique (genetic) abilities when stage settings change, other actors fill in and the scene shifts, or those roles and the scene disappear entirely.

16th. Besides the nature preserve, our homeowners association has cul-de-sac streets, lawns, a cabana, and a swimming pool as property owned jointly for the benefit of the community. If people respect the common good, these commons work well, because resources are available that some wouldn't or couldn't have individually. Historically, livestock was kept on such property, but greedy folks increased their herds for personal gain and overgrazed the commons, ruining it for all. Today, a different kind of selfishness damages the nature preserve with free-ranging pets, gardens, trash, and privacy fences.

More importantly, the tragedy of the commons now describes the entire Biosphere, wherein humans dump wastes that pollute all life. No cost is involved, because air, water, and land dumpsites are unregulated common or public property. Societal and personal costs are rising rapidly. Increasing storm damage in a climate warmed by the dumping of greenhouse gases, and increasing rates of skin cancer because spray-can gases puncture life's protective ozone layer are examples. The tragedy of the commons that once had local repercussions for local communities now threatens an entire planet.

17th. I never tire of seeing colorful encounters of the green anole kind. These lizards are easy to watch, as they sit with apparent confidence on conspicuous perches like my woodpile. I'm watching two of them signal for space right now. One, about five inches long, nose to tail-tip, displays its red throat fan and does push-ups that signal "mine, all mine," meaning his territory. The smaller anole is an inch shorter and threatened by the woodpile owner. He is traveling an elevated highway from the garage end of the pile to woods on the other end. Both better be careful, because screech owls catch tardy anoles at nightfall—those that spend too much time contending.

Territory is a defended suite of natural resources, spatially and temporally defined by sufficiency relative to the cost of ownership. Wild creatures can't afford to defend more than they need, because their energy expenditures (costs) would exceed energy gains (benefits). Larger areas are defended or more time is spent defending only if necessities are scarce. The ultimate cost is one's life, which is why natural selection employs only those actors who adjust their cost: benefit ratio to unity (stability) or temporarily needed benefit (growth, repair, reproduction). Cultural selection is, of course, a different matter altogether.

18th. Native hunters either sit and wait for prey to appear or search actively. The sitters wait at places they've discovered by experience to be profitable, such as animal trails or water sources. If one spot doesn't produce, they move to the next one. Trap-lining is what ecologists call this practice of visiting several known food sources, much as human fur trappers check lines of animal traps, but it's really comparison shopping. Anoles and screech owls are sit-and-wait predators that shop sequentially at places like bird baths and feeders, garbage cans, porchlights, and flower gardens.

Prehistorically, we too hunted by sitting and waiting along game trails or at waterholes and salt licks that attracted prey. The bottom line was cost:benefit, as it has always been in nature. But modern hunting doesn't have to be beneficial, because it is subsidized by fossil fuel energy. We sport hunt and fish for prey we don't need and often don't use, funded by coal, oil, and gas, translated into bullets, bait, and cars. Energy used for comparison shopping ("trap-lining") among stores and garage sales is obtained in the same remote, impersonal way —so far from the fossil fuel "kill" that we ignore the net result.

19th. Giant scalybark oaks are a unique feature of my home. I don't know another place with so many originals. I am in awe of these ancients that tell me of long-gone community members, including red wolves and first Americans. Large ones average eighteen inches in diameter, but a goliath is thirty-five inches through and seventy feet tall —perhaps a state or national champion. Based on the ages of those cut down during house construction, I figure it takes a scalybark close to 150 years to grow to average size. Inside the ravine, especially on creek terraces protected from storms, fire, and cutting, scalybarks are easily identified, but on exposed scarps where naturally stressed and burned or unnaturally cut and regrown, they are squatty and multiple-trunked—quite different-looking survivors.

20th. Our nature preserve exists partly because it's a narrow, steep-sided ravine with a floodplain in which houses cannot be built according to city ordinances. As "unusable" land, the city tax rate is low and my homeowners association doesn't mind that at all. Ravine walkers comprise only about three percent of association members. Some children play in the woods, but mostly when it is cool and the poison ivy and snakes aren't such a threat, according to their mothers. I've seen parents with children only a dozen times in twenty years. The nature these kids know is mostly second hand and controlled by culture on television, the internet, or in zoos and arboretums.

Some in my community would like to build an outdoor nature education center on abused land that could be restored to seminaturalness. It would be about half of a fifteen-acre public site that already includes arboretum gardens, a demonstration composting area, and a meeting house. We'd like for people to receive messages from the wild, not the usual messages about human control. Nature centers have been popping up all over recently, and I'm glad because their main users are schoolchildren for whom they are often the only near-heritage learning experience.

21st. The sun has reached one end of its annual journey across the sky and begins to retrace its steps, or so it seems from the vantage of an orbiting planet. Days will become shorter, giving me less mental feeding time outdoors. Young nocturnal animals will profit, for they must practice how to live on their own. Despite the forest's verdure, I am always a bit melancholy as the sun retreats southward. Late June through early August brings more stops than starts, contributing to my mood. Headwater creeks stop running, leaves begin falling, and birds stop singing through the day, while schools vacate, groups cease meeting, symphonies cease playing, and neighbors depart for vacation. Yet my mental drought is not as severe as the season's physical one, for the year's hottest, driest time is just ahead.

22nd. A subtle change in the forest is softly audible, but I am drawn to what is underfoot, because it is hard to miss the first flowering Turk's caps. They are scarlet splashes in the green understory of low moist spots. As if better advertising were needed, Turk's caps attract orange and silver, Gulf fritillary butterflies and ruby-throated hummingbirds. This wonderful wildflower grows by runners beneath the leaf litter, forming tight colonies. There isn't a more striking exhibit in the forest shade of summer—in fact few others this time of year. Leaning over to look closely, I recover a freshly shed screech-owl feather and hear it again, the soft rain of dropping cedar needles.

23rd. The ravine's first trails, surely made by native mammals, probably were used by first Americans about ten millennia ago. Then came livestock trails used by horseback-riding settlers in the mid-1800s, and used a century later by walking suburbanites, I suppose, though I never saw anyone else in the 1960s. Next came trails made by construction equipment, traveled by people on motorcycles in the 1970s. All-terrain vehicles were another stage a decade later, then mountain bikes in the 1990s. Industrial technology added changes in transport at a faster and faster pace, but fossil-fuel use declined with the advent of bicycles—a surprising turn of events in a play with an unnatural history of just the opposite.

24th. Sitting and waiting is something I learned from the wild. This afternoon I sit in deep shade by the creek, my back against the prone trunk of a gnarly scalybark oak that came down in an ice storm a few years ago and now slowly returns to the earth that produced it. I can smell and feel the process. It is warm in the late afternoon, a good time to be patient. But I am not like native predators whose hunger dictates waiting time, although I do seek food for reflection, which is necessary for human survival. I think about humanity's interest in the wild and its messages.

Reading historic accounts such as W. J. Holland's *The Butterfly Book* (1898) and Anna Comstock's *Handbook of Nature Study* (1911), I muse about their combinations of emotional and rational expression, since today's science literature often indicates detachment and preoccupation with statistics and mathematical abstractions. Despite worthy contents, it can be really boring. The nineteenth century French naturalist, Jean-Henri Fabre, fired as a teacher because he allowed girls to attend class, said, "Scientists fear lest a page that is read without fatigue should not be the truth."

Some modern biologists seem to speak less with the wild than with computers, indicating their particular distance from nature. Some send graduate students, who may employ undergraduates, to get the data. Does modern science figure that distance from one's subject enhances objectivity? How much distance without divorce from reality? Have scientists forgotten about sensory experience? They seem to dismiss the intuitive right side of their brain, and so may sacrifice life-knowing ties to distant ancestors who were more strongly shaped by nature.

I think too about the writing of favorite naturalist-authors like Loren Eiseley compared with modern nature writing that may look without seeing and hear without listening. Too often it is experiential trophy collecting—artistry that fails our whole brain and teaching elders. I'm disappointed by the missing messages. Where is Eiseley's universal voice? A half-century ago he cautioned that "we are too content with our sensory extensions." I'd like to see reason and emotion come together again.

25th. Two young broad-winged hawks who've been walking on the edge of their nest, begging for food, jump and climb to nearby branches, exercise their wings, and peer down at me, but return to the nest to be fed. They're branchers stimulated to leave home by parents withholding lunch. Parental luring is purposeful behavior. Screech-owl parents fly close to begging nestlings at the cavity entrance, displaying the food they carry, and then perch in full view, holding temptation. One took a stored rusty lizard from its nest cavity and held it ten feet from the owlets. To me, raptor departure antics suggest the behavioral conflicts of dispersing human offspring, who also come and go depending on their energy (money) supply.

26th. Pastures in and around the ravine used to be cactus country, advertised by yellow flowers in May and June. Livestock helped to maintain the grasses while dispersing broken prickly pear joints stuck to grazing skin. Common along fencerows was Christmas cactus, a pencil-stemmed prickly pear with red fruits for December celebration. Flat-padded Lindheimer prickly pear grew head-high—the western movie variety—while Engelmann and plains prickly pear hugged the ground, and plains pincushion and pineapple cacti were prickly knobs on stony soil. That was before suburbia transformed the diverse, self-sustaining natives into costly monocultures of imported, watered, fertilized, pest-treated, crew-cut San Augustine grass.

27th. Tickletongue, pepperbark, and toothache tree are folk names for prickly ash. It's not a very big tree, up to six inches in diameter and eighteen feet tall, but it's very instructive. When I have a toothache I chew the inner bark to numb my gums, because its alkaloids produce an analgesic effect without destroying tissue. Black willow is another dental tree in the ravine and provides headache relief as well. First Americans, equipped with the wild's messages, told Anglo pioneers about these medicines and many others that came from or were copied from nature.

Curious about such wealth at my doorstep, I review positive and negative values, aside from ornamentation, of the seventy plants I normally enounter in a year (see appendix). Some have many uses, for instance twistleaf yucca as food, fiber, soap, and medicine. Others, like red mulberry, are positive resources at one time (berry food if ripe) but negative at another (poisonous if green), and a few, like western soapberry, are helpful and harmful simultaneously, depending on how they're used. Altogether, forty-four percent provide material resources. Only eighteen percent are poisonous. And the rest? Who knows, but why disregard or waste the potential?

Utility is a worthy reason for conserving wild diversity, and other important considerations are aesthetic, ethical, spiritual, and recreational. However, as I pause to admire the festoons of feeding insects at a blooming tickletongue, I'm struck by connection as the one reason behind all others. The linkages this tree and its pollinating-giving/feeding-taking insects display are the ultimate validation! Without these services, we would have no goods—no food, medicine, building materials, or other resources, because we simply wouldn't be here.

28th. Gulf fritillary and queen butterflies decorate blooming western ironweed along the sunny path behind my house. The two butterflies are southern, mainly tropical in fact. I'm uncertain if any stage of either species overwinters regularly; yet they appear by late June each year and occasionally earlier, especially in the recent warmer years. After hard south winds in mild winters, I've seen them on Valentine's Day. Both produce one or more summer broods. They must winter some years and not others, when they ride the south winds and re-colonize, and I'll bet they'll stay longer as our climate grows warmer.

What a potpourri of travelers the ravine has to offer! Some come from the tropics and reproduce but don't remain in winter, while others only visit sporadically. And there are northerners of annual and itinerant types that like our winter better than summer. Also, some semi-permanent residents immigrate from east or west, but emigrate when the local going gets tough. Fifteen thousand years ago, most came from the north and east until a progressively hotter-dryer climate admitted more southern and western species. We've always been a mix of differences, and that's one measure of success.

29th. Surely the ravine's most abundant lizard is the little brown or ground skink, a four-inch lover of leaf-litter. My gridwork of pit-fall cans, sunk in the ground, traps skinks I have marked along with new ones, allowing me to estimate 125 per acre. Like all window-eyed skinks, the species has a wondrous transparent patch in its lower eyelid through which it sees when the eyelid is closed, protecting the eye while crawling in leaf litter. Screech-owls confirm the skink's abundance by listening and then diving into leaves to catch them, apparently using only their ears for guidance. In twelve minutes at dusk this evening, two adults deliver eight skinks in succession to their brood of four nestlings.

30th. "Notice of appraised value," is what today's property tax letter says. I owe the city, county, and school system more money than last year. According to them, I own a suburban house on a suburban lot and an adjacent "empty" lot. I chuckle, because the empty acreage is full of life. According to me, I pay for the privilege of saving a life-support system that belongs to everyone. I'm the temporary steward of a wooded refuge that houses gas, water, shade, and delight providers who are also noise and dust screeners and science, music, humanities, and art teachers—and who have much more acting experience than any humans.

✳

Peace comes within the souls of men when they realize their . . . oneness with the universe and all its powers . . . *Black Elk*

✳

July's Heat Is On

On the heels of spring rain comes the driest month and an abrupt shift to hundred-degree weather—a change in life as dramatic as anything in the ravine's annual cycle. The creek dries to a few pools, and the nightly katydid chorus takes an eight-month holiday, replaced by a black cricket ensemble. Wildflowers become wildfruits. Small, quiet, fall-drab songbirds begin to dribble southward, while migrating purple martins flock by the thousands. There are fewer appearances than anytime in the growing season, and dropouts forecast the year's end.

✳

1st. A Gulf Coast toad sometimes roosts in the soil of potted plants on my patio. When I water, it comes to the surface, walks to the edge and jumps onto the concrete. During the day I move it between pots, but it's always in the original abode the next day. Obviously, home is the right place to live. When I move pots into different configurations, keeping them all in their original partial shade, the toad disappears for a day or two, or for good, or emerges from a new pot in an old position. Apparently, proper microclimate is a factor in choosing shelter, as it is with me, and directions to that place are readily learned.

2nd. Circling through the yellowish haze of air pollution above the Dallas-Fort Worth airport, I look down on lines of cars converging on and diverging from clearings of concrete, asphalt, and glass. They are culture's harvester ants. A car takes me home to those other lines of black bodies moving along cleared trails, gathering greenery and returning it to their own city center. Their atmospheric costs are minor, since ant vehicles balance energy spent in travel to energy gained from the harvest. Natural selection does their "thinking," but we think and yet we separate from nature without thinking about it.

3rd. The south wind gives way to a calm, humid ninety degrees despite rainless days. As I trim vines and branches from the preserve trail, I think again about automatic sprinkling systems, swimming pools, reservoirs, and how our summer climate is increasingly humid. I literally run water. Biting deer flies give me fits, because I only wear shorts. But I am entertained and instructed by a green anole that jumps a good three feet off a pepper vine, hackberry butterflies in a territorial fracas above my head, and hedge parsley seeds stuck tick-tight to my legs. All are edge inhabitants—signs of the disturbance a trail makes in a nature preserve.

4th. A black female tiger swallowtail emerges today from a chrysalis formed on June 10 by a caterpillar that was brown through at least the last two developmental stages (instars). Some books say that only early stages are brown, others say that brown caterpillars turn green and then brown again before pupating, but none say why. Couldn't brown remain that way in summer broods for better camouflage among the season's drying and dying leaves? The eastern tiger swallowtail is a widespread, presumably familiar butterfly, and on Independence Day I have the freedom nature offers to ask how to live and, whether answered or not, to be delighted.

5th. Smooth sumac berries are red ripe, and Mexican plums are pink with faint hints of blue ripeness. Gulf fritillary butterflies lay eggs on yellow passion flowers. Hummingbirds have returned to feeders, including an adult male rufous, my birthday surprise, reminding me that migrants have begun to move southward, and our growing season is winding down. Summer resident birds sing sporadically, but northern mockingbirds mimic them all—all the time—telling me who's on stage and who's not. Mockers are chanticleers, and this evening they speak a lot of purple martin.

6th. The daytime din of green cicadas marks high summer. If the sky is clear, the droning begins an hour after sunrise at about seventy-five degrees. Gretchen and Mark once collected the cast skins of eighty-six cicada nymphs in ten minutes, all from the previous night's emergence. Instead of selling lemonade, they painted the skins and set up a stand to sell their art. Since they too have grown up, transformed, and flown away, I leave cicada skins hanging on the house in autumn and winter to remind me of summer. One by one they fall, counting the days to the beginning of next cicada season.

Cicadas have many predators. This morning they include a family of red-bellied woodpeckers with three fledglings that flush and fly-catch the big green bugs, as they do to other aerial insects. And any nymph or adult that moves within a few feet of the ground surface is fair game for a yellow-bellied racer or greater roadrunner. Copperheads trail and eat the nymphs at night. Ringtails, gray foxes, spotted and striped skunks, armadillos, and our Labrador retriever catch and crunch cicadas with seeming glee, like a human eating popcorn at the movies.

A screech owl delivers so many cicada nymphs to his three motherless chicks that the ten-inch-deep natural nest cavity fills up with uneaten bodies, boosting a single survivor to entrance level. After fledging, I count at least a hundred rotting cicadas and the bones and leg bands of both siblings who died and fed decomposer insects. They died because they were too small to control their body temperature and tear up food into manageable bites. Only the female parent broods and feeds nestlings directly, but she was gone too long and presumed dead.

7th. Early summer flowers from latest spring include purple clematis, eggleaf skullcap, low petunia, yellow passion vine, and roughstem sunflower. Also, there are late spring reminders, such as green dragon's red berries. American beautyberry blooms alone among trees and shrubs. Junipers drop needles slowly, quietly—without fanfare. July continues to replace storm- and insect-damaged leaves that began to regrow in the May-June rainy season, but rain is now hit and miss, so today's gallery displays represent June's momentum.

Western ironweed in purple and Turk's cap in scarlet are new ad-

ditions. Turk's cap's bright "turbans" of tightly wound petals are special favorites of hummingbirds and butterflies, but they don't open,
so hummers pierce them to extract nectar. They are the first place I
look for zebra and Julia butterflies, wanderers from subtropical south
Texas, whose populations must be large, the south wind strong, and
summer wetter than average for them to appear. Turk's cap too is near
its northern limit in the ravine, and summer is a fitting time for tropical ambience.

8th. Texas horned lizards, usually called horned toads or horned frogs,
are gone from the ravine, perhaps because they require its missing
grassland, although they're extirpated from all of central Texas for
mysterious reasons. I first caught these spiny, endearing creatures as a
youngster at my uncle's house in what has since become the horned-
toadless, Dallas-Fort Worth megalopolis. Gretchen and Mark had the
same fun here, catching and keeping horned toads that in their hey-
day became Texas' official reptile. We always let them go when school
started, because we knew we couldn't keep them over winter.

The ravine's last baby hatched in July 1975, and the last adult was
seen in 1978. Not only did horned toads disappear because of suburban sprawl and reforestation, they also vanished when exotic fire ants
invaded and we dropped pesticides from airplanes on everything below. Yet the fire ants prospered and began to kill native ants and other
insects that horned toads eat. Whether they were poisoned, fire ants
ate their eggs, they starved for lack of native ants, or succumbed to
triple jeopardy, we don't know, because landowners are frightened by
laws that protect this state-endangered animal and deny us permission to study private land where horned toads used to live.

I think of Californians who named the grizzly bear as their state
symbol and promptly exterminated it. But Texans haven't completely
eliminated their state reptile yet, for I hear sundry reports round-
about. The species remains in south Texas despite exotic fire ants
and in arid country west of fire ant range. Meanwhile, as we employ
more pesticides on target, harvester ants are returning and, if we can
save wild landscapes, we might reintroduce horned toads. Since the
only other lizard like it is Australia's thorny devil, we used to have

something very special, and might again—a challenge for an informed and reconnected generation.

9th. Yellowing Ohio buckeye leaves began to fall a few days ago, and enough have now dropped to disclose tan, golfball-sized fruits dangling from the trees. Two saplings I transplanted from Ohio for comparative study begin their yearly die-back two weeks later than Texas cousins, and they leaf out equally later in the spring. The green-leaf season for our own Ohio buckeyes is March-July, although the plants usually take several weeks to go completely bare. Their strategy is to store the solar energy of earliest spring and avoid the hot-dry summer in preparation for next year's start ahead of arboreal competition.

10th. As I clean filters on our common-property swimming pool, a Carolina wren with four eggs flushes from her nest between the gate post and breaker switch panel. She drops to the floor, scoots along it, flutters up a six-foot wall, and exits over the top. In all these years I've found only one natural Carolina wren nest in a creek-bank root tangle. Instead, I find nests in places such as a front door wreath, hanging flower basket, ceramic pot, bicycle basket (the old days), the underside of a seat in an overturned canoe, the cranny of a second floor balcony, clothes pin bag, pants on a clothesline, old parrot cage in an entryway, wicker fishing creel, and metal bucket hung on a garage wall.

Moreover, it is rare to see the same Carolina wren nest again in the same place, whether it was successful the first time or not. At my house, this has never happened within a year and only twice between years, although one or the other or both of two edificial sites are always used. I have no precise record of total nest number, but I know that only twice has a banded individual reused an old site. That's partly because many if not most Carolina wrens don't live longer than one nesting season, and also because the species may avoid competition for cavities and predator perusal of known sites by choosing temporary, hard-to-reach, and diverse physical structures.

11th. A half-eclipse of the sun is expected this afternoon, and I'm poised to see how it affects wild messages. I've read about lizards stopping dead in their tracks, butterflies "freezing" on flowers, and other dramatic events during total eclipses. I'm watching a green anole, a

Ravine forest in winter and spring (same scene)

Ravine forest in summer and autumn
(same scene as previous page)

Creek in spring   Scalybark oak in spring

Creek in autumn   Sugarberries in autumn

Mexican plum

Southern plains trout lily

Plateau spiderlily

Polyphemus moth

Great purple hairstreak
on goldeneye

Gulf fritillary on Turk's cap

Gulf Coast toad

Smallmouth salamander

Rusty (Texas spiny) lizard

Yellow-billed cuckoo

Inca dove on nest

Eastern screech owl with nestlings in box

Young Virginia opossum

Ringtail in owl nest box

Baby eastern cottontail

Nine-banded armadillo

thermometer, the sky, and listening to cicada song at the 2:15 P.M. peak. The clear day darkens as if overcast, the air temperature drops one degree, my subjects are unfazed, and a previously unseen black witch moth flies from my front porch. This tropical visitor is cryptic in shades of brown, gray, and violet when resting, but impressive when flying because of its six-inch wingspread. What a surprise! How can a naturalist be disappointed?

12th. To celebrate Henry David Thoreau's birthday (1817), I ambled for an hour in mid-morning, 1965, along half a mile of trail and surveyed butterflies. Hackberries, questionmarks, and silvery checkerspots were everywhere, including five questionmarks that sipped fresh skunk scat on the path. Gulf fritillaries, buckeyes, and pearl and phaon crescents were less common. Goatweeds, sleepy sulphurs, snout butterflies, giant swallowtails, common wood nymphs, Julias, bordered patches, viceroys, and red-spotted purples were scarce. Altogether, I noted sixteen species, compared with birthday celebrations of twelve species in 1975 and ten in 1985 and 1995.

Weatherwise, July is the most stable time of year and late enough for immigrant tropicals; but, over the four decades that I've lived here, there were differences due to climate, suburban sprawl, and reforestation. Grassland shrinks extirpated wood nymphs, while increased sugarberry trees and a warmer climate may have introduced empress leilias. Reforestation meant fewer species in fewer habitats, but some dynamics were cyclic, such as no buckeyes in 1975, present in 1985, and gone again in 1995. The butterflies taught me about the repeated pattern of a few common and more rare species in any community and predicted an equilibrium of about ten species in mature forest.

What can I suppose Thoreau might have learned at Walden in his New England century? His cutover forest, a mosaic of crop, pasture, and urban land with remnant woodlots, probably housed a diversity of butterflies, something like my 1960s scene. And probably they had increased in species richness, as much of the original forest was cleared and replaced by other habitats. But in the century after Thoreau's death (1862), New England's forest recovered to nearly eighty percent of its original cover, as people moved from farms into cities.

Then I'll bet butterfly diversity declined toward its original forest condition.

13th. One of my banded female cardinals has finished her third nest of the year, six feet high in a roughleaf dogwood by our front gate. She flushes every time anyone walks through, although I leave the gate open. Constantly disturbed, she is one angry bird. I watched her fly off the eggs to join her mate chasing a blue jay and quit incubating to drive another female cardinal from a feeder twenty-five feet away. If a pair of jays had been there and she chased one, she surely would have lost eggs to the other. So, today, I'm amazed when three hatchlings appear. While feeding them, she sings softly. The youngsters fledge after seven days.

Only cardinals that nest in April and May "read books" that say they fledge offspring in nine–eleven days. When summer arrives, and the heat builds, our suburban cardinals produce fledglings after a seven–eight-day nestling period. Another nest, seven feet up in a Mexican plum, has hatchlings with a soft-touch father and no-nonsense mother. As the male arrives with a crushed cicada, a banded month-old fledgling from the pair's second nest flies in, begs, is fed, and the nestlings go hungry. I see this happen several times, although dad does feed his nestlings when the beggar is absent. Mom feeds only the nestlings, who also leave on the seventh day.

Is the male the more efficient parent, because he feeds a more independent offspring that has a head start on survival and better chance of passing on his father's acting ability? But why nest again so quickly, if one's earlier fledglings compete with nestlings and reduce the likelihood of nestling survival? Presumably, the more youngsters produced, the greater the chance that any genes will be passed on, although among birds generally, later offspring don't survive as often, presumably because they have less experience when food becomes scarce. Nature's decision-making process is interesting and confusing, especially if I haven't seen or heard enough messages.

14th. I wonder how long it took for the ravine's earliest humans to learn about weather cycles, since they had no written language. I too kept no written record during the two decades I needed to discover that city weather differs greatly from weather in the country, where my region's official recording station is located. Only in 1985 did I begin to enumerate events in the ravine and verify that summer thunderstorms drop relatively little rain (twelve percent of the average annual precipitation), because they are so spotty. Tropical storms add some (six percent), mostly in late summer and early fall, but by far the most rain (eighty-two percent) is produced by colliding air masses from north and south as seasons change in spring and fall.

15th. Purple martins have been flying around in small flocks, rather than pairs or family groups as they did last spring, for this is assembly time and the start of autumn migration. An hour or two before sunset, the flocks coalesce on conspicuous perches before roosting in the tallest, thickest trees. The usual cheerful twittering of their dawn foraging becomes the dusk cacophony of thousands. One evening, I estimated forty martins per minute flying across the full moon. Another mid-July evening I figured five thousand massed together on wires at a shopping mall, where Nancy and I came for a movie but gave it up in favor of the really big show.

From now until early August, purple martins assemble on utility wires at that same shopping mall situated at the busiest intersection in town. In the midst of a month-long, hundred-degree heat wave, I estimated twenty-five thousand martins, the biggest flock ever. Where did they all come from? Some, surely, came from the north. Several were killed in the traffic. Why did they choose such a dangerous place? If it is attraction to flying insects concentrated at lights, there are dozens of other spots with less human congestion. Perhaps it is the planted live oaks used for roosting. Now that essentially all our martins nest in suburban nest boxes, they may simply ignore culture's downsides.

16th. Among permanent resident birds, titmice, chickadees, woodpeckers, blue jays, crows, and screech owls raise only one brood a year, and stay in family groups through July, gradually learning, though sometimes not soon enough. Today, four titmouse fledglings apparently encounter their first birdbath and jump straight up when they touch the water, one after another like popping corn. Then one leaves to search for insects in a bunch of dead oak leaves, where it is caught by a hidden black ratsnake. The trials and tribulations of youth are many for all animals, including humans, because youngsters are in-experienced—a major drawback to independence.

17th. Sometimes several wildlings tell me about naivete, and today they are a flattened screech owlet and flightless fledgling yellow-billed cuckoo on the street, and a starving baby raccoon eating spilled sun-flower seeds at my feeder in broad daylight. The birds speak very clearly, but I'd forgotten that my neighbor trapped and dispatched a raccoon family from his attic, apparently leaving one escapee to fend for itself. Certainly the juvenile period of life can be double jeopardy in suburbia, where youngsters lack both experience with danger and instinctive avoidance behavior.

Why, then, do screech owls prosper in suburbia? Vehicles as cul-tural predators and weapons such as pesticides account for ninety percent of the dead eggs and owls I find. Yet thirty-six percent of fledglings survive here each year compared to thirty percent in the countryside, and, among breeding adult females, the long-term, sub-urban-rural contrast in annual survival is an average sixty-two versus fifty-three percent. Regardless of added cultural hazards, the advan-tage is explained by more food and less natural predation in suburbia, where seventy-five percent more nests are successful in fledging one or more owlets each year.

18th. Nothing squawks quite like a yellow-crowned night heron. This otherwise austere bird nests in April, high in the branches of creekside trees, two or three pairs within a few hundred feet, never packed together in huge rookeries like other herons. The birds stand immobile as I pass by on the trail. Even if I stop and stare for several minutes, they remain slimly erect, limb-like, transfixed, easily missed by those who don't know them. By mid-June, grown nestlings walk about in the nest tree but freeze if approached. Tonight at dusk, three of these speckled, recently graduated youngsters fly over my house, squawking in unison, going out to dinner together, their nightly quest for aquatic insects, crayfish, and maybe a frog for dessert.

19th. There is a major ruckus at a hollow oak log by my house. Blue jays are mobbing something on the ground. I look, expecting to find a house cat or snake, but see nothing. Then all is quiet. An hour later the fussing picks up again, and I find what must have been the original cause for alarm—a six-foot black ratsnake, coiled, sunning in a clear spot next to the log amid Virginia creepers. It might have been the reason why four screech owl eggs vanished last spring in a nearby nest box. I don't know, of course, but that is natural, and I'm reassured to see a really large snake again in suburbia and know we have help keeping exotic rats in check.

One summer, eight black ratsnake eggs from a neighbor's compost pile hatched into nine-inch babies, each of which I marked—by clipping particular scales beneath the tail—and released at intervals in the ravine. The next spring I found number two, an inch longer, in a neighbor's flower bed only one hundred feet from its release point. Other neighborly ratsnakes of my acquaintance were coiled in a cooking pot in a kitchen cabinet, in a cardinal nest beside my house (having eaten two northern cardinal and one brown-headed cowbird eggs), and crawling on my patio mobbed by fussing songbirds and a wide-eyed, silent screech owl with an incubating mate nearby. When I displaced the snake, the songbirds turned their fury on the owl.

Suburbanites especially dislike large predators, so most snakes don't live long enough to grow to full size. Big ones range too widely, increasing their chance of crossing paths with us. My human neighbors consider all snakes dangerous, or just plain bad, although most are not. Perhaps we've kept an intolerance that originated in prehistoric circumstances of threat from or competition with these predators. In any case, snakes in suburbia are killed by humans with tools such as guns, cars, and hoes, which separate us from reprisal, so we can afford to remain ignorant and unselective. By contrast, natural predators make body contact during predation and must use careful judgement.

20th. The creek below my house has almost dried up, as it does most summers. This morning I watch two thirsty armadillos walk in tandem toward the creekbed, where they scratch among loose rocks. They stop a few times to scarf up with great crunching sounds grounded dying or dead cicadas. They don't bother a black vulture family of four that walk into a shrinking pool. The buzzards drink, bathe, and fly ponderously into creekside elms to preen. Then they fly over to a neighbor's chimney and arrange themselves around the top, apparently to dry off in the sun, for their wings are spread. I'll bet they're refreshed in the escaping air-conditioning.

21st. Twenty years ago the nearest house was two hundred yards away. Although we had forest, grassland in the form of abandoned pastures bordered the trees on two sides and housed critters that I can only reminisce about today. Great Plains narrowmouth toads used to buzz from rain pools, Texas spotted whiptails dug for termites, greater roadrunners cooed on our rooftop, and least shrews scurried while tarantulas traipsed. I'd pick up flat rocks and sometimes find a narrowmouth toad and tarantula rooming together! Presumably, the toads ate pesky ants while the tarantula deterred toad-eaters with threatening fangs and irritating hair—another symbiosis and message about mutually beneficial living.

22nd. July presents more carbon copy weather than any other month —puffy white clouds, light south breeze, high in the middle to upper nineties, low in the middle to low seventies, and local thunderstorms. Yet the forest's gallery is always changing, this time with bright fruits. Bloodberry, balsam gourd, Carolina moonseed, and green dragon berries are red, while Indian cherries are reddish but will turn as black as falling Mexican buckeyes. Pinkish blue Mexican plums are surrounded by the deep purple of dropping mustang grapes. Roughleaf dogwood berries turn white along paths framed by rusty red smooth sumac berries. We animals who eat fruits, dispersing seeds in the process, are attracted to the color of reproduction.

23rd. The mercury reaches a hundred degrees for the first time this summer. More often, though, it's 100 at the official recording station in open prairie, and ninety-five at my house. Still, it's plenty hot. By late July, natives are acclimated or hidden away from high temperatures, and humans are hiding behind air-conditioning. In 1998 the ravine was in the midst of a drought when it was hit by a record 105 degrees and ten weeks with 100 degrees or more on some days each week. Only two and a half inches of rain had fallen in the normal ten-inch May–June period. Herbaceous plants were dead or dying, some trees leafless, and the ground was so dry that a few trees on steep slopes fell over, uprooted from shrunken, cracked soil.

Although we stay relatively cooler in the ravine, we're warmer at night because the leafy tree canopy seals heat in as effectively as it keeps heat out. Leaves reflect sunlight and transpire (release) heat-holding water, keeping the air cooler in the day, but they don't transpire at night. Beneath the July canopy, the daytime temperature averages five degrees lower and the nighttime four degrees higher than the official temperature. Before automatic lawn sprinkling systems and swimming pools became widespread in the 1980s, mid-day July humidity averaged thirty percent. By the 1990s, however, humidity had doubled, so the hot spell of 1998 felt more uncomfortable than the forty-seven consecutive days of one hundred degrees or more in 1980.

El Niño in late 1997 and early 1998 was replaced by *La Niña,* so July was only halfway to the end of summer. Afterward, a serendipitous combination of cold fronts and moisture fed by tropical storms brought twenty-six inches of rain over three months. This more than doubled the average rainfall we didn't get earlier. Dormant plants were stupefied! Spring wildflowers bloomed or rebloomed profusely, so October looked like May. Oaks grew a foot or two of new twigs with leaves, while leafless ashes acted like it was springtime all over again. Although 1998 turned out to be our hottest year until 1999, life was rejuvenated by the extraordinary fall rains.

24th. Listening to the hum of insect multitudes on a summer morning, I give life's richness and provisions some retrospection. How are they linked? Is the pattern of species number and community function positive and linear or does it increase ever more slowly toward dynamic stability? The insects say that it is a matter of time and space transitions from more to less stressful environments. Early and at maximum stress the habitat houses few species, and the play adds actors at a regular pace. Eventually, more stage space (habitat structure) is added, which reduces physical stress and houses more actors, including some who slow things down by storing more energy in larger bodies that live longer and reproduce less.

The few actors on simple stages take great hits from geologic processes and weather so their provisioning is erratic and often reversed.

That was the situation when a tornado and bulldozer hit the ravine and is true for similar situations anywhere. But in the two decades between tornado and bulldozer, the ravine's trees and shrubs had grown large, which buffered the community against storm and drought damage. Stand-in actors like sumacs filled in for lost leads such as elms and sugarberries until the leads could regrow and be joined by supporting cast members. Growth patterns revealed that community function increased rapidly and linearly at first but slowed down as the tree canopy began to close.

25th. An afternoon thunderstorm's cool moisture triggers a rush of bird activity and deposits a migrating spotted sandpiper in the creek. Autumn's first black and white warblers, blue-gray gnatcatchers, warbling vireos, and empidonax flycatchers arrive. Black-billed cardinal youngsters and chickadee children join these early signs of seasonal change. All migrants feed ferociously, as befits the increased metabolic demand of travel and twenty-degree temperature drop to seventy degrees in the last hour. Springlike air stimulates a pair of yellow-billed cuckoos to copulate and a male ruby-throated hummingbird to court a female, who ignores her suitor and punctures Turk's cap blossoms for sustenance in the chilled air.

26th. Cicadas are notably fewer, and so are new blooming plants of any kind. I have a sudden twinge of sadness; summer's annual merger with fall does that to me. Yet flameleaf sumac begins to flower this week, a way of having insect pollinators all to itself, since no sister species reproduces within a month of this date. These large showy shrubs and vines use time to avoid competition in their shared space. Fragrant sumac flowered in mid-March, poison ivy in mid-April, and smooth sumac in mid-May. Now it is flameleaf's turn, and by late August it will be evergreen sumac's. This last species doesn't live here but is only a few miles away, an accident of dispersal at its eastern range limit.

27th. If I were a true-to-form yard owner, I would be out watering, because it hasn't rained in four weeks. But I've screwed down the sprinkler heads and don't mow San Augustine grass that came with the property as required by our homeowners association. Once in a while I do water by hand at dawn to keep the wild soil-holders alive, for they protect the hillside from erosion. I don't use chemical bio-cides or fertilizers, but I do throw coffee grounds out the front door along with spent bouquets, leaves, and limbs from walks, driveway, and deck. However, my yard-woods is hidden from folks who might object to the wild look.

Why put organic debris in the trash to fertilize a landfill that can't use it and then buy chemical fertilizer for a yard? Besides recycling nutrients, leaf mulch insulates, providing benefits that one doesn't have with disintegrating chemicals. Twigs and sticks hold leaves in place on my hillside. Furthermore, this wild yard-woods would be less a daily delight without its burrowing insects, earthworms, slugs, snails, and their snake, skunk, and armadillo predators, all dependent on natural ground cover. And my house guests from afar would be disappointed, for they all ask to see armadillos.

Perhaps the fertilize-water-cut-and-bag-grass routine displays dominance and signals social status. The suburban lawn could be a medieval mindset leftover from the time when European rulers had closely cropped fields, because they had large grazing herds that revealed their wealth and status. Perhaps the fields became lawns and gardens that showed off castles and mansions and were emulated by house owners who could afford to do so. Another theory, more believable to me, is our ancestral need to expose and deter natural predators and human enemies by surrounding ourselves with open lands instead of wooded hiding places.

28th. Often I lament the fate of our gossamer-winged dragonflies and damselflies, the most ancient of aerial predators—the insect equivalents of many birds. Locally, they are called snake doctors or devil's darning needles, reflecting myths about these three-hundred-million-year-old members of the Biosphere. Sky-blue "damsels" are demure, tending to sit on vegetation, compared to bold, blotched "dragons" that cruise back and forth, hawking insects over ravine trails. These elders are increasingly scarce in my neighborhood, because their immature stages (naiads) live in tranquil water that is increasingly rare in the flash-flood-prone environment.

29th. Walking just ahead of me on the trail, Cinder, our black Labrador retriever, steps right on an unusually large common garter snake that flattens, displaying its bright coloration. I pick up this outsized female of thirty inches. No sooner do I release her than I catch and measure a twenty-inch male apparently following her track, and a few minutes later another similar-sized male appears. For mating? It seems early. The female is not gravid (in reptiles, equivalent to pregnant), although young are born about now through September. My earliest record is a brood of eleven on this date. I'm perplexed but happy to see these beautifully marked creatures, each with an orangish red midback stripe flanked by bright yellow stripes.

Their ribbon-snake cousins have the same color pattern in this area. Eastward, both species have all yellow stripes, except in western Florida where the stripes are bluish. Upon capture, both species writhe, spreading a foul-smelling repellent fluid from anal glands. Surely this deters natural predators and, just as surely, the bright colors advise predators to leave these snakes alone after attempted predation that connects color to repugnance. Noxious or toxic creatures often have such warning coloration, and two or more species with repellent features may converge in coloration, increasing the likelihood of teaching predators. I think the regional resemblance of garter and ribbon snakes is an example of this. It is called Mullerian mimicry.

30th. So typical of July, we are still without rain. Clay soil cracks are wide, annual grass is brown, some leaves yellow and fall or drop green if damaged by aphids. Shrubs like coralberry are drought-deciduous. Other plants like Turk's cap are lax or have curled leaves in the heat of the day, adaptations to reduce leaf surface area and water loss. Resident birds pant in the shade with open bills and flopped wings. Tawny emperor butterflies nap on the somewhat cool brick of my front porch, while fox squirrels spraddle over tree limbs, looking like squirrel rugs. Midday is siesta time for animals, including humans in most of the world's cultures except mine, which is too busy feeding its appetite for growth.

31st. Getting up an hour before sunrise, I almost always glance down at my birdbaths, because a family of eastern screech owls may be drinking and bathing. The creek is dry except for two small, spring-fed pools. This is the time for owlets to disperse from their parents' home range. They scarcely beg now and, in any case, their begging is no longer disguised by rasping katydids that disappeared a week ago. June bugs and cicadas are waning, but there are plenty of moths and black crickets to eat. The eastern screech's defensive descending trill signals summer and fall, when owlets are moving all around, in and out of everybody's turf.

On her dawn run, Nancy hears one down the street. His rough, low-pitched trills are unpracticed and immature. Territorial boundaries are reaffirmed by established males and declared by male newcomers. Is he one of "ours?" She can't see a band in the low light. Two pairs nested in Owl Hollow this past spring. One clutch was predated, and its owners left. The other pair, together for five years, includes a female banded as a nestling only a third of a mile away. Ten weeks ago, they fledged one owlet, who could be this singer, dispersed about seven hundred feet from his birth place. If so, he has vacant acres to proclaim, practically on his natal doorstep. I'll keep an ear on him.

The motive of science is the extension of man . . . till his hands should touch the stars, his eyes see through the earth, his ears understand the language of the beast and the sense of the wind, and through his sympathy, heaven and earth should talk with him. *Ralph Waldo Emerson*

August, Prelude to Autumn

A hot-dry time in the old ravine is August, but the year's second monsoon may begin near month's end, kicking off a new wildflower season with frostweed, goldenrod, and rain lilies visited by new generations of butterflies. It mostly depends on hurricanes that move inland as tropical storms or early cold fronts. Rain or not, summer's signature sound of cicadas ceases. Resident birds molt feathers, little yellow hornets pester patio users, green june bugs buzz, and ironclad beetles are underfoot. Perseid meteors turn the night sky into a wondrous pinball machine.

⟩⫯

1st. Rounding the corner of my house, I spot a two-foot mountain (Texas) patchnose snake rooting among leaves under coralberry bushes. It is shopping at my lizard grocery, a moist place where eggs are found. Patchnoses have a distinctively enlarged nose scale for digging out lizard eggs, and they eat the egg layers too. They are thin snakes, colored light tan with a yellow mid-dorsal stripe bordered by two chocolate brown stripes from head to tail, and hard to see, even when crawling slowly. I'm lucky to glimpse this one, which vanishes before my eyes, aware that my size and movements are to be avoided.

2nd. I don't check nest boxes now, because no one's home. The last screech owls finish nesting in mid-July, and they don't use cavities as roosts or food storage lockers in hot weather. Foliage roosts are cooler and insects so plentiful that there is no need to store. Today, though, I notice honeybees going in and out of a box, and I dispatch them because of potential danger from aggressive Africanized bees that spread into our area in 1995. Bees and wasps don't invade active owl nests, because the owls and cohabiting ants keep them out. After fledging, if the ants don't stay, their bee and wasp cousins often arrive. Someone's always knocking in the guild of tree-cavity dwellers.

3rd. Another early cool front brings another migratory surge, including an Acadian flycatcher killed on the street and a rufous hummingbird at my feeders. The typically belligerent rufous chases an adult male ruby-throat. A few purple martins pass through, while white-eyed vireos linger in fall territories and yellow-billed cuckoos feed late nestlings. Resident Inca doves give the tail-up display and "ca-growl" call, preparing to nest again, and northern mockingbirds feed the advance guard of dispersing black crickets to their third broods of fledglings. Autumn is in the air, but summer isn't over by any means.

4th. While turning over his compost pile, a neighbor digs up nine snake eggs buried a foot down and gives them to me. They hatch into black ratsnakes August 19–21. Last year, on August 13, he called when he found three hatchlings and several eggshells in the same warm compost. Had those youngsters lingered because of the warm refuge — eighty-three degrees compared to sixty-six in outside air after a cool front? Heat from decomposition and retained moisture make compost ideal incubation and hibernation places for reptiles, similar to deep organic soil in the forest. Fortunately for these snakes, my neighbor appreciates the importance of sharing stage space with native actors.

5th. I've been watching large flocks of cattle egrets flying overhead in characteristic V-formation. They come from a rookery, a communal nesting place in short dense eastern red cedars at the edge of the industrial park, about a mile to the east, and fly west to feed among livestock. Unlike heron and egret relatives, these white birds dine on land, eating insects kicked up by large native and domestic grazers and browsers. Flights reach a peak in early July but decline now, as fledglings accompany their parents and the families roost closer to pastures. Today there are only a few small flocks and some families walking around in suburban yards eating black crickets.

Cattle egrets flew from Africa to South America and northward to Texas, arriving about 1950. They exchanged elephants and rhinos for our cattle as pasture hosts, and adopted uniform-age woodlots for rookeries in place of the African savannas created by elephants. Then they attracted native egrets, herons, and anhingas to their rookeries. But we dislike rookery odors and noise, so we employ air cannons to scare the birds and emulate elephants by bulldozing the trees. Unlike nature's selective tree removal, however, we clear the ground, so cattle egrets will establish new interracial neighborhoods in the nearest uniform-age woodlots we inadvertently created for them by bulldozing in the past.

6th. At 6:30 this morning I sit in darkness on my patio, substituting ears and nose for eyes. I am serenaded by a male screech owl's descending trills, echoed by a dispersing youngster. As the elder soloist moves away, perch to perch, singing, heading downhill toward the creek, my attention shifts to clicking Mediterranean geckos, truly vocal nocturnal lizards, and to junipers, locally called cedars, in woodland above the creekbottom forest. Cedar's pleasant, pungent odor typifies a cedar break, or brake, both names applied by Anglo pioneers because their woodland was an abrupt shift in the prairie landscape and a barrier to traveling on horseback or horse-drawn wagon.

Unblended into this scented musical is the noisy prelude to rush hour traffic on the divided four-lane highway a mile upwind, and barking dogs touched off in succession by joggers passing fenced yards. My newspaper is thrown by an adult from a truck that wheels through the cul-de-sac, and I remember with nostalgia my growing-up days of delivering newspapers by bicycle. A neighboring physician leaves for the hospital, beckoned by an ambulance siren. Essence of just-cut yard grass mixes with aroma of fertilizer laced with biocide— not so sweet! This mix of natural and unnatural history shifts strongly to the unnatural, as the human workday takes over.

7th. Big green cicadas are gone. A few lingered the past few days, not venturing to sing until late in the morning—later and at a higher temperature than in June, when these insects began to proclaim summer. Other smaller cicadas are later-day singers, but I miss the big green chorus, whose bodies litter the ground. Nancy and I are walking Ginger, our yellow Lab, on the street. It is nature's trash-recycling day, not culture's, although my suburb begins voluntary recycling in 1997. A half-grown armadillo nonchalantly cruises cicada bodies in a front yard, a glance away from suburbanites driving to work passed landfill garbage.

Green june bugs emerge as if to fill the vacant cicada niche. They don't sing but buzz loudly, flying in daylight like cicadas. They're a stout inch in length, velvety green with golden orange along the edges, and second cousins to the ubiquitous brown june bugs of spring and early summer—and they're replacement food for any critter that munches on short fat insects. Also just emerged is an attractive inch-and-a-quarter-long, white-mottled, black beetle that crawls nonchalantly, getting stepped on but seldom squashed by joggers who mumble about hitting stones. It is the ironclad beetle, an ambling fortress—the insect world's equivalent of an armadillo.

8th. Any one of the ravine's mostly natural populations is cyclic, while its human counterpart grows linearly. Eastern screech owls, for example, fluctuate from a peak of eighteen to a low of ten nesting pairs per square mile every four to five years, and thus from peak to peak every nine to ten years. Their ups and downs are caused by the usual planetary connections—weather and numbers effecting resources and predators effecting survival effecting reproduction—and send the same message about wildlife's ten-year cycle as northern bobwhites do in Illinois, lynx in Canada, and willow grouse in Europe.

In the past four decades, my human neighbors have doubled in number, sprawled over ravine wildland, and erased three-quarters of its green, calling it progress. They've mostly missed wild neighbors, who continually remind them that populations always rise and fall around a size supported by the Biosphere's interlocking cycles. Otherwise, they crash, sometimes to zero, as did several very instructive human civilizations before ours. The owls sing that while the unnatural use of fossil fuels may permit short-sightedness, nature is only patient and not permissive.

9th. When he heard scratching at his back door this evening in 1988, a neighbor opened up to greet a porcupine who may have smelled his salty sweat on the door handle. Then the beast slowly waddled off into the woods. I'd seen a couple of roadkills close by but not a live porky in the ravine. This is not their original home, and they'd been around only about five years. They expanded eastward across Texas during the great 1950s drought, apparently seeking greener pastures. I would really like to see a live one here but I never have, nor have I found any porky roadkills since the mid-1990s. If porcupines have disappeared, it's probably another example of dynamic flux at a species' range margin.

10th. Freshly minted eastern tiger swallowtails and pearl crescents have just joined the year's butterfly medley, an eight-month, aerial kaleidoscope. I've missed their brightness in August's relatively quiet colors. My records for twelve March-appearing species suggest that subsequent generations, except the last, emerge rather synchronously, almost within a two-week period. Second broods are focused in the

last week of April, third broods a month later, and fourths in the first week of July, but fifths may appear anytime, August to October, or be omitted entirely depending on fall rain and the regrowth of food plants.

11th. Whether walking in the ravine or on the street, I marvel at the aerial excellence of the wind masters. There is no disguising my love of hawks and vultures, especially when they sail on rising thermal winds. This year's young broad-winged hawks left for the tropics yesterday, riding an early cold front with cousins behind parents who had already departed. I'll miss their morning greetings. Our nesting individuals depart a month before the first big passage of northern broadwings and return in the spring a month earlier, because their act is nicely tuned to our particular scene.

12th. Once in a while some traveling exhibit reappears, representing a very long cycle, reminding me that I may try to understand seasonal and annual events but can only marvel at the longer ones. I am myopic about celestial messengers that teach about humanity's minute role in universal time. Very early this morning I watch Perseid meteors streaking out of the northeast. They are debris left behind by the comet Swift-Tuttle that passed through our inner solar system five years ago and won't be seen again for a century. Even more instructive and awesome was the comet Hale-Bopp in the spring of 1997, last seen by the ravine's first people 2,400 years ago!

13th. Nancy and I often get "what's it" questions about native neighbors. Most folks have no idea who it is that crawls into their lives, and some don't care. They only want to eliminate the intrusion. Wild things are low priority in busy lives that involve but don't acknowledge natural partnerships. Today, though, a neighbor reported a brightly ringed snake dead on the road and identified it as a poisonous coral snake with bordering red and yellow ("kill a fellow") rings, by contrast to the harmless milksnake's red and black ("good for Jack"). The resemblance, called Batesian mimicry, protects milksnakes but only from natural predators.

Someone heard that Nancy squashed a brown recluse spider in our bathtub. "What do they look like?" "Light tan, spindly looking spiders, body and extended legs about quarter-sized with a darker violin-shaped mark on the back." "And what are those little brown bugs with so many crawling legs? Do they bite? I called the exterminator!" Nancy explains that they're millipedes that enter our houses seeking moisture in the summer dryness. They are harmless and, in fact, helpful to the woods by eating and thus recycling dead vegetable matter. "Pick them up in your fingers—they don't bite—and toss them outside. Then smell your fingers, which have the interesting, harmless odor of an anti-predator repellent."

She and I talk of a time when humans knew the wild world around themselves, because their lives depended on it. As personal safety and the tribe's general knowledge increased, people began to depend on others for information. Then came books, and now computers, to replace the tribe's verbal inventory, and we depend on money to buy information. We've lost primal knowledge about nature, although we've moved to suburbia in search of nature's services, such as fresh air, shade, and greenery. We've forgotten that those services and thus our lives are permanently attached to snakes, spiders, and millipedes.

14th. All week people are sniffling, and allergists are telling them it's mold spores. The mold count is high, to be sure, but what about cedar elm pollen? It is the only leading tree in the ravine that flowers in late summer. Cedar elm can be impressive, averaging sixteen inches in diameter and sixty feet tall—lots of pollen, especially when you add its abundance to size. This tree co-dominates streamsides and leads all trees on lower north- and east-facing slopes, even registering on the hotter-dryer south- and west-facing slopes and scarp edges. Few others of the mature forest are invasive, but cedar elm ranks high in ability to colonize after disturbances. I can read human history in the ravine's rows of cedar elms, junipers, and sugarberries marking former ranch fencelines.

15th. A dark little snake only three inches long with a white neck ring wriggles across the trail. It looks like a newly hatched ringneck snake, a rare species locally, but its belly is only a few shades lighter than its dark brown back, not bright yellow with black spots like a ringneck. It's a newborn rough earth snake. DeKay's (brown) snakes also begin life with a neck ring, but only the true ringneck retains its ring into adulthood. The DeKay's ring is connected light spots that fade with maturity, as does the rough earth snake's youthful ring. All three species live secretive lives in leaf litter, eating earthworms and slugs, although adult ringnecks switch to eating small reptiles. What is the significance of the neck ring, anyway, and why do the young of some species lose it while others don't? Why advertise the vulnerable head? The answers are missing, like the answers to most of my questions, and that stimulates continued searching.

16th. Although some unusual species live in the ravine, none are threatened or in danger of extinction. Of course, we think snakes are threatening, which is why they are in danger. Some, such as copperhead and eastern hognose snake, seem to have been extinguished here after decades of unrelenting persecution. Other animals—in fact, most of them—don't find permanent refuge because of city growth. Nationwide appraisals of endangered native animals list urbanization among the three most serious human impacts, and I figure that includes preempted land, cars, pets, poisons, and power tools in the arsenal of cultural weapons.

17th. When frustrated dragonflies lay eggs in my birthbath and our community swimming pool, I know that summer drought is extra tough. There's no damp soil at least six inches deep and no mud in the creekbed. Leaves drop green and brittle, sucked dry by aphids, and turn yellow, brown, and fall from sugarberry and red mulberry. Leaf miner and tent caterpillar food is not replaced. Fruits and nuts drop prematurely, but "horse apples" are on schedule. They are the softball-sized fruits of osage orange (*bois d'arc*) trees, locally called bowdarks. In an exceptionally dry summer the forest is "winterized." I can see right through it!

18th. During this driest period of the year, we may stroll on the limestone bed of the river normally fed by our creek. What water remains is in pools. This river is dammed into the reservoir downstream, but well above that the low water level discloses what we came to find— fossil sea urchins, ammonites, nauteloids, clams, oysters, scallops, and other marine creatures. They tell of a distant time and an asteroid or meteor impact that shifted scenes and casts of actors from ammonites and dinosaurs to mammals, and eventually to humans who commandeer the most stage space in the shortest scene of the great play.

Because they're in even greater danger, red-shouldered hawks and blue mistflowers in the remnants of floodplain forest cry out that my species has already drowned most of their home permanently, not cyclically as befits the life of this seasonally flooded habitat. The dam is scheduled to be raised again to impound even more water for more suburban sprawl, and their forest will disappear completely. They ask if we strollers realize that we disrupt the natural cycle of water renewal that depends on forest vegetation that shields the land from erosion and extends the reservoir's life.

19th. Inca doves are knocked back by cold weather and predation but little-affected by summer drought. They numbered only two adults and a fledgling last February. By June the pair raised two more youngsters. Today they have a third baby, and another pair joins them with another offspring. Later, the flock may number ten or a dozen with ongoing flux, since Inca doves nest every month except January. Their lives are a sequence of messages that, before suburbanization, natural predators were population regulators, not exterminators, winter was tough but survivable, and to cycle was certain.

20th. *1990*: My suburb just finished erasing a four-tenths of a mile by fifty-foot-wide section of our nature preserve's streamside forest in order to plant a six-inch diameter sewer line. The city had a utility easement and needed to remove a sewage lift station that overflowed into the creek. I agreed completely about ending the pollution but not the needlessly wide swath of destruction. I showed the mayor, city manager, and a construction company official how to save heritage values, but that pre-destruction field trip was only public relations on their part. Fortunately for the rest of us, the forest would teach about healing.

1991: Sixteen species of woody plants are growing in my twenty study sites around each of the year-old sewer line's twenty manholes. Most are in the shadiest, most litter-covered and hence protected spots. Sugarberry and cedar elm are native dominants that total fifty-four percent of all seedlings and saplings, but exotic chinaberry is among the top ten species. Flameleaf and smooth sumacs are successional opportunists, averaging taller than the other woody plants, indicating a quicker growth response to the increased sunlight. They weren't part of the original forest, so their seeds had to be imported by birds, who are registered nurses in the healing process.

1999: There are still sixteen tree and shrub species, but half the study sites are covered by exotic Japanese honeysuckle, and most sumacs are dead. The sugarberry and cedar elm lead has dropped to thirty-six percent which, with the demise of the sumacs and arrival of seedling and sapling box elder, red mulberry, American elm, bur oak, pecan, black walnut, and eastern red cedar, indicates that forest recovery is underway. But the rampant honeysuckle, plus chinaberry and invading Chinese tallow, nandina, ligustrum, and others from suburbia are setbacks, indicating that the preserve needs rehabilitation therapy if we wish to save it.

21st. At midday a curious, soft warbling in the treetops is traced to northern cardinals. The song is new to me, and apparently to others too, for I can't locate any written description. Interesting that such a familiar bird is so unfamiliar. I notice that warbling youngsters are beginning to molt feathers, and their black bills show some red. The adult male sheds too. I've seen enough stray feathers around lately to know that this is close to the peak of summer molt for resident songbirds. Eastern screech owls peaked a few weeks ago but still shed body feathers. Young of the year will acquire a semi-adult look in another month, but no adult wing and tail feathers until their second summer.

Feathers become frayed and faded and must be replaced once or twice a year by songbirds and once by eastern screech owls. Worn gray screech owls may fade to brown. I guess that molting adult screech owls can't fly well enough to catch the extra food needed for dependent offspring, which is why they finish nesting before molting. Few flight feathers are shed while there are hungry mouths to feed and, if they are, those mouths are from late replacement nests. Multiple brooded cardinals normally produce offspring in mid to late summer, so it is understandable that their molt is later. Perhaps the soft warbling signals molting and is so narrowly seasonal that it's easily missed.

22nd. Frostweed has started to bloom, a "school bell" for autumn insects. After our first hard freeze, frostweed will reveal its name, but now the clusters of white flowers on three- to six-foot stalks in sunny openings are hopping with bugs, especially sparkling butterflies. A ten-by-ten-foot patch in my yard-woods holds a beauty pageant for hairstreaks—gray, red-banded, juniper, dusky blue, and great purple —and there are eight other butterflies, large and small, plus "bodyguard" wasps and bees. There is no more concentrated diversity of form and color anywhere that I've seen, not even in the tropics.

23rd. Summer drought continues, so I begin to water yard-woods study plots in different ways to learn how much rain stimulates the leaves of dayflowers and spiderlilies to grow. It's at least an inch in one to three days, simulating a tropical storm. White-eyed vireos and Carolina wrens, the only dawn singers, join hummingbirds drinking and bathing in my water droplets. Why don't the neotropical migrants leave? Great-crested flycatchers have! The smaller birds must know something I don't, because three days later a real storm arrives, supporting the suburban folk adage that rain happens when we water lawns or wash cars.

24th. A greater roadrunner busily flips and pounds a small snake of some kind, a signal that hatchlings of egg-laying species and the recently born young of live-bearers are out and about. It's just a month after I found newly hatched lizards, which are suitable food for the baby serpents of late August. Tonight, a hatchling ratsnake climbs our front porch bricks, apparently trailing Mediterranean geckos, although it will switch to eating rodents and birds when it grows up. In so doing, it will compete less often with roadrunners, who now eat more grasshoppers and crickets than lizards or snakes. Reduced competition among predators and their tandem cycles with prey are important stabilizing features in wild neighborhoods.

25th. Despite the heat I try hard to think of fall, since prairie goldenrod begins to flower on dry slopes. It tells me to watch for tall goldenrod on the lower hillside, a more definite sign of seasonal change. American beautyberries are newly ripe, and a cool front brings a brief morning nip, but this afternoon's high of ninety-six erases thoughts of fall. Prairie goldenrod blooms two weeks before western ragweed, flanked later by tall goldenrod, so both showy yellow plants are blamed for hayfever. But they are insect-pollinated, which means their pollen isn't windblown and, therefore, not so allergenic. It is ragweed's inconspicuous flowers that employ a breeze, as my nose always knows.

26th. Sunrise fills the sky with red. The day is hazy and slow. Animal activity drags, including my own. Sunset is spectacular, for the full moon glows red. Afterward, a screech owl follows me, flying among perches, as I mow the trailside, exposing black crickets. The owl makes beeline dives and sings like a distant whinnying horse between sorties. The atmospheric haze, red sun, and now red moon are caused by smoke blown in from massive forest fires a thousand miles away in Yellowstone National Park. The haze remains for five weeks in this summer of 1988, lowering air temperatures and reinforcing messages about the Biosphere's inclusiveness.

27th. Little yellow hornets that feasted on a road-killed fox squirrel now may tug at my bare toes, as I rest on my patio. The appearance of these mild-tempered insects, nature's tiny garbage collectors, is as characteristic of the season as the swarming of black field crickets, whose car- and foot-smashed bodies are everywhere. There is plenty for scavengers to do. Spotted-wing scorpionflies will finish off insect carcasses, as the last bugs fall with the first frosts. The insect world parallels my backboned world, but moves energy along and recycles nutrients with special vim and vigor because of its vastly greater numbers.

28th. Eryngo and snow-on-the-mountain have showy blooms that confirm the end of the prairie summer. Instead of the name eryngo, I prefer purple thistle, although the plant is actually a wild carrot. My name calls attention to the rich lavender and prickly thistle-like flowers and leaves. Snow-on-the-mountain is a relative of the poinsettia but with snow-white, green-centered leaves around its inconspicuous flower heads. Both wildflowers grow tall enough to stand out and seem unbothered by the seasonal drought. I regret that the ravine's remnant grassy patches have disappeared, because purple thistle and snow-on-the-mountain are gone with them.

Nancy and I often remember the missing by cutting bouquets in the countryside. Most of the plants are prairie disturbance indicators encouraged by livestock grazing or roadside mowing. Two weeks ago we brought purple thistle indoors, and today, for the first time, we notice a marvel of camouflage and secrecy, an adult green lynx spider resting quietly below the top flowers. It is three inches between toe-tips on spiny legs, supporting an inch-long greenish gray body—not small by any means—and a beautiful blend into the thistle's spiny green lower flowers. I take it outside to patio plants, whereupon it jumps to safety and vanishes.

29th. During a dry spell, if a cold front triggers an inch or more of rain on lawns or other open ground, Drummond's rain lilies will appear in two to three warm days, or a week in cool weather. Miraculously, out of nowhere it seems, they are blooming. The single snow-white flowers on leafless stems up to a foot tall are a botanical resurrection that may occur after any extended dryness from June to October. Often they form eye-catching colonies, so it amazes me that yard mowers just cut right through them as if they don't exist. Rain lilies are "weeds" in suburban lawns but to me a pleasing reminder that natives can survive our monocultural mania.

Copper lilies have the same flowering regime but occur locally only along highways. A botanist colleague thinks this species could be an historic import brought by Spanish explorers-missionaries from temperate South America via Mexico. Its local distribution seems to follow the old Spanish trails, except where soil has been moved around by construction. Copper lilies bloom in what corresponds to early spring in the temperate southern hemisphere, and there are no reports of the plant in the six thousand miles of intervening space. If they were responsible, the Spanish of five hundred years ago were only human, insofar as introductions are concerned.

People have a tradition of importing aliens. Even first Americans carried and traded animals, plants, and seeds. Considering that to move domestic and unintended organisms among continents and islands is human, our capacity to alter faraway landscapes is both fascinating and disturbing. I point to modern society for self-service that threatens the Biosphere but acknowledge that we have learned from successive generations of ancestors whose introductions, intended more for personal survival than for pleasure, became agents of extinction by outcompeting, overeating, or poisoning native organisms.

30th. Gazing upwards on this clear night, I marvel at my cosmic community, the Milky Way. Venus is Earth's nearest planetary neighbor, the bright evening planet in the lingering southwestern twilight. It is an instructively hot place, too hot for familiar life—so shrouded in thick, insulating, greenhouse gases, that we can't see its surface. Venus sends an important message, as Earth's own greenhouse layer thickens. It connects me with all times and places just as surely as fossils do. Last week I looked again at Venus, and just shook my head, as I listened to endangered Atlantic right whales from a boat on the Bay of Fundy, Canada. The whales asked me why today's humans are so forgetful.

31st. This morning Nancy and I are driving when we see Mississippi kites take off from a woodlot behind a truckstop. I simply can't resist these graceful birds, so I pull off the road and walk over. Soon the aerial acrobats are swooping and circling, some flapping, most sailing near ground level over the gravel parking lot. We are surrounded by whirling gray bodies with lighter gray heads and peering yellow eyes, as the kites breakfast on grasshoppers and black crickets, caught and eaten on the wing. After twenty minutes of refueling, the flock moves southward, spiraling high in the rising thermal wind.

This night, more migrating Mississippi kites roost in trees by our house, followed by Carolina wrens in a patio hanging basket a half-hour later. Wrens need more activity time, because they require more food per unit of body mass. They must forage harder, which includes later. Kites conserve energy by soaring, and their greater size means less skin surface area through which to lose heat and more mass in which to store energy as fat. Furthermore, kite food, even insects, comes in less-frequently-caught, larger packages, an additional savings. The kite's lifestyle is geared to longevity, the wren's to brevity with lots of replacements.

The kites lay two eggs per clutch once a year, compared to the wren's four to six eggs each in several clutches. Wrens lose more eggs to predators but produce more offspring per pair, more of which die before breeding. These are nature's life-history strategies: large body, long life, low reproduction versus small body, short life, and high reproduction. Both schemes work, as shown by both birds' abundances and broad ranges. I'm like the kite, except that my cultural drop in death rate diverges from my naturally low birth rate, creating an exploding population. The kite and wren warn that I could be the first long-lived strategist to self-destruct.

A land ethic changes [our] role from conqueror of the land community to plain member and citizen of it . . . the conqueror role is eventually self-defeating. . . . *Aldo Leopold*

September Vacillates

Summer may linger on, but Labor Day weekend is often the last extended hot weather, followed by cooling rain that stimulates spring wildflowers to jump-start and black crickets to disperse, and beckons Rio Grande leopard frogs to their annual songfest. Tree sap begins its run back to winter in roots, seeping through breaks in the bark, and inviting the year's last butterfly drinkers. Against the backdrop of an orange harvest moon, great horned owls hoot about the prospect of nesting, while northern songbirds arrive for their year-end vacation.

1st. This was our forty-seventh and last consecutive hundred-degree or hotter day in 1980, our first summer in Owl Hollow. But I missed the message. First 1990 and then ensuing years became the Earth's hottest. Message repeated! How much climatic warming is due to nature's interglacial period and how much to culture's greenhouse gases is uncertain, but we know we're major culprits. We can't change nature, but we can change ourselves; and, indeed, a quarter of us now have a world-view consistent with balance in the Biosphere. That quarter, however, is offset by the larger fraction of folks who are ignorant or in denial, and we're good at denial when greed is involved.

2nd. One summer at Butterfly Hollow we had periodic rain beginning in late July, and everything was green on this date. Yellow-billed cuckoos even stopped forecasting. Flameleaf sumac, low petunia, and Turk's cap flowered vigorously to the enjoyment of insects, including a northward migration of snout butterflies by the thousands and the vanguard of southward-moving monarchs. Black field crickets swarmed. But today in another summer we'd had only one brief rain in ten weeks, so the woods lost life to death, inactivity, and migration. Even so, eastern screech owls sang their horse-whinny trills, proclaiming the dispersal of offspring—for them September's character despite the weather.

3rd. On our patio sits a twenty-two-inch concrete birdbath cast from the fossil footprint of the three-toed, bipedal carnivorous dinosaur called *Acrocanthosaurus.* It was a gift from Nancy to remind me who lived near here when the ravine's limestone was the silt of a shallow sea bottom one hundred million years ago. Down the patio slope is a foot-high homemade birdbath of similar color and diameter and, nearby, an artificial three-by-five-foot pond. All birds, reptiles, insects, and mammals bathe or drink at the birdbath, or drink at the pond, but only permanent residents are used to using bigfoot.

Insects, anoles, downy woodpeckers, chickadees, titmice, and house finches also drink at my hummingbird feeders. An acrobatic anole climbs down a wire from the porch roof to one feeder. Like short-billed birds, wasps, and bees, it can't get anything when the level of sugar-water drops. Either these animals benefit from the extra energy or use hummingbird feeders as water sources in dry weather, because all of them recheck the availability of reachable liquid. Since I supply water otherwise, I'll bet they're as hooked on sugar as I am—in other forms.

4th. Big spiders in big webs typify autumn. One rotund species, the Christmas-tree orbweaver, loves my front porch and eats its web before dawn, reweaving it each night. It is brown and named for the mark on the underside of its abdomen. The black and yellow garden spider is our family favorite, the children's "Charlotte." Hatchlings hang small webs by late April, but inch-long females are especially prominent now in two-foot webs with densely woven vertical "ladders" in the center. If disturbed, they bounce, vibrating the webs rapidly, increasing their visibility.

The garden spider's dense center weaving and vibrations signal large mobile animals like birds to avoid the web, so its owner doesn't have to expend energy in repair that could go into producing eggs. Bright body markings and trampoline behavior enhance the visual effect. The Christmas-tree orbweaver avoids predation by being relatively somber and nocturnal. By reweaving its web each night, using energy from eating the previous night's web, it is a natural recycler, which is more efficient than repairing breakage, especially if it hasn't caught anything recently.

5th. Most of the forested ravine consists of the backyards of house lots, and I'm happy that many property owners like trees as much as I do. Some have modified the forest, but the total only amounts to about five percent of the area. In one backyard, junipers are forbidden. In another, most everything below tree canopy level—shrubs, rocks, tree trunks, and other ground cover—has been removed. The owner rakes the ground free of fallen leaves, so it is bare at all times and subject to drought and erosion. Are these folks afraid of something or just civilizing nature?

Our distant ancestors lived in trees, so we may have an inherited affinity for forest; although I occasionally feel claustrophobic, surely a protective mechanism left over from closer ancestors who lived in savannas. I can understand the need to see a long way and to believe that nothing dangerous is hiding in vegetation. Maybe that's why I like views from trees, mountains, and my roof. My guess is that most people came to enjoy the trees, not realizing long-inherited phobias, while some want to show nature who they think is boss.

6th. Autumn flocks of migratory birds usually are small and contain only a few silent individuals of a few species. They can be inconspicuous unless one looks for noisier foraging groups of chickadees and titmice soon after a cold front changes to south wind. Among the migrants, however, blue-gray gnatcatchers are fussy. Yesterday was muggy and still, but the wind shifted in the late afternoon and we had a thunderstorm with nearly two inches of rain. This morning chickadees and titmice bathe, chatter, and adjust feeding matters in dripping oaks, emulated by migrant gnatcatchers, flycatchers, and warblers.

Watching mixed foraging flocks here and in tropical forests, I've noticed that resident birds are more than consorts. They are flock organizers and leaders that chart the course that seasonal species follow, and they are first to sound alarm about predators. Wintering white-throated sparrows, for instance, let resident northern cardinals mob eastern screech owls, while they watch and presumably learn. Even when given their own agendas on a field trip to a new site, my students tend to flock with me. There is a survival advantage in accompanying those who know about local danger and when and how to find resources in unfamiliar places.

7th. Some people like nature, because they appreciate ancestral connections. Others prefer a shopping mall. My close friend and colleague, Jochem Burckhardt, not a biologist but a naturalist, recognized his heritage and truly felt the wild. He would stand by a big tree or on a cliff, raise his arms, take a deep breath, and exclaim, "*wunderbar!*" (wonderful). Jochem died tonight, as the waning moon, Venus, Mars, Castor, and Pollux lined up, southeast to northwest, directing his spirit to sail with the wind along our walking-talking paths from the *Philosophenweg* in Heidelberg and Bavarian meadows to the southwest's mountain islands—a spirit that is always with me.

8th. Black field crickets attain adulthood these days and, triggered by rain, fly into suburban lives, much to human consternation. Because they are attracted to lights, swarms are crushed beneath street lamps, on sidewalks, and under store windows. They invade buildings to become fodder for commercial pest exterminators. Natural predators are treated to a repast to match earlier feasts of june bug and green cicada.

Raccoons linger, licking up the freshly smashed food, and one itself is smashed on the road. A greater roadrunner snatches so many crickets that it affords the leisure of prolonged drinking and bathing in my bird bath, followed by preening and sunning in a dead oak, where it is mobbed by songbirds who remember what it ate last spring.

9th. September rain following summer drought stimulates male tarantulas to begin nocturnal wandering in search of females. As I sit on my patio listening to and smelling wild things, a big, black high-stepper traipses by. I wish him well, because tarantulas cannot abide reforestation or suburbanization. Most folks won't miss them—spiders rank with snakes as undesirables—but I will, for they were favored pets in my grade school days and are part of our landscape heritage in fact and folklore. My European friends and colleagues think of Texas as a land of tarantulas along with rattlesnakes, horned toads, and armadillos—and cowboys of course.

10th. Three young raccoons flush from a street drain during a thunderstorm. They race up a big oak and huddle high on a limb, bleary eyed. A few migrant birds fuss, but only briefly. Resident birds take a silent look and leave. Normally, when songbirds gather to mob predators such as these, or owls in particular, permanent residents are involved twice as often as migrants in autumn and five times more frequently in spring when they are nesting and have a reproductive commitment. Today's residents recognize that small, soggy raccoons pose little threat, whereas the transient birds don't know that.

Another time, strolling down Owl Hollow, I flush an eastern screech owl that flies into a thicket of saplings. A mob of songbirds quickly forms, so I sit down to learn about the drama. The songbirds pester the owl for sixteen minutes, led by a male northern cardinal who approaches within two feet. He's backed up by a female and two black-billed fledglings, a pair of Carolina wrens, three chickadees, an American robin, and a migrant blue-gray gnatcatcher. Only the male cardinal gets close, and he also makes the most noise. Other birds stay behind him, the residents giving vocal support, while the gnatcatcher is mostly and uncharacteristically silent.

My experiments with taped screech-owl songs and freeze-dried

specimens indicate that mobbing is visual assessment, vocal warning, and teaching. Danger is signaled and only incidentally deflected, although jays and crows can displace an owl. Birds eaten by the owls, especially males of permanent residents, mob most frequently and intensely. All others tend to be minor fussbudgets or onlookers. Mobbers use seasonally specific songs and plumages as cues to their act, hardly bothering with fledgling owls in cross-barred plumage, but recognizing the vertical breast steaks of adults as danger signals.

The parallel among humans is parents telling their children to stay back—the incident I witnessed of moms clubbing a snake to death in the street in front of "fledgling" softball players. As a transient member of their community I looked on from the periphery, though afterward tried to educate the mob. Another time neighbors called me to extract a black ratsnake from their kitchen cabinet. Behind me they formed a line of defense, holding children back, as I bagged the harmless but angry invader and told them why I don't kill snakes. Those were learning situations that I hope mattered.

11th. When sap runs back into tree roots, it may seep through breaks in the bark, inviting butterflies and beetles to drink the sugary fluid. I relate to these gatherings, since real maple syrup is my elixir. Late this afternoon, four hackberries, two goatweeds, a wood nymph, a questionmark, and two green june beetles tank up at a sap bar. A male hackberry displaces his drinking buddies only a few inches, but he can't stand passersby. He chases a Wilson's warbler, a ruby-throated hummer, and me every time I pass—three times! I know, because the second time I catch and mark him with extra-large white spots on his forewings.

An hour later he's still there with a red admiral, red-spotted purple, and the june bugs—and he chases me again. Apparently, he owns the bar and I'm unwelcome near it. I watch for another half hour. The warbler and hummer are catching small insects attracted to the sap and occasionally flush the hackberry and his drinking companions, but I don't bother them. Maybe I'm the closest thing to a black bear his instincts "remember." A bear could displace everyone and loves sugary tree sap like the rest of us. Could this butterfly deter a bear, if it wanted that sap? Not likely, and I remain perplexed.

12th. Provided with shelter and a garden of insects and lizards to hunt, yellow-bellied racers learn to live in my house. Anytime, one may spend a few days in the English ivy around the big Shumard oak beside my front porch. One summer a hatchling lived in a weep hole between the bricks by the patio, and another larger racer stayed in the "basement" of my water meter in the driveway, coming and going through the hole used to open the lid. Both remained several days. I watched them watch me from time to time and heard the meter reader shout and drop the metal lid on the concrete one morning, after which he and the racer disappeared for good.

13th. Ginger sniffs a beeline into the woods and catches a half-grown Virginia opossum that feigns death. The critter is limp, eyes closed, jaws open, tongue hanging out, as she retrieves it and lays it in our garage. We leave the possum and, after our walk, it is gone. Several times before, other natives have "played possum" in response to my handling or the dog's. Such death feigning seems to stimulate predators to put prey down because of its sudden change from active defense or attempted escape to passivity. Then, when the predator is distracted or away, the captive departs, leaving little doubt that death feigning is lifesaving.

Friends want to hold death-feigning female screech owls that I take from nests as I examine nestlings. When they relax their hold, the owl suddenly flies away. Studying these situations, I note that screech owls open one eye very slightly, and I wonder if possum-playing possums appraise odors and sounds before exiting. I've seen tentative tongue-flickering (odor testing) by small snakes that roll upside down while death feigning. If captors are still, there is a gradual or rapid righting of the body and slow or quick escape movement. My lesson is to lie down quietly if attacked by a grizzly bear five times my own weight. But will I have the fortitude of a screech owl held by me, 450 times its weight?

14th. Any big autumn migration is rare enough that today I'm overwhelmed. Yesterday's cold front turned around as a northward-moving warm front, a "stop sign" to migratory birds. I can't even count the Wilson's warblers. There are over a hundred in the nature preserve with perhaps twenty-five to fifty each of American redstarts, black-throated green and Nashville warblers, empidonax flycatchers, Baltimore orioles, and lesser numbers of black and white warblers, yellow-breasted chats, yellow-throated and red-eyed vireos, great-crested flycatchers, whip-poor-wills, and yellow-billed cuckoos. I estimate thirty passage migrants per acre, six times the density of birds in the breeding season. It's an experience in biodiversity as the spice of life.

15th. Once in a while, during a thunderstorm, a night-migrating water bird is forced down or mistakes a wet suburban street for a creek, lands to rest and refuel, and can't take off because it must flap-run over water to gain momentum. This often happens near dawn, the usual time for cold-front storms. The few, live, uninjured water birds brought to my attention are mostly rails, rarely grebes, and once a white pelican—a real wrestling match. If unharmed, all are released into appropriate habitat. This morning, though, it is a misguided sora rail so badly smashed by a car that I can't even save the specimen.

Teenagers are rushing to pre-school events, and adults drive to work just as maniacally fast. Many clutch drinks or talk on cellular phones. Confused water birds are "dead ducks," as are any land birds that fly low over the street. Toads that forage for earthworms on the wet pavement are unintended targets. Opossums, armadillos, and snakes are particular car meat. Nancy finds a dead female opossum with eight babies in her pouch, confirming in an unhappy way that this critter breeds so late in the year. One September I counted a roadkill every five days on our two-mile walk, the numbers correlating positively with overnight rainfall.

16th. Another fifteen minutes until sunrise, so I'll head home along the trail. A swamp rabbit, one of the last of its kind, jumps ahead into thick woods. It's a rare sight. Swamp rabbits are skulky anyway, but scarce since they began to decline when the forest area started shrinking. Half again larger than eastern cottontails, they need more space and cannot abide lawns and shrubbery. They require lowland forest with permanent streams and ponds and may escape predation by swimming and diving. Tonight, as the harvest moon rises, I re-walk the same area of trail, hoping to see the elusive creature again but have no luck.

17th. The creek below my house is dry except for one small seep smothered with southern shield ferns. This lacy species has fronds up to two feet long and grows mostly on north- and east-facing banks of the creek, where the outcropping limestone drips water. Those below my house are dark green and thriving despite only three rains all summer. I'll bet the fern seep is fed indirectly by lawn water that drains into cracks in the limestone, hits a waterproof layer, and runs laterally until it emerges in the creek bank. If suburbia fosters this native, it is a novel turn of events but slight compensation for the many species lost to sprawl.

18th. From Owl Hollow to my office and classroom is a nine-mile bicycle ride through former tallgrass prairie, then cropland, now industrial park. This landscape differs dramatically from my forest home. It once was home for such messengers as nesting Swainson's hawks that are migrating overhead today. I gave up bicycling as being too frightening, when the road became a four-lane divided highway connected to an interstate highway. I think about cars now that I drive by the circling hawks, whose messages I might understand better at a bicycle's pace. Yet, with a car, my horizons are broader than those of pioneer naturalists.

The pioneers were mostly concerned with describing an amazing diversity of new species in a new world. Travel limitations didn't allow them as much study of lifestyles, which in my day verify our universal interdependency. Now we know that the real meaning of biodiversity is Biosphere, wherein life-sustaining goods and services are produced and shared, unless they are abused or destroyed. Certainly the utility of gas-powered vehicles has been considerable, although electric cars would be an added advantage, since they'd reduce pollution and require me to slow down and stop more often for physical and mental recharge.

19th. Hurricane Gilbert, strongest Caribbean storm of the twentieth century, hits the Mexican coast near Texas, bringing sustained drizzle in 1988. This "second spring" excites wildflowers. Goldenrods, frost-weed, low petunia, and Turk's cap bloom in the ravine—yellow, white, blue, and red—as do white snow-on-the-mountain, purple thistle, and pink prairie agalinis in surrounding grasslands. American beautyberries and gum bumelia berries are so numerous that it is fruitless for mockingbirds to defend them against flocks of white-winged doves and American robins, not to mention the many passing migrants. But they try anyway. Rainfall's tunes have really enlivened this particular September scene.

20th. On sunny hot middays the only birdsong is a lovely warbling rendition of house finch, another species at the eastern edge of its natural range. Males are beautifully colored like spilled strawberry jelly on their heads and breasts, but females and juveniles are brown striped —not very notable except for song. Besides hummers, house finches love my hummingbird feeders best of all and bathe constantly in big-foot, my dinosaur-footprint birdbath. Strangely, they don't usually stand out otherwise, and I don't know why. Now, however, little else is vocal in the ninety-degree heat, and I need to hear what the finches have to say.

21st. Easy to miss because it is scarce and blooms mostly at night is Lindheimer four-o-clock, named for the father of Texas botany, Ferdinand Lindheimer. From two small populations in the ravine, I planted seeds at my house to keep an easy eye on this plant, and found that it is a five-o-clock; for, even on cloudy afternoons, the pink flowers don't open much earlier. If the sky is clear, blooming begins closer to six and ends about eight the next morning. As nights grow shorter and colder, flowers open progressively earlier and stay open later, suggesting a switch from nocturnal to diurnal insect pollinators that may be more numerous in the warmer daylight.

Some botanists say the plant isn't native, but I know of populations in wildlands far from human habitation, all with rose-pink, fall flowers. First Americans may have traded for seeds or brought them from Mexico, where the species blooms from spring to fall in several colors and is said to be medicinal. However, the uniform rose and essentially autumnal blooming of our plants suggest nativity. If primal people transported it, is this species introduced or natural? What about trout lilies moved about by those people, copper lilies brought by Spanish explorers, or any seeds planted anywhere by other animals?

Do we industrialists make a difference? Yes indeed! Equipped with fossil fuel energy, we've abruptly accelerated the pace and widened the scope of introductions, so exotics now endanger natives. Among other actors, only some bacteria use fossil fuels, but in doing so for millennia longer have stayed in tune with the Biosphere's concert. Humanity's increasing effects are traceable, directly or indirectly, to a change in actor power in the last fraction of a "second" of the play of life. Because they required "hours" for development, nature's checks and balances don't fully compensate for unnatural history.

22nd. Acorns are dropping like hail, and black walnuts are miniature eight balls on the ground, except where fox squirrels have opened them, extracted the "meat," and produced halves with owl faces. To-day's seed dispersal agents are blue jays, crows, red-bellied woodpeckers, and the squirrels, all contending loudly at particular trees. Is their cue the most, largest, or best-tasting nuts? Everybody is storing in preparation for winter. Crows fill their gullets but fly too far to see. Blue jays put theirs in the ground or, like red-bellies, in standing dead-wood at edges. Squirrels cut and carry nuts, or cut twigs then race to the ground and plant the nuts, patting the soil in place with one hand and then the other.

A tree's adaptive strategy is to produce lots of nuts (seeds), sacrificing some to hungry animals while others are planted, forgotten, or unneeded by the planters and germinated away from competition. If a tree produces larger or more nutritious seeds, it may attract more seed-dispersal agents and be planted more often. Humans select large, tasty pecans for cultivation, so why shouldn't wild nuts be large and flavorful because of other nut-eaters? I'll bet the ravine's earliest people learned to be selective as they gathered the bounty; and, by accidentally dropping a few nuts here and there, helped to plant today's tasty forests.

Curious about how fast and far away forests might travel, I follow the "gardeners" from trees to storage spots. Birds are easy. Their nuts are stashed within about three hundred feet, many aboveground. Some are eaten later, while others germinate, a few after falling from arboreal depots into leaf litter. Squirrels operate the best travel agency. In an hour up to five of them run multiple trips from one especially rich pecan tree. A homeplace squirrel plants within a hundred feet, the others go anywhere beyond to maybe five hundred feet in all directions, but especially along edges. Given ten years for planted trees to reach maturity, I estimate that this forest could expand a mile in the twenty-first century—if it still has the room to expand.

23rd. The season's first "blue norther" arrived overnight to announce the autumnal equinox. The cold front dropped the air temperature from seventy-five degrees at midday yesterday to forty-eight at sunrise today. There are no hummingbirds at my house but neighbors reported several juveniles and females feeding ferociously in the late afternoon yesterday. Between about 5:30 and 7:30 P.M., as the wind stiffened and darkness closed in, two hummers perched on feeders and stayed all night. At 7:30 A.M. today, a neighbor touched one and, finding it unresponsive, took it inside, where it began to fly within a few minutes. As this day dawned in bright sunshine, her outside bird woke up and departed about the same time.

She didn't know that hummingbirds are torpid at night. Their heart rate slows down, so their metabolic demand for food energy drops. Otherwise, they are too small to store sufficient fuel for overnighting under environmentally stressful conditions. Those hummers were simply doing the natural thing, albeit in an unnatural situation. I'd never heard of roosting in exposed places, let alone feeders, so I examined the sites. Not surprisingly, I guess, those feeders were on the south side of the house beneath an overhanging roof. The hummers simply exchanged their usual secluded foliage for cultural protection, as Carolina wrens do on my front porch.

Hummers usually stay around local feeders into the first week of October, rarely until the last week. Black-chins leave before ruby-throats, but many hangers-on are often the difficult-to-identify juveniles and females. I go by the ruby-throat's proportionately shorter bill and more deeply forked tail—questionable features unless I get a

rare comparative look. Anyway, ruby-throat males are definitely staying later in recent years, several times into December, and in a few
years rufous hummers remain all winter. I'd like to know how much
of the change is due to increasing numbers of feeders in suburbia and
how much to increasingly warmer winters.

24th. *El Niño* is supposed to bring a warm-wet fall and winter. After
three weeks of hot dry days, unusual so late in the season, this morning dawns drizzly. Is it *El Niño*'s signature? Or is this the remnant of
yesterday's cool front that expelled hummingbirds, then stalled, and
returns today as a warm front, stopping the first southbound ruby-
crowned kinglets, brown thrashers, and northern flickers? I sit on the
front porch, welcoming the rare gloom, and try to hear what increasingly warmer autumns are saying. That familiar winter birds won't
come this far south? I hope not; for home must include sprightly kinglets, "wicking" flickers, and the occasional deer-like snort of a brown
thrasher.

25th. It is really dark at 7:00 A.M. this morning, yet we're a month
away from switching our clocks back an hour. I hear chirping crickets and geckos, some cawing crows, and lots of nuts falling from the
trees. Every minute another plop. The brown seed pods on Ohio
buckeyes have begun to split and drop their shiny black "eyeballs." I
wait for a hint of the "southward-moving" sun. By December it will
rise almost in front of me. Darkness, relative quiet, and great-horned
owls heighten my sense of season. I hear the first booming hoot of the
female—"hoo-hoo, hoo-hoo, hoo"—followed by the lower-voiced
male's resounding "hoo, hoo." It is the beginning of their nesting year.

26th. Is loud natural noise quieter than loud machine noise? Perhaps noise level is not as disconcerting as noise frequency in suburbia. Crashing limbs and trees in storms and rumbling rocks in creek
floods are more frequent, as we remove stabilizing wildlands. Once
roads and houses fill the space, as they do in the square mile around
my house, the frequency of machine noise is maximized by cars, delivery trucks, lawn mowers, garbage trucks, hedge trimmers, leaf blowers, and the like. All power tools have increased. Both noise level and

frequency damage hearing, unless we live behind permanently closed windows as some do, but which is the more destructive to our psyche?

27th. From my second floor deck, designed for small-time living in the tree canopy, I watch a migratory whip-poor-will flycatch just before dawn. It must have arrived overnight. Like a real flycatcher, it returns to a dead tree limb between sorties. As dawn breaks, other passage migrants flit about, and the whip-poor-will disappears. I've seen our nesting chuck-wills-widows flycatch from tree perches and wonder how often trees are used, as compared to the ground, where all nightjars nest. Then, an arriving sharp-shinned or Cooper's hawk flies overhead, the songbirds freeze, and I crane about trying to confirm something they already know.

28th. A neighbor calls to ask about downy barn owl chicks in his deer-hunting blind in a tree—would I come and take them? Another tells me about some in his duck blind in the reservoir. What an adaptable species is this monkey-faced or white owl, as some folks call it. Natural cavities in trees, cliffs, and dirt banks are usual places for nesting, but the species will accept grain silos, house and barn attics, and nest boxes, including those on poles in the water intended for wood ducks. When rodent populations are booming, our barn owls raise at least two, possibly three broods a year—exceptional for any bird of prey.

The barn owl may have the broadest natural range of any large avian predator on Earth, for it nests on all continents except Antarctica and on most large islands. Its diet is often studied, since it is an inveterate rodenteer, and rodents cause crop damage. I once proposed that barn owl studies be coordinated worldwide to include population and biocide assays, because the bird's broad range makes it an ideal Biosphere barometer, and its acceptance of nest boxes makes barometric readings easy. I couldn't think of a better creature for understanding the collision and the rapprochement of natural and unnatural history.

29th. Stimulated by heavy rain, plateau spiderlilies just sprouted two leaves about two weeks behind the single new leaves of hill country dayflowers. Although spiderlily appears later now, it blooms a month earlier in the spring, because it grows gradually, harvesting the sunlight of warm winter days. It is a stay-put perennial that utilizes last year's energy, stored in fleshy roots, to get started. The dayflower is an annual with seed energy sufficient only for the quick germination needed to secure a position in shifting edge habitat. It won't grow again until spring.

30th. Rio Grande leopard frogs have been singing a week already and are laying eggs in the creek's shallow pools. Summer's last brood of Gulf Coast toadlets leaves as the first leopard frogs arrive. I always think of frog choruses as announcing springtime, but this species breeds between late August and early October, coincident with the first big autumn rains and cool nights. On sunny forty-five-degree and warmer winter days, its tadpoles eat algae in the pool-bottom ooze. They overwinter in the muck, often beneath skim ice, but perish if their pools freeze completely.

Smallmouth salamander is another autumn breeder that takes advantage of less-used resources. It migrates to the creek's pools in mid-October or later. Its four-legged, bushy-gilled tadpoles feed on tiny aquatic animals that eat algae, so more time is needed to generate the longer energy transfer after autumn rains. It is a northern species, whereas the Rio Grande leopard frog is tropical. I'm not surprised that this salamander breeds in autumn, but I am amazed that a tropical frog breeds now when it could be frozen out. Is it because this is also monsoon time in the tropics?

⁂

The fairest thing we can experience is the mysterious . . . the fundamental emotion which stands at the cradle of true art and true science.

Albert Einstein

CHAPTER 5

Autumn IS WINDING DOWN

October, the Last Green

Color begins to decorate the forest's trees and shrubs as the pace of cycles quickens—almost spring-like. Migrating monarch butterflies are timepieces, and the last summer birds leave for the tropics, although hurricanes may surge inland and become tropical storms, temporarily stopping all movement. Thousands of geese, cranes, gulls, and white pelicans wheel overhead, bound for warm Gulf Coastal waters. Summer gives up slowly, but October reaffirms autumn with the last flower-feeding insects and first fog-shrouded mornings.

1st. Autumn's southbound parade of songbirds has passed midpoint. I expect nineteen species this week, up from five in late July, but headed down from twenty-one in mid-September. By month's end, all will fade into the distance. The color guard of warblers, not so colorful now, has traveled south already. Blue-gray gnatcatchers, empidonax flycatchers, Baltimore orioles, and Wilson's warblers—common fall migrants—are strung throughout. Thrushes, catbirds, and Nashville warblers come at the end with kinglets, yellow-rumped and orange-crowned warblers, blue-headed vireos, brown thrashers, and northern flickers, who take a break for winter residency.

Before dawn a cold front rains migrants at my door. A summer tanager eats roughleaf dogwood berries, and a gray catbird catcalls from beautyberries. Yellow-breasted chats, northern yellowthroats, and mourning warblers search for insects in goldeneyes. Wilson's and orange-crowned warblers peruse possumhaws. An out-of-place marsh wren forages with the chats and yellow-throats, its familiars from a marshland summer. Some birding neighbors "hound" the marsh wren, because they haven't seen one before. I hope they're as interested in its message about the ravine's safe harbor as they are about the messenger.

"What about your life list?" the birders ask, "since you've been so many places." I answer that I keep records of messengers and especially of their messages to remind me of nature's basic principles, as I try to compromise my life with natural history. Once I did a lot of name and specimen collecting but that was partly youthful insecurity, when trophies were proof of ability, and partly a time when my science needed the vouchers. Slowly, though, I learned to learn with patient looking, listening, touching, and smelling, although I don't decry listing that is learning or specimens that represent necessary messages.

2nd. Almost every year a sharp-shinned or Cooper's hawk stays for the winter and eats mostly the abundant and naïve offspring of permanent resident birds. The hawks quickly learn that such food is concentrated at bird feeders and seem to visit several in rotation, like humans on shopping trips. I know one female sharpy personally, a bad biter if I catch her to check her band. I don't always see her right away, but I know when she arrives because blue jays suddenly become quiet, in contrast to loudly pestering the migrant crows that also move into our neighborhood grocery.

Eastern screech owls begin to eat more birds, as insects and reptiles become less active on cooler nights, but are not pressured by the arriving hawks, since avian prey is two to three times more abundant here than in the countryside. Of twenty-two common songbirds in ravine and rural habitats, thirteen are more common and their populations more stable, year-to-year, in suburbia. These include such favored lunches as northern cardinal, blue jay, house finch, house sparrow, and northern mockingbird among permanent residents, and American goldfinch, yellow-rumped warbler, white-throated sparrow, and dark-eyed junco among winter residents.

My censuses show that permanent residents have increased, while winter residents cycle with the severity of the winter (more in harsh weather). The raptors have no long-term influence on their numbers. Seventy-five years ago a study of the avian prey of eastern screech owls in New York found the same thing; so the message, like the Biosphere's other fundamentals, is time honored. Why would any predator destroy its livelihood and thus itself? The problem here is a decline in summer residents (neotropical migrants), also unrelated to raptor numbers, but to numbers of the only predator that reduces or exterminates unintended prey by damaging or erasing wildlands.

3rd. While playing in our yard-woods, four-year-old Gretchen finds a copperhead and calls me. I don't know it now (1968), but it is almost the last one I will see in the ravine. I catch the fifteen-inch creature, colored like oakleaf litter, mellow rusty bands on a tan background, and take it to a communal winter den a half-mile away. Others haven't gathered yet, but last year I counted sixteen sunning on and around this east-facing, limestone ledge in what will eventually be named Owl Hollow. Twelve years later, we move within two hundred feet of the site, which has been bulldozed. I have mixed feelings, because copperheads are potentially dangerous to small children yet unaggressive and at home where I am an intruder.

4th. Glancing down I see a body feather shed by one of this year's screech owlets, now independent and growing adult-style plumage in time for winter. The feather is a reminder of unhatched owl eggs — a message about pesticides put in soil, transferred to plants that feed insects that owls eat — a message about energy flow and human cost accounting. We think of land, water, and air as cost-free, but who ever heard of anything without effect — something for nothing, as we like to say? A gust of wind blows the downy feather ahead as I walk, a message that people need to travel farther on the trail of planetary understanding.

5th. Autumn has been unbelievably wet this year, courtesy of several tropical storms spun off of hurricanes in the Gulf of Mexico. Wildflowers rebloom, including the usual false garlic, but also Mexican hat, standing cypress, and Texas marbleseed. The outburst, transferred to insect energy, induces many summer resident birds to remain for weeks past their normal migration time. Southward-moving monarchs are stalled by south winds that deliver our first-ever malachite butterfly and many immigrant zebras and Julias that bounce about in the lilting flight so typical of their tropical family. This experience is new to me. Is it a precursor of increasingly stormy weather associated with climatic warming?

6th. I forgot to close the garage door last night, and this morning a sleepy, black-haired opossum peers up from the bottom of my garbage can. Is my dog sympathetic to an unusual compatriot, or was she just sleeping that soundly? Holding the possum by its prehensile tail, I put it in a tree so the Labrador retriever won't pester it. I know possums are good climbers, because they take up temporary residence in natural tree cavities and screech owl nest boxes, first depredating any eggs and nestlings. I used to see only gray-haired Virginia opossums, but increasing numbers of a black-haired variety arrived during the 1990s. Are they common (tropical) opossums, who've joined the northward push of tropical butterflies, birds, and armadillos?

7th. Overhearing autumn's last overhead conversation of chimney swifts, I realize that they are about as suburbanized as I am. I can't think of another native with such a wide distribution that has so completely switched to house habitat. The swifts know what I will feel tomorrow—a temperature drop of forty-eight degrees. Today's falling air pressure cues their foraging in preparation for the change. At 7:00 P.M. one migrating flock roosts in a neighbor's unblocked chimney after diving in and out several times, apparently checking the hospitality, and stays two days before moving southward.

8th. A late-passing Nashville warbler bathes with an early wintering ruby-crowned kinglet as the seasons change. Earliest winter sojourners have returned, so I anticipate the next group of "snowbirds" —white-throated sparrows and orange-crowned and yellow-rumped warblers. Dark-eyed juncos, followed by American goldfinches and cedar waxwings, bring up the rear, unless we have an invasion of pine siskins, purple finches, and red-breasted nuthatches. I hope to see old friends, banded in years gone by, because fidelity to a winter site is as usual as it is to a nesting place, if resources are supportive. Wild actors operate on the principle of "why change what works," although both nature and culture are full of surprises!

9th. Seasonality is astoundingly rapid from my perspective of being away for a week. In just that time goldeneyes began to bloom beside the paths, frostweed and goldenrod faded, Turk's cap flowers became red fruits, and the year's last broods of butterflies emerged. Sumacs always initiate the forest's palate of autumn colors, and flameleaf sumac shouts its name now, while smooth sumac is quietly purple. Poison ivy stands out sufficiently in red that I can spot and pull its runners from the path, but fragrant sumac is just beginning to turn shades of yellow, orange, and scarlet.

Goldeneyes bloom profusely only after there is a real nip in the air. They decorate edges, particularly fencelines, trails, and temporary openings created by treefall or bulldozer. I'm grateful for their successional tendency to fill barren spots with golden cheerfulness, often accompanying frostweed and, like it, growing six feet tall. Butterflies love the flowers too. Today's eager feeders include dogface sulphurs with characteristic French poodle images on their forewings and a dozen migratory monarchs. Altogether, it is a fantastic, golden autumn day.

10th. Several thousand monarch butterflies roosting overnight is an unbelievable sight, surely one of nature's greatest marvels. It is most likely about now but not every year—seldom in fact, because there must be a coincidence of large migratory population, a sudden switch from a north to a south wind, flower food, and mature broadleaved roosting trees. At about 4:00 P.M., if it is cloudy, cool, or windy, or later until dusk (7:15 P.M.) under clear, calm skies and falling temperatures, monarchs assemble in pompom-like clusters beneath leaves in the lower canopy. Next morning, around 8:00–9:30 A.M., as the sun strikes them and the air warms toward sixty degrees, the pompoms become confetti blowing in the wind.

The fall migration of monarchs peaks this week, although individuals will drift by through November, nearly all preceding the first freeze (average November 20). Even the last ones are usually a few days ahead of a mostly leafless tree canopy (average November 28). Obviously, roosting monarchs avoid exposure to the night's lowest temperatures. Right now the nightly minimum averages four and a half degrees higher below tree canopy level than in the open. After deciduous trees are leafless, there is only one degree of difference. Thus does the fall passage of monarchs avoid harsh conditions, another instructive example of fine environmental tuning.

11th. An eastern screech owl banded as a chick, now established in its lifelong adult home, is always a special instructor. Such a recapture only happens once every few years, so its message is bound to be interesting. Suburban owlets disperse about a mile on average, so today's recovery of a three-year-old female in an exurban setting, five miles from suburbia, is special. My longest local record is nine miles, although a single remarkable one is ninety. The few (four percent) over three miles are almost all from suburbia into the surrounding countryside. Only one rural owl ever moved to town, which is quite different from the human trend.

When asked why one young screech owl in a thousand—the number of nestlings I've banded—traveled ninety miles when others stayed close to home, I answer that long-distance dispersal may only appear to be rare because the individuals are outside my search area and not easily found, or it could be truly rare, because few survive long trips through hostile territory. But such movement allows individuals to colonize new areas and perhaps spread novel genes into other populations, increasing variation that may increase survival as environments change.

Because suitable nesting habitat is patchy, our screech owls comprise semi-isolated breeding populations, and suburbia is a potentially important source of recruits for the rural environment. Many resources are better in town, so the city owls are denser and more successful nesters than their country cousins. This, together with less habitat, causes crowding, which stokes the suburban-to-rural supply line. In ecological terms, the suburban owls constitute a source population that may help to support a rural sink population, and that's a reversal of my expectation.

The human contrast is no surprise in view of suburban sprawl. Country folks shop in the city and move there in increasing numbers in response to increasing opportunity, which is why cities consume the countryside. A few wealthier folk reside in the country but make money in the city, so they aren't a true rural population. Certain ur-

ban birds, such as cattle egrets, grackles, and doves, use city roosts or nesting places and feed in cropland but most stay put, since travel costs can exceed food benefits. Because of their cultural resources, cities attract people in basically the same ways as they do the few native animals that can live there.

12th. On this day in 1999, the Earth's human population is estimated to reach six billion and still growing! A journalist interviews local folks about the event. The report is that although things won't be the same, we won't feel it much in my community. I shudder. While hearing the conflicting messages of wild population cycles versus rampaging human population growth, I consider how suburbia's wealth of energy buffers it from direct experience and hence understanding. Much of nature is as foreign to my human neighbors as are the people from third world countries whose numbers explode—those from whom we take the energy we use to distance ourselves.

13th. At dawn five blue jays harass two late, migrating chuck-wills-widows, probably because chucks sometimes eat small birds. It's the wrong season for baby jays, but the mobbers remember, just as they remember to sound alarm at empty screech-owl nest holes. Afterwards, while drinking at the birdbath, the jays mimic white-eyed vireos and American crows. Vireos? They're no threat! And crow calls? Jays know their sister species also eats birds and mobs predators such as hawks, so they may be trying to discourage predation or perhaps competition at the water. But no wintering hawks have shown up, unless the jays know something I don't, which is quite likely.

14th. As we pass them on the street this morning, European starlings on a utility wire imitate red-tailed hawks. They forage in the countryside and might have seen or heard a redtail there, because the ravine's wintering individual isn't back yet. Do starlings differentiate among potential predators? After walking the dog home, I return alone to the garrulous starlings without evoking mimicry, while on another day with our Labrador retriever, they mimic. I'll have to try this with blue jays. Despite their tendency to evict native nest-cavity users, I have to admire starlings who learned to trade their European hawks for ours after being introduced here a century ago.

15th. Behind the huge old Shumard oak that Nancy and I have climbed on the preserve's west ridge, an orange harvest moon beckons. It is time for our annual tribute to the greatest that expire first and the least that will inherit the Earth. We howl in behalf of wild dogs, first as red wolves howled here a century ago. And we do so in mourning, because red wolves are gone forever from the wild except as faraway, subsidized reintroductions from zoos. Then we yip and howl for coyotes who run through the ravine but can't stay, because the area is too small. Finally, we rejoice by barking for the resident gray fox. Our howling tree is a hundred feet from a house whose owner said—kidded, we hope—that she would shoot any such varmints.

16th. Bewick's and Carolina wrens respect each other's separate stage space when nesting, but in fall and winter I may see a Bewick's wandering in the woods. This small, gray fellow inhabits savanna, shrubland, and yards with plantings, while its larger, rusty cousin is a forest elf. A city street two hundred feet from my house and our forested commons isn't crossed by Bewick's wrens in spring and summer or by Carolina wrens any time. I think Bewick's is the more venturesome, because it is a successional species that must prospect for new transitional or patchy habitat or a suburban surrogate, as its present home slowly vanishes during reforestation.

17th. This year's last Carolina wren nest just fledged three youngsters —a record late date. The pair's success is a testament to persistence and flexibility, which are important traits in a fast-changing environment such as suburbia. They chose a hanging basket in a sheltered alcove by the southside front door of a house on a street named Elysian Lane. Five eggs were laid by September 17, and three hatchlings appeared October 2, staying in the nest a record fifteen days. Local Carolina wrens may raise three or four broods a year, but previous last nests have all been started by late August, suggesting that today's parents lost several earlier attempts, and, as wrens do, kept on trying.

18th. Ah-hah! Blue jays have started imitating red-tailed hawks, announcing the return of our usual wintering individual. Often it is relatively small-bodied, so I suspect it's a local nester, not one of the big guys that comes south from northern prairies. This is a bit early, since migrant broad-winged hawks are still passing through. Does the new arrival forecast a cold winter? Our woolly bear caterpillars are no predictors, for they're always all-black. Buffered by culture, I don't need to make special preparations but look for messages of seasonal significance in training for those of long-term consequence.

19th. By 10:00 A.M. the air temperature has risen thirty-two degrees to a very comfortable eighty, and the sun shines brightly. A common garter snake eats an earthworm in my front yard-woods. I find a fatter individual sunning on a log, possibly full of worms, a salamander, or a frog, since rain over the past three days stimulated small-animal activity on the ground surface. Snails and slugs are also out enjoying the feast of fallen leaves. Rain and nighttime temperatures in the fifties triggered the first seasonal migration of smallmouth salamanders to breeding pools in the creek and reinstated the chorus of Rio Grande leopard frogs.

Warm sunshine also exposes a lumpy eastern hognose snake, resting after an amphibian lunch. It spreads its lower jaws and anterior ribs, becoming cobra-like during a dramatic, hiss and sway, antipredator act. Superb defense, I think, except against people, who somehow believe that harmless hognoses are poisonous copperheads. If the hognose's performance fails, it will feign death, but I put it down and walk on. How I wish people would appreciate that defensive posturing is bluff and physical attack is so much more costly—often at the expense of life—that it is rarer in nature. They invariably hack up hognose snakes, considered to be the most dangerous serpents outside the Garden of Eden.

20th. The open ground and rooftops are covered in white frost, although leaf litter in the woods is brown, protected by the partly green tree canopy. It is thirty-two degrees at 6:00 A.M., the earliest freeze ever (1976), but I see a late-lingering yellow-billed cuckoo eating one of those winter-flying moths that generate their own heat by "shivering". Thus reminded, I check on six polyphemus moth caterpillars I've caged on the twig of a scalybark oak. They're inert but alive in thirty-four-degree air beneath the protective tree canopy. I put them in our unheated carport closet and, within a week, they all spin cocoons.

These caterpillars remain ensconced all the next spring and much of the summer, emerging as moths in late August, although there are adult polyphemuses flying in the spring. Whose caterpillars did they come from? Did my handling and the closet delay the captives' transformation, because acting cues were missing? Early spring polyphemus moths, emerged from autumn's caterpillars, typify the species' life cycle. Normally, they produce an early summer brood, whose caterpillars stay cocooned during the hot-dry mid-summer and sometimes the fall, tuned into prime time the following spring.

21st. Continual overcast with drizzle or rain and warm air have been our fare lately. It's interesting to see lizards and butterflies, as well as birds, foraging in the drizzle, but what else can hungry critters do? How hard must the rain be to dissuade them? The added weight of water brings down lots of dead leaves and a deluge of acorns that might be dangerous to small beasts. At four this morning a norther blows through, dropping the temperature to forty-five, bringing sunshine for Nancy's birthday and a celebratory stroll on the new leaf- and acorn-crunchy carpet. We are on the upswing, but lizards and butterflies drop out of sight on the cool end of the seasonal seesaw.

22nd. Next morning we take a misty ramble amid drifting yellow leaves and through slanted rays of sunlight magnified by water vapor. Ballooning spider hatchlings waft by on the gathering breeze, "unstructured, unafraid voyagers—youngsters that will become web-tied timid adults," says Nancy. It is the natural way, even with humans, whose roving teenagers display instinctive dispersal tendencies and cause parental consternation but whose conservatism increases with age. Today's gallery and living museum is magnificent to behold and affords new opportunities for learning, so we've paused for a moment to look at ourselves.

23rd. The forested countryside of Appalachian foothills is a potpourri of fall color that turns completely green as I fly back to Texas. Our growing season is a month longer than the Midwest's, nine degrees farther north in latitude, though our floral diversity is but a remnant. No yellow shagbark hickories and tulip trees or real red oaks. We have the leftovers barely hanging on at the western edge of a once vast deciduous forest that covered the ravine and sent its sugar maples, sweetgums, and magnolias all the way to Guatemala. But that was a cooler-wetter, glacial time fifteen millennia ago. Today, only the sugar (bigtooth) maple remains in central Texas—in a few hospice canyons.

24th. Scalybark oak, cedar elm, Mexican plum, Eve's necklace, western soapberry, and Mexican buckeye are among our first trees and shrubs to hint of yellow. Sumacs and Virginia creeper are already reddish. Black haw and roughleaf dogwood turn purple. Shumard oak will be the most brilliant of ravine reds but is a month and a frost away from glory. There is color here despite the few kinds of woody plants that produce it, but only if we've had plenty of rain and cold nights followed by warm days. Many years our autumn gallery is subdued, the color not so coincidental as up north because multiple Indian summers confuse this forest.

25th. White-throated sparrows are back for the winter, singing their sweet-sad melodies on mild mornings. Gretchen called them "little brown birds with snow tucked under their chins." Both sexes are either white- or brown-crowned, but the dominant white-crowned individuals arrive first, then the brown-crowns that stick primarily to the woods, hardly associating with dark-eyed juncos. Later, the white-crowned morph moves into shrubland or departs entirely. Spatial separation of the two plumage types doesn't happen while nesting, nor do the birds mate according to crown color, so their winter segregation must reduce competition for increasingly scarce food.

Dark-eyed juncos show a similar survival strategy. Black-topped males arrive first and dominate later gray females and juveniles but thin out quickly. Winter really hasn't arrived yet, so it is primarily the females and youngsters that endure it. Then, in early spring, males return from somewhere and briefly command the dwindled food supply before leaving ahead of their potential mates and offspring. At my experimental millet patches, dark-eyed juncos and white-throated sparrows usually forage apart or at different times. If together in bad weather, the smaller juncos take the more dangerous periphery with females and youngsters outside any remaining males.

Wintering Harris sparrows are no lesser messengers about reducing competition. Those with the blackest heads and chests get the center food relative to others with browner heads. As revealed by individuals we band and recapture in subsequent years, brown-heads become darker and rise in social prominence, but some never do achieve the social rank of the blackest heads. Meanwhile, forest redevelopment gradually replaces shrubby Harris sparrow habitat, and the blackest birds drop out first, leaving winter seeds to browner heads, until all Harris sparrows that remain are subdominants in increasingly small flocks that finally disappear entirely, evicted by natural succession.

26th. A series of cold fronts has kept things mostly cloudy and cool, but on this mid-morning the southeastern sun warms the front of my house to seventy-six degrees. That brings a gathering of five green anoles, who are brown, on cedar siding, beneath which they spend autumn nights but not the winter. Their number includes the big male from my tree-canopy deck, the female from patio plants, and three youngsters from who-knows-where. They and I bask and watch Io moth caterpillars eat the last redbud leaves and depart to the ground in a train of red- and white-striped bodies—the seasonal wind-down of coordinated cycles.

27th. While digging woods soil for potting, I unearth the naked brown pupa of a sphinx moth—a "squeaker!" What nifty defensive behavior. It is done by moving hard body segments against one another as the creature flexes. Foregoing cocoons, sphinx caterpillars burrow in soil where they transform into unclothed pupae with unique external loops that will house the moth's long, flower-probing tongue. Soon the squeaking pupa transforms into a tersa sphinx. I release it to feed on blooming asters and lay eggs that overwinter and hatch into caterpillars that will transform into next year's squeakers.

28th. Our house is overarched by oaks, so fallen acorns and leaves are plentiful. These days they are swept from the deck, patio, front walk, and driveway at least twice a week and scattered in the woods to resume nature's recycling of nutrients and reseeding. The forest's fall obscures our travelways, and rolling acorns spill unwary human visitors, but tannic acid from crushed leaves and acorns rebalances the limey soil's acidity. In study plots away from my house, seven new acorns per square yard is the daily average, and many have been eaten by weevils.

Beetles are the most abundant of familiar creatures, and the most numerous beetles are weevils. Some have long, decurved, chewing-drilling "snouts" specialized for eating acorns. Of one hundred acorns I examine, a third have weevil drill-holes and were dead when they fell, but last year none had holes, and two years ago twenty-two per-cent—a possible three-year cycle. Weevil larvae eat the acorn's energy-rich insides and transform into snouted adults that emerge and may invade my house through cracks and crannies, seeking warm winter quarters. Since they are only two-tenths of an inch long, I'm im-pressed by these mighty mites whose predation on oaks might be prodigious.

Yet there are twenty-six mature Shumard oaks, seventeen scaly-barks, and one plateau live oak in the half-acre closest to my house. Half the Shumards and a third of the scalybarks are multiple-trunked, former sprouts from the stumps of trees cut by humans long ago. Nine have died from heart-rot fungus in the last twenty years. Three of these have fallen in high winds and three others were leveled by ice storms. Since weevils, fungus, ice, humans, fire, wind, lightning, and drought kill trees, it's remarkable that any oaks survive for centuries. Acorns are their messengers about the Biosphere's cyclic connections and the long-term outlook necessary to appreciate them.

29th. Suddenly, I wake up to the fact that hackberry and tawny em-peror butterflies, the bouncers and buddies of tree-sap bars, are gone. Practically overnight the bars are taken over by questionmarks and red admirals, who will overwinter as adults. Swallowtails, hairstreaks, fritillaries, and others have expired too, just as winter broods of sul-phur butterflies emerge. A black and yellow garden spider hangs dead beside the shrunken empty egg sack in her web. Spotted-wing scor-pionflies appear, indicative of this time of dying, for their life cycle is timed to eat the bodies. They're end-of-season recyclers.

30th. Mediterranean geckos stowed away on trans-Atlantic ships, transferred to trucks at Texas Gulf Coast ports, and arrived here in the 1950s. Substituting the brick walls of suburban houses for their native rocks, geckos neatly filled the missing role of nocturnal climbing lizard. Any evening at dark, I see and hear several, chasing and squeaking, grabbing moths from lighted windows, baleful in my flashlight's freezing ray. As the temperature drops, their activity does too. Between fifty and sixty degrees only a youngster or two is out, because small bodies have more skin surface area per unit body mass and pick up heat from the bricks more readily than large bodies. Any colder and all move inside through weep holes in the bricks and other crannies.

31st. Fog is the essence of seasonal change, itself always changing, produced by cold air filtering slowly over the ravine's lingering biotic warmth. Quiet fog invites ambling at dawn. The diamond strings of orb web spiders shine high in the trees, some so far over my head that I never saw them before. Small birds flit in shrouded treetop flocks. I hear muted scolding and find recently arrived kinglets and warblers in a flock with residents. They mob something shadowy that disappears inside an armadillo hole. Then the flock drinks and bathes in fog-water droplets condensed on the last tree leaves of summer.

Nature is a mutable cloud which is always and never the same.

Ralph Waldo Emerson

November's True Gold

Autumn's first frost early and first freeze near month's end are assurances of forest gold. The sun is low in the sky, its golden light diffused by fog at dawn and later accented by sulphur butterflies and the last blooming goldeneyes. The hermit thrush's single ringing note and white-throated sparrow's lonely melody add to seasonal melancholy. Woolly bear caterpillars hurry to winter retreats, and at fissures in the bedrock serpents lie about in sunlight that pushes hard through the chilling air of even this salubrious time.

1st. Jupiter, Saturn, and the crescent moon are aligned vertically in the dawn, an auspicious event, as I await the first peek of the sun. By mid-morning, when the air has warmed into the seventies, a butterfly festival begins at the last remaining patch of blooming goldeneyes and asters. It is spirit-lifting to be among a dozen different species, complemented by one of the last passing monarchs at this small alcove in my gallery of living art. A spectrum of color is massed against a backdrop of western soapberries dressed in autumn gold and, overhead, migrating sandhill cranes provide the right kind of music.

2nd. Day and night the water birds stream by, riding the north wind, heading to reservoirs warmed by electrical generating plants on their shores and to the Gulf Coast. Snow geese are abundant but the once common Canada geese stay farther north, seduced by green lawns and ice-free water. Instead, Canada humans head south. Winter numbers of water birds and people have increased in response to more built habitats. Park and golf course keepers fuss about grass-grazing, pooping geese, and fishermen wail about cormorants eating hatchery-raised fish released in reservoirs. What do they think the birds do with more food and space—something fundamentally different from what people do?

3rd. I've been very fortunate. Seldom have I been unable to submerge myself in the wild physically and mentally, even for a short while. It's hard to remember when I haven't taken a few minutes to replace culture's hustle with nature's slower nurturing pace. But I just had surgery, so I'm limited to window watching; although, thankfully, at home in Owl Hollow in the healing forest. Our species "grew up" in the wild, where we're most at home—instinctively—but only recently have we awakened to the fact that injured or ill folks repair more quickly in rooms with windows looking on greenery rather than building walls or parking lots, as so many hospital rooms do.

4th. A neighbor is "weed whacking" the border between his property and our nature preserve. American beautyberries have purple berry clusters there, and Texas asters have white blooms, or did before today! I'll bet he's antsy about the naturally smooth transition that's developing. The definition of his property versus our commons is razor-sharpened, because electrical and gas-powered weed whackers are so convenient, so conducive to dominion. All power tools are. Hand tools are less destructive, because they require more personal energy, which requires more forethought.

5th. An unusually early freeze last night killed the last lingering green leaves. Sugarberries, white ashes, and red mulberries were most affected, while scalybark and Shumard oaks show a bit more color this morning. Within a few hours the air temperature approaches seventy degrees as I stroll along the creek, where pools of shallow water were muddied by raccoons finger fishing for crawdads and tadpoles last night. I walk upslope through Owl Hollow along thin-bedded layers and eroded ledges with deep cracks, fissures, and flagstones. This spot is a perfect snake den, where I sit with the wild, basking in afternoon sun.

6th. On a mellow autumn afternoon, the season's first yellow-rumped warblers are foraging in trees that still have a few leaves and, doubtless, hidden insects. Yellow-rumps are warblers of autumn and early winter. When their insect and berry supplies run out during prolonged freezing spells, they push south, reappearing in the spring on magic-making south winds. I don't find other part-time winterers yet but flush a poor-will, a small resident cousin of the larger migratory chuck-wills-widow and whip-poor-will. Poor-wills supposedly hibernate, a strange thing for any bird to do; but, rarely, I may startle one on mild autumn and winter days and wonder what we really know.

7th. When they first return for the winter, hermit thrushes sing their single, high, ringing notes. I guess it's a territorial proclamation, since hermits are spaced at about five-acre intervals through the forest, and never seem to utter anything else except scolding calls until late March or April when they rarely offer the beautiful dawn and dusk carols I love to hear. White-throated sparrows also sing on this sunny but cool damp dawn, and I hear the first tinkling bells of a winter wren. Then a cold front blows in and drops the air temperature eighteen degrees in the first five minutes of a forty-five-minute downpour that cancels my serenity.

8th. Great-horned owls hoot in the evening countryside, but not here anymore. Instead, I hear the barred owl's "hoo-haw." When the ravine area was mostly ranchland and its trees were fewer and younger, great-horned owls commanded the night and red-tailed hawks the day. As suburbanization accelerated in the 1960s, the ravine's forest recovered from cutting and grazing in places where building was prohibited by steep slopes or floodplain. Great-horned owls and redtails like open country so, by the mid-1970s, they left the ravine to nesting barred owls and broad-winged hawks, who choose forest and abide less space because they are smaller.

The succession of wildlings happens as habitat changes, but unless there is severe storm damage nature gradually slows down to longer cycles with less change between the highs and lows. Not so the succession of suburban folks who move in and out according to the dictates of personal income, regardless of local resources, because their livelihood is subsidized by outside energy. Temporary and hence unconcerned, too many do not contribute to human or natural community stability, despite the fact that their democracy and Biosphere depend on it.

Human turnover averages five percent per year in my subdivision, compared to two percent of our resident eastern screech owls. Only half of the eight houses on my cul-de-sac have original owners. One house has had four owners, another three, in fifteen years, so I count heavily on the owls and other natives as neighbors. At least our nature preserve is secure; and I feel fortunate, because natural history is an important psychic aspect of home. Tonight, among bright stars and musty falling leaves, hoo-haws from barred owls blend in an autumn mélange of familiarity, security, and sensory delight.

9th. Indian summer means sunny sixties to low eighties for several days between cold fronts and the peak of fall color insofar as there is any peak. Our most spectacular tree, the Shumard oak, doesn't really glow until after all others, and some trees such as white ashes are bare already. Yet it's a good time to be out, to find and eat the first fallen, native pecans and try to locate wild turkeys attracted to the wild nuts. These largest of native land birds are also the wariest, and even more so now that hunting season has begun. We may need better perceptive talent than our own to find them before they find us and sneak off quietly through the woods.

So we take our Labrador retriever along the Balcones scarp west of the ravine. As she trails off the path, clucking breaks the silence, then the aerial explosion of flushed turkeys that fly like World War II bombers. Great dark bodies with white-bordered tails weave and glide through the trees. What a thrill, because wild turkeys are impressively huge—our largest land bird—and strictly North American. Like so many wonders, though, we wiped turkeys out of this natural range early in the twentieth century. By mid-century we were wealthy enough to reintroduce them, not for any intrinsic value but for hunting, which eliminated them to begin with.

10th. Starting out this dismal morning, two cups of coffee strengthen my resolve. I'm testing my tolerance by a walk in cold gray rain to experience why a screech owl moves into a tree cavity in this weather. Shivering, despite a water-resistant but not waterproof jacket that mimics the screech owl's water-resistant but not waterproof feathers, I toss the coffee grounds into the woods and retreat to my own cavity. I "feed" the trees about fifty-two pounds of grounds yearly, or close to half a ton in twenty years, only a possible economic benefit to the forest but a certain one to Mayan friends in northern Central America.

Coffee connects me to the fate of fall's migratory birds, since it is now grown in sunny clear-cuts as well as forest shade in tropical America. But species such as the great-crested flycatcher and wood thrush can't find a winter home in a tropics without trees. Furthermore, sunlit coffee must be sprayed with pesticides, replacing the avian pest-control service, and chemically fertilized, a service formerly provided by the native shade trees. These and costs such as the loss of erosion control may exceed added income if a realistic cost:benefit analysis is made, as I noted firsthand in the destruction of Honduras after hurricane Mitch.

11th. Reading back over field notes, I am amazed at the surprises I've forgotten. Each day offers so much. For instance, this evening in 1976 brought rain, then sleet, and finally snow to the tune of thunder and lightning, all in one hour. Overnight, the air temperature dropped forty-five degrees to freezing. Two inches of snow covered the ground by dawn; and our two yellow-billed cuckoos, the latest ever summer resident birds, were gone. Did they die or migrate? They'd been seduced to stay late by abundant berries and warm, Indian summer weather.

Such singular events are noteworthy, but it is repeated patterns or changes in them, verified over years, that are the critical messages to remember. Ordinarily, the theater's directors dismiss actors such as late-lingering cuckoos because they don't perform properly in altered scenes. Occasionally, though, those actors survive and reproduce genes that allow their offspring to act in new scenes such as warmer environments. New parts for seasoned actors or their replacements result from natural selection, which can keep things on track or redirect the play.

12th. From the immediate perspective of natives, it's a matter of tolerating humans, who created suburbia only recently. But is there a benefit? That question stimulates my continuing attention to what eastern screech owls have to say about my neighborhood's quality, compared with a younger, smaller suburb five miles away and a rural site five miles in another direction. In fact, suburban owls produce more owlets per nest, are denser, and their numbers are more stable compared to those in rural forest, while owls in the younger suburb are intermediate. Have I uncovered a paradox?

Livable space is certainly scarcer in suburbia, but food is more abundant, and natural predators are less numerous. The wetter, warmer climate fosters food supplies, and there is permanent water in yard sprinklers, birdbaths, and lily ponds. More importantly, perhaps, food and water are more dependable. Again, I measure intermediate values in the younger suburb, suggesting that resources increase in certainty and amount during urbanization. That's different from forest development, wherein dependability increases but amount cycles below an early maximum.

During natural community construction, food is most plentiful early but fluctuates greatly. As the habitat develops, food declines somewhat but becomes more dependable (stable), and that may be the key to success. Of course a native species must be able to live in a

relatively small area of habitat, survive the scarcity of some resources such as tree cavities, and tolerate or avoid human traffic, tools, and toxins to take advantage of suburban largesse. But if population stability is a good criterion of prime place, I've certainly learned something new about suburbia.

13th. Until 1972, houses in Butterfly Hollow had septic tanks. Ours nourished five species of native trees, whose measurements indicated that they grew at twice the forest's normal rates. But the human population of my suburb doubled in size during the 1960s and 1970s, which meant that too many septic tanks seeped too much polluted water into creeks, which drained into a reservoir that was another city's water supply. Eventually, a regional sewer system was built with neighborhood pipes under streets and collector lines in the ravine. Ditches dug for the new lines damaged reforestation temporarily but reviewed scenes over past runs of the play.

Ridgetop ditches had two to three inches of dark brown organic soil above a foot of light tan chips and small flakes of limestone overlying a foot and a half of larger slabs and rock chunks. That was the root zone for most plants. In the ravine bottom, however, the six- to eight-foot-deep ditch sliced through a creek-made "layer cake" of angular rock chips alternating with soil, signifying respective periods of slope erosion alternating with quieter water. Tree roots grew throughout the profile with growth rings in their cut ends, indicating that the exposed layer cake was three centuries old, recent erosion coincided with suburban sprawl, and forest giants remembered a deeper ravine in a quieter time.

14th. We have a new estimate of the annual worth of the Biosphere's essential goods and services, such as climate regulation, flood control, oxygen production, soil formation, and water supply. That value, thirty-three trillion U.S. dollars, is twice the cultural world's annual economic output, and fourteen percent of it is the work of forests. When asked to comment, one ecologist said, "I don't see much hope for a civilization so stupid that it demands a quantitative estimate of the value of is own umbilical cord." I disagree, for I've found that people learn best in familiar terms and might appreciate natural values translated into money.

Nevertheless, I'd add at least three additional calculations for a realistic evaluation. First, the Biosphere's annual negative value to culture requires counting losses from floods, tornadoes, and other natural catastrophes. Second, we must assess the negative value of human folly that triggers and exaggerates catastrophes, for instance building houses in floodplains and cutting trees on slopes. Third, culture's adverse impacts on nature's positive life support must be accountable. Perhaps a net value compared to the gross will be sufficiently scary to awaken humanity before its real nightmares begin.

15th. Hoping no one will see, I walk from my front door through a hundred feet of woods to the preserve's main path and blindfold myself. My hearing, smell, and touch are out of shape and need exercise. Downhill I go, across a rocky slope and creekbed, ambling by touch of trailside vegetation and spider web, crunch of creekbed rock and leaf-litter, pungent odor of juniper. I navigate by lizard scramble, sparrow rustle, kinglet chirp, and the softness of butterfly wings and falling leaves. Astonishing what I've tended to lose in our so-called age of information—so strictly visual and electronic.

16th. Cold air is heavy and falls, displacing warmer air, so the ravine bottom is colder than my home hillside, especially before sunrise. Creekside trees grow leaves and wildflowers bloom a week later than their hillside counterparts in the spring, and the trees turn color and lose leaves about a week earlier in autumn. Yet the disadvantages of a colder, shorter growing season are offset by water availability and protection from storm damage. Tree rings show that creekside trees grow somewhat faster than hillside trees in the more limited time they have available each year, reminding me about the principle of compensation.

17th. A soft, cool drizzle by night is autumnal for sure. I forget about seeing Leonid meteors this year and remember a night thirty years ago when the sky seemed to fall with Leonids. September and October followed the summer dry pattern, so the novelty of November rain stimulates a few green plants to linger, beckons the winterproof leaves of some spring wildflowers, and signals Missouri violets to pop their seed capsules. In the rain, our overage, droopy-faced, Halloween pumpkins have a decompositional leer, as they provide food for small, decomposer animals that recycle "pumpkin pie" into forest soil.

18th. Because of suburbia's heat and the forest's protective canopy, first freezes average a week later at my house than at the official reporting station in a rural setting. We've already had 260 growing days because of clear *La Niña* weather compared to 249 freeze-free days on average each year, so I'd left potted plants on the patio. Big mistake! Last night it froze. I hadn't paid attention to wild forecasters, who knew what the human reporters didn't. Local birds fed like crazy before nightfall yesterday, and flocks of winterers arrived. Their remote sensing equipment is millennia old, while humanity's dates back only a few decades.

19th. Among the migratory crowds, the largest single-species flocks belong to American robins. They arrive this week, stay a few days, eat berries, and leave. Since Ashe juniper berries are larger and darker than eastern red cedar berries, they should be favored, but I can't detect a preference. Some robins remain in winter as do cedar waxwings, who are equally voracious berry eaters, and some will travel on with the hordes that come north next January. A relatively small but constant number will stay to nest. American robins are consummate yard birds —suburbia's most familiar messengers across the continent.

20th. The ravine's galleries are painted autumn yellow, winter gray, spring green, and summer brown. Most tree and shrub leaves turn yellow, and the low-angle sunshine reflects yellow. Autumn broods of appropriately named sulphur butterflies are peaking now and will dominate an autumn butterfly fauna that includes some darker, over-wintering, orange and brown, leaf-winged species. Cloudless sulphurs with three-inch wingspans are particularly striking, as they dance among the sun spots and falling leaves. Dainty, sleepy, and clouded sulphurs, and a late alfalfa, little, or dogface may join the party.

Yellow flowers began with goldenrods in late August and continued with goldeneyes in October. Then white frostweed came along, followed by white asters. Actually, white is the dominant flower color of earliest spring and latest autumn, whereas yellow dominates in late summer and mid-autumn. Blue is third in annual frequency but chiefly a spring color, while red is scarce throughout the growing season. Current yellows attract sulphurs and bumblebees, by contrast to spring whites visited by brown and bluish butterflies, honeybees, and sphinx moths. Courtesy of these insect pollinators, flower colors rotate in the ravine's seasonal galleries.

21st. Dense fog pervades every nook and cranny, silencing the land. I love the woods on such early mornings. As I pass a crimson and gold Chinese tallow tree, I consider whether to allow its beauty to perpetuate its weediness. It is an escapee from cultivation that can take over disturbed places. Shumard oaks are just as beautiful in scarlet and burgundy, as are scalybark oaks now past their golden peak. But nurseries push the easily grown (weedy) Old World exotics because of a European gardening tradition that represents civilization, by contrast to natives that symbolize a wild world that should be tamed.

22nd. On the peak of an abandoned shed silhouetted against the sunset, looking like hunched, leftover Halloween witches, are three roosting turkey vultures. As I return home, lines of black clouds appear behind them, backed by a sunset, a tapestry of orange, blue, and black on the horizon. An eastern spotted skunk pokes along the trail ahead of me. After yesterday's rain, the path was plowed by what seems to have been a skunk squad with help from armadillos. The wild creatures know that a trail made by humans is a way to riches. I'm constantly amazed at the natives that use my paths and amused by coyotes who deposit scat (feces) right in the middle as their sign of ownership.

I am only the latest in a long line of trail makers, users, and transformers that once included marine worms, in the ocean-bottom silt of today's bedrock, and mammoths hunted by humans. Trails are a natural fact of life, but not suburban-style trails. We don't need to conserve energy, worry about predators, or concern ourselves with stabilized routes to reuse to make a living. We seldom walk very far anyway (one neighbor drives two hundred feet from house to swimming pool!). Natural trails made and repeatedly used by large mammals, including primal people, do not parallel creekbanks and become flooded, or run straight up and down hillsides and become gullies, but follow a diagonal or zig-zag (switchback) track.

All animals are instinctive trail followers, as trails afford the least cost in finding resources. After repeated use, trail following becomes subconscious and may be odor-marked. Pets follow trails in the house and yard, and humans have their own routines. Birds fly trails through the air and perch in the same spots. It is survival strategy. Natural trails are tested and reused if productive and safe. The same was true of city streets and country lanes before cars, although property ownerships modified them. Some modern walkways are for show, as any park or college campus reveals, since we are the only animals that afford inefficient trails.

23rd. Some open rocky places on the ravine's trails appear lifeless from repeated trodding, but scraggly black stuff is gathered here and there. I like to call it instant algae because, after a few minutes in a glass of water, it turns green and emits oxygen bubbles. It is nostoc, slippery and photosynthetic after rain, not a true alga, a plant, but more closely related to the first bacteria that invented oxygen manufacture by photosynthesis using water and carbon dioxide about four billion years ago. Nostoc's ancestors totally transformed the Biosphere, making our green terrestrial world a familiar way of life.

Nostoc's harsh environment reminds me that life was more difficult and totally aquatic before bacteria and algae made oxygen, some of which was ionized and became an atmospheric ozone shield against damaging (mutagenic) ultraviolet radiation. Before then no life could live on land. It was just too dangerous. Are we returning to those days? Holes in the ozone layer over Arctic and Antarctic regions are growing, caused by chlorofluorocarbon gases wasted from our spray cans and air conditioners. And human skin cancer increases accordingly, especially in near-hole places like New Zealand, where I personally felt the message.

24th. Damp, cold, and gray, unusual for more than a day here, remind me of Selborne, England, and its naturalist-parson, Gilbert White. Nancy and I have walked many trails used by him three centuries ago, a time when swallows were thought to hibernate in the mud. Beechwood, alder-lined creek, cobblestone street, and thatched-roof houses made us feel that he walked with us. White's classic, *The Natural History of Selborne,* says, ". . . the life and conversation of animals is a concern of much more trouble and difficulty [than labora-tory study] and not to be attained but by the active and inquisitive, and by those that reside much in the country."

25th. Caterpillars are scarce so late in the year, but sometimes the plump green ones of Io and polyphemus moths show up, rapidly gob-bling any remaining green leaves. Io larvae are protected by stinging spines, red and white striped warning stripes, and group traveling be-havior that accentuates the warning, but a polyphemus should be a juicy morsel for birds and easy prey in the mostly leafless trees. Per-haps heftiness protects this three-and-a-half-inch-long, inch-and-a-quarter-wide behemoth—essentially the bulk of a small songbird—although I'd think the chance of a sudden freeze might dismiss both actors from this late-season scene.

26th. Carving out its winter roost hole in the same dead ash it drilled three years ago is our frontdoor downy woodpecker. That earlier hole near the broken trunk top was used by Carolina chickadees for nest-ing but rotted away afterward. The current hole is nine feet high in the current stub. This downy knows what's coming. Although we haven't had a deep freeze, two days later the temperature drops from seventy-two to twenty-five degrees, accompanied by sleet and snow and the year's first frostweed frost. Watched by a planning pair of chickadees, the downy's chiseling has continued until the cavity hides him completely by the time of cold bluster.

27th. By Thanksgiving most deciduous trees are bare, or almost, but seedlings and saplings remain green a bit longer, having been pro-tected from early frosts by the former canopy. Their leaves are larger than those of the canopy trees, an adaptation for gathering light in summer shade. Now they alone soak up the limited sun of this old year. Cultured versus native pecans are distinguished by their respec-tive broad deep-green versus narrower light-green leaflets. Along a quarter-mile of the creek, eighty-eight percent of the young pecans I count are cultivars planted by seed-dispersing animals that unwit-tingly remake the forest.

28th. The forest stage rotates 180 degrees in time, its seven-and-a-half-month green set replaced by four-and-a-half months of brown.

But the timing changes these days, as the theater's thermostat is reset at higher temperatures. Some props have been here but hidden by others now in storage, while some moved in from suburbia. Green mosses suddenly reappear. Southern shield ferns have been joined by exotic holly ferns, renegades from suburban gardens. In the mild, moist stillness of the last falling leaves, mosses and ferns shed their reproductive spores, speaking of life before seed plants and much longer before humans, whose unnatural history vies with nature for theater management.

29th. My suburb just completed a parks survey which included nature in only one of twenty-two categories. A citizen proposal to have an outdoor center for nature education wasn't included, and the generic nature area was checked by only thirty percent of respondents, ranking seventh among eighteen facilities. I had suggested that we do a nature-for-tax swap with citizens who own wild acreage. Each landowner who protects natural values and permits nature education would pay no taxes on the acreage concerned. If protection were afforded but no public use permitted, taxes would be reduced by the value of natural services rendered to everyone. But these ideas were rejected by a city council with only culture's script to read.

30th. November ends as it began with Jupiter leading Venus in the southwestern twilight. In my reflective state of mind, memories of Cinder and Ginger, our successive Labrador retrievers, are loving ones. We all roamed the ravine together, discovering new acts in the play of life. The dogs instructed us beyond our ability to hear and smell, greatly extending our understanding, as their ancestors did for ours over the last ten thousand years. Both labs have long since returned to stardust and new beginnings on our sunrise slope, the direction of life's expectations.

To be kindred means to share consciously in the stream of life.

Paul Shepard

December Is Finally Leafless

Autumn lingers a week or two longer, as diehard oaks slowly become winter skeletons and the ground receives a freshly woven carpet of leaves. Dawn voices are the calls of winter birds in small foraging flocks with their resident hosts. Peeping chorus frogs, the ravine's Christmas bells, announce the season. Flowers are gone, but in freezing weather the forest floor looks like a chocolate birthday cake, decorated by white candles of frostweed frost. Without screening tree leaves, the night sky is full of star pictures and noisy with sounds readily carried in the cold, dense air.

❧

1st. Tree leaves are adrift and strawberry bushes are garbed in scarlet, their red fruits eaten by sucking bugs that mimic ants. I sit on a rock by the creek, waiting and watching. Northern cardinals stop by for their nightcap. Four males and three females take turns at a pool, males first. The impending winter calls them together, when only a few months ago they spent so much time and energy staying apart. Winter means less food, fewer hiding places, and occasional frozen water—imperatives for cooperative eyes that are more likely to find scarce resources, see danger, and survive.

2nd. Dusk is a magic time of bright stars and hooting barred owls in near-freezing air. The Pleiades are overhead. A Virginia opossum drinks at my pond and repairs to an old fox squirrel nest in a fifty-foot eastern red cedar. It forsakes nocturnal foraging, as does my neighbor armadillo, whose current burrow is beneath frozen brown Turk's caps fifteen feet from the house. A pair of Carolina wrens chortles and roosts on my front porch, nestled together in an upper corner. White-throated sparrows drink and bathe, while the tiny shadow of a winter wren sings a tinkling song like icicles falling on rocks.

3rd. When occasionally asked what traits allow native animals to live in suburbia, I answer that they are small to moderate in size, so they don't require a lot of space and aren't so likely to be noticed. They like edges, eat a variety of foods in a variety of places, including our feeders, and can use our houses for roosting, nesting, and food storage. They are nocturnal, behaviorally inconspicuous, or beautifully colored, cute, or innocuous, so we don't persecute them. The cadre of jays, opossums, robins, rabbits, doves, squirrels, swifts, crows, finches, martins, and raccoons is widespread in suburbia.

Moreover, our nature-culture mix invents new suburbanites from among range-marginalists such as western kingbird and house finch, colonists such as white-winged dove and great-tailed grackle, and generalists such as American crow and common grackle. The dove and great-tailed grackle from subtropical Texas use cities on their march northward because of urban warmth and the uniform structure of planted vegetation selected for nesting. Grackles choose planted evergreens as safe communal roosts and fast-food parking lots for eating. And the highly intelligent crow is no surprise to those who once hunted it as a varmint and only recently stopped the persecution.

Citified species may add new habits, such as nocturnal foraging for insects at lights by the usually diurnal cattle egret, killdeer, and introduced house sparrow. Moreover, killdeer now nest on flat, graveled rooftops together with common nighthawks. Heat doesn't bother these two, for they typically nest on naturally exposed gravel bars; but hatchling killdeer feed themselves and can't fly, whereas nighthawk chicks are fed until they can fly. So the baby killdeer just run off the roof, flutter-fall to the ground, and begin foraging. Clearly, those actors can play many roles, allowing them to take advantage of cultural opportunities.

4th. Only five times in thirty-five years has the ravine experienced more than two days below freezing. Today ends the earliest such spell. The landscape thaws at 11:00 A.M. after fifty-nine hours, and fox squirrels decide to get up. Pushed here by Arctic air, the season's first cedar waxwings settle on possumhaws and "whine." They eat the berries just as furiously as the squirrels dig for buried nuts. Under a cloudless sky the bright sun warms the air three degrees per hour to forty-eight by mid-afternoon, whereupon red admiral and question-mark butterflies appear. Someday I'd like to find just one hibernating butterfly. With glycerol as the antifreeze in its blood, how sheltered must it be?

5th. Patches, my pre-dawn writing companion, is our house cat who enjoys the wild through windows. Other domestic felines roam the ravine—about one for every five houses in my neighborhood—despite rules against it. People don't let dogs run loose, so why cats? Some don't buy a license requiring a rabies vaccination, so how can I know if a cat is safe? When we had a rabies outbreak and trapped seventy-three cats in the ravine, only fourteen had identification. We caught one cat per two-and-a-third acres, which is partly why ground nesting birds don't live here anymore. Domestic cat density was five hundred times the density of native bobcats, who can't live here anymore.

Neighbors complain bitterly if their cats are missing, and I suggest they ask the coyotes about it. Many owners cannot accept the fact of their pet's fur amid coyote tracks. "We need to call animal control," they say, and I respond that they are animal control—out of control. Some who've lost roaming cats still let replacements range. Obviously, these folks don't mind their cats killing the small native animals that our nature preserve is supposed to protect. Based on the local density of free-ranging cats and their free-range predation rates elsewhere, I estimate four thousand wildlife kills per year in the ravine.

6th. Time to empty my garage of two months of stacked and stored recyclables—152 pounds of unsolicited catalogs, 47 pounds of newspapers, 55 pounds of glass and plastic containers, and 14 pounds of aluminum and tin cans. We and our Labrador retriever retrieved most of the cans and bottles while walking everyday routes on city streets. Recycling is voluntary here but facilitated by the city. Recently folks were asked if they shop for products made with recycled material, and one in six said they did.

The approximately half-pound of trash per mile we pick up annually is a message of missing information about the Biosphere's rule that everything goes somewhere—nothing just disappears. Suburbanites are used to others picking up after them, as their throwaway mind-set grows with their materialism. Their concept of "once is enough" illustrates the separation from the natural reality of cycles. Personally, I find disposable cameras hardest to take, since repeat photography reinforces my understanding of nature's seasons and the conflicting linear changes made by humans.

7th. Eastern screech owls are roosting in tree cavities and my nest boxes for the first time since last spring. They like to be out in nice weather too, hiding by day in evergreen foliage, but when rain turns into sleet or snow or enemies threaten, inside they go, sometimes together as a snugly nestled pair. Early this morning two crows fly hard on the tail of an owl heading toward a tree with a nest box on the opposite side. The owl does a 180-degree turn around the trunk, directly into the entrance hole that it couldn't see upon approach. It depended on memory (learned behavior) as humans do, causing me to muse about the term "bird brain."

8th. A temperature in the mid-twenties or colder for several hours is necessary for frostweed frost, which is the plant's sap, breeze-whipped and frozen into white swirls as it exudes from cracks in the dry stem. Last night it happened for the first time this season, and today frosty white "candles" decorate the forest floor, previously "iced" with a new carpet of chocolate-brown leaves. Frostweed ornaments the holiday woods together with red possumhaws, blue juniper berries, and clusters of white western soapberries—a personal view that contrasts with the increasingly garish Christmas light displays of suburbia.

My ancestors mimicked the summer they missed when decorating for Christmas. Green trees, wreaths, and red berries gave cheer to people forced indoors by harsh weather and brought good luck according to legends dating from Roman times. Lighted candles on Christmas trees broke the gloom before electricity in an age when the trees were not put up until Christmas eve and gifts were homemade. Now folks buy gifts, employ plastic Christmas trees, and commercial and suburban lighting and other decorating begins before Thanksgiving for merchandising and winning prizes.

9th. A clear blue sky gives way to shifting cirrus clouds, strong south winds, and flocks of foraging songbirds. Kinglets, titmice, and chickadees demolish clusters of hanging dead leaves, looking for secreted insects. A hermit thrush finishes off Indian cherries and moves to American beautyberries but contends with mockingbird ownership. I'm watching as I rake leaves from our driveway into the woods. Underneath the leaves I uncover earthworms. No wonder screech owls

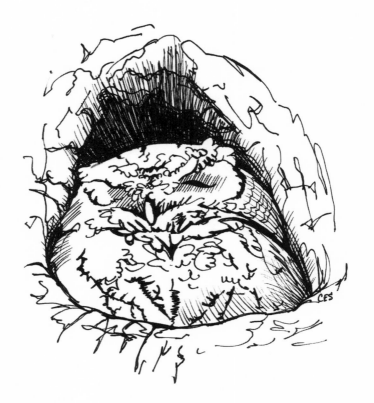

dive into the leaves when they hear hidden crawling food. Overnight, a cold front drops the temperature fifty-four degrees, unleashes the season's first cedar pollen, and deposits purple finches at my door.

10th. Blue-headed (solitary) vireos have been here two weeks, but if the weather becomes severe, they'll head farther south. The past few days one has been roosting inside a dry cluster of curled leaves on a Shumard oak twig tip. It sleeps at dusk, about the same time as Carolina wrens roost on the front porch and a downy woodpecker enters its newly chiseled tree hole. I stand motionless on my upstairs deck, watching the tiny vireo peering around through eye-ring "spectacles." It fusses a little before disappearing into the leaves. What does it hold onto in there? Until a winter storm tears the leaves off, they are its nightly protection on the south side of the house only ten feet from my own bed.

11th. Cast off skins of cicada nymphs, a cardinal's nest fallen beneath a cedar tree, and shaggy mane mushroom splotches on the ground are stark reminders of the green year gone by. Yesterday's sixty degrees and bright sunshine induced a mountain patchnose snake to bask, but by dawn it's a dark twenty-nine degrees, and I'm unlikely to see it again until March. The sun rises directly in front of my house and never gets more than five fists above the horizon, for we are only ten days away from the shortest sunlight of the year. The last sights of warmer days and creatures and the darkness make me sleepy. This time of year I feel torpid, as do so many wild brethren.

12th. Our influx of American crows began in the early 1980s and grew through the 1990s. Winterers number up to eleven in a flock, and several such groups are scattered in the ravine. The breeding population increased from zero to about one pair per thirty-five acres. I think the crow family at my house stays in winter and invites migrant cousins to join them in suburban luxury. These scavengers peck at squashed squirrels and pizza crusts on the street and pecans and acorns in lawns, and drink at birdbaths and garden pools. They haven't gotten into trash bags yet, but I'll bet they will soon, because they already follow raccoons and dogs that open them. No suburbanized native is more sagacious.

13th. An American woodcock, dressed like dead leaves, nonchalantly probes for earthworms on the creekbank, where I sit contemplating water's odyssey. First Americans drank from and bathed in this creek, and Anglo settlers dug wells here. Their descendants switched to treated public water drilled from the rocks, then pumped water from reservoirs that drowned wild landscapes. Moderns buy even more distant water in plastic bottles, which many throw away. I wonder what the Biosphere charges us to pollute or overuse local water and import water mined elsewhere, bottled and exported, and for the pollutants released in water processing and transport.

14th. A neighbor family has lived in the same woods on the ravine's eastern rim for forty years. Their back deck has a tree growing through it and raccoons who look in their picture windows. No effort is made to subsidize a yard, so they receive unending solicitations for ground clearing, tree cutting, mowing, trimming, and similar cultural maintenance. Another neighbor keeps only a winding path through shrubs that others think should be a lawn, because she wants to experience the seasonality of natives. A third family grows bluebonnets and other wildflowers in their front yard and foregoes mowing until the city threatens them.

Recently, only a quarter of my suburb's citizens, who completed a questionnaire on community values, rated natural beauty as a reason for living here. They specified the hills, ravines, and wooded aspects, but not the wild lives that help to construct and maintain these living landscapes. Among features of quality of life, they rated natural beauty fourth behind school system, housing, and public safety. Thus do most of my neighbors value cultural creations above nature's, perhaps not knowing or remembering that all are gifts from a world that people did not create.

15th. During three afternoons of repairing, replacing, and relocating screech-owl nest boxes, I was pleasantly surprised to see the sleeping male of a pair that nested the past two years. Another box had an owl that flew out as I climbed up to find Inca dove and northern mockingbird feathers. A third had a freshly beheaded brown rat, and the lid of another had a pile of ringtail scat comprised of chinaberries and

rodent hair. Half the boxes had fox squirrels or their nests of shred-
ded cedar bark. One housed a female with four tightly packed, full-
grown youngsters—a very late date to stay home—but some squirrel
children may be like some human children who return to parental security after hard lessons on their own.

16th. Mild, windy weather tells me that I have a day or two to do some
outside caulking and touch-up painting before the next blue norther.
While mending cracks in cedar siding, I find sunflower seeds stashed
there by titmice and chickadees, all on the south side away from winter's direction. This instinctive storing enlivens my afternoon chore.
It results from the cold-season demand for more food combined with
feeder surplus and opportunity. The use of my siding is like blue jays
and fox squirrels storing acorns in patio pots. It is adaptive substitu-
tion of culture for nature, and helps to explain why certain natives are
suburban fixtures.

17th. A thunderstorm, complete with singing robins, followed by a
light snow, celebrates Gretchen's birthday. In another year, snow accumulates to eight inches. A third year brings a dust storm, the evening of which we write personal Christmas notes as we listen to the
carols of a hooting great-horned owl on the chimney. The children's
upbringing in the woods contributed in a major way to their love of
the wild. Curiosity about other lives meant a constant relay of natives
in the house, and our delight in those different looks and lifestyles had
a lot to do with learning to appreciate all the neighbors we've known
around the world.

18th. Two yearling male sharp-shinned hawks sit about thirty feet
apart this morning. They've just arrived for the winter but will be
pushed out by an older female who's here for her third winter in a
row. She'll not tolerate another sharpy in this territory and will give
these youngsters about twenty-four hours to get out of town. Yesterday she flew in suddenly, scaring a bunch of house sparrows under
low-lying fragrant sumacs. She landed on top of the thicket, grabbed
some stems, and flapped hard, bouncing up and down for three minutes trying to frighten the sparrows out, but to no avail. Ten seconds
after she flew off, they all split in the opposite direction.

A sharpy's daytime hunting strategy is like an eastern screech owl's at night. It sits immobile, slowly peering about from a relatively se-cluded perch inside the tree canopy, never in the open. When food comes into view, the hunter takes off in a dive toward its quarry, fly-ing low, dodging tree trunks if necessary, or in a beeline if close by. Surprise is the major element in this sit and wait strategy. Chases are few and short. If the hawk or owl makes no catch, it again flies low, usually beneath or through the low tree canopy, and rises sharply and abruptly to another perch, where it becomes immobile—waiting.

Besides hiding the hunter, the arc-like flight pattern obscures nests. There is no simple trajectory an eye can follow. Hunting sharpies are so inconspicuous that twice I've unwittingly released songbirds I just banded into waiting talons, and once I did the same thing near dusk for an eastern screech owl. Those hunters were attracted to the alarm cries of handled birds. One Inca dove disappeared in a puff of feath-ers. Another time a male cardinal bit and fought, forcing the hawk to release it. My inadvertent help was unnatural, of course, but even natural hunts for vertebrates are no more than about fifty percent successful.

19th. Every year bare trees surprise me with previously hidden con-nections, such as bird nests, wasp galls, lichens, mistletoe, beetle bor-ings, burls, squirrel gnawings, and woodpecker holes. Tree leaves feed gall-wasp larvae, whose adults feed birds that also eat mistletoe berries and nest in the lichens and holes. Beetle grubs and termites eat wood, aided by digestive bacteria, and are eaten by woodpeckers, whose holes are used by other animals, some of whom eat the hole makers and users. And this is only part of the grazing food web, named for the multiple-path, energy relay that begins with sunlight translated into greenery.

Energy transfers don't stop there, however, for the grazers are tied to decomposers by their wastes and their dead, and these creatures are responsible for cycling nutrients back to everybody. Because humans are grazers, decomposers such as fly maggots, beetle larvae, snails, slugs, millipedes, fungi, and especially bacteria are relatively unfamil-iar. In the ravine they live mostly in the dark world of wood, leaf lit-ter, soil, and pond sediment, assuring that our green world doesn't end with a tree's death in a storm or the forest's temporary demise in a tornado or fire. Our world only ends if trees are bulldozed and the ground is covered with asphalt or concrete.

20th. The brown rat that I found stashed in a screech-owl box a few days ago is one of suburbia's unnatural subsidies. Owls belong here, but exotic rats, house sparrows, sunflower seeds, and sugar water don't. Raptors and other predators prosper because of food supplies introduced or enhanced by culture, but they also thrived in more natural surroundings when the ravine was part of a ranch with native prey populations. Again, the sequence of scenes in life's play is that energy flows from simply structured, energy-loose communities such as ranch pastures and suburban yards to more complex ones that store energy, like the ravine forest.

Grasslands produce edible energy fast, storing very little of it, because they have little wood; whereas forests grow slowly and sequester energy for centuries in tree trunks. Young growing and annual garden and crop communities are more productive of edible energy than older and perennial ones, which is why we eat more grass seeds (wheat, rice, corn) than tree seeds (nuts). Suburbia, subsidized by fossil-fuel heat, cold, fertilizer, and water, includes yard and garden grassland that exports rat, sparrow, and seed energy to the ravine, which houses predators who use that food in their own energy import-export business.

Eastern screech owls, for instance, emigrate from suburbia to the country, taking city energy with them, while wintering sharp-shinned hawks import energy from northern nesting places and export it back in the spring, exchanging some at stopover sites. Exchange rates have not been measured, because the necessary studies are very difficult, but we know that the food quality of winter habitat for migratory songbirds, and thus the amount of exportable energy, determines nesting success thousands of miles away. As always, the Biosphere's fundamental message is that everything is connected to everything else.

21st. Each year at the winter solstice I declare a time-out from holiday hustling just to "be." I try to reserve an hour in the wild at dawn, noon, and dusk. Most years the ambience is autumnal. Normally, there is no sustained winter until after Christmas. We've had a few light freezes and one twenty-four degree low so far this season, but red and bronze leaves still fall from Shumard oaks and Indian cherries, and strawberry bushes remain scarlet in leaf and fruit. Orange-crowned and yellow-rumped warblers and blue-headed vireos are other autumnal reminders.

Dawn is a mild fifty degrees. A Carolina wren sings a few verses. Five American crows emerge from their cedar roost, cawing disconsolately in light rain until a hawk zips by and they awake with alarm. At dawn and dusk these crafty characters won't appear or retire if they can see me watching, but they sneak in and out, one by one, as I look from my own hiding place. The clouds part briefly at noon, and I'm treated to the vocal repertoire of a barred owl. I don't hear him at dusk, but a winter wren warbles. The rain begins again, the wren's song continues, and my spirit is at home.

22nd. Downpours started yesterday. Four inches in an hour created an eight-foot-high washout of the creek and continued today with four more inches. It is 1991, and the ravine experiences its greatest flood in my time. Logs move like matchsticks, boulders like bowling balls, smashing streamside trees. Gone are a ten-foot-high earthen dam and a swinging water gate, relics of ranching days. Cultural refuse rides the crest toward the lakefill. The reservoir rises forty feet for three months, drowning houses and parks. Some folks debate how much destruction is due to human folly, but the answer is clear to those who appreciate that humans belong to the Earth and not the other way around.

23rd. Before suburban sprawl did them in, I'd hear peeping Strecker's chorus frogs. They are December breeders, remarkable for the fact that they sing when stimulated by cold rain despite being cold-blooded, perhaps because their pond water is warm relative to the air. I never measured it but got chilled searching for them and for smallmouth salamanders on rainy nights before suburbia surrounded the ravine, filling or draining temporary upland ponds and flooding pool life from the creek. Strecker's chorus frogs used to announce the holidays by sounding like hundreds of tiny sleigh bells tinkling in the wind.

24th. On Christmas Eve, legend says that other animals talk, but I hear them year-round. Winter messages often concern severe weather that influences survival in a way that my human neighbors and I haven't related to for decades. Today in 1989, an Arctic express delivered a temperature of two degrees below zero, the coldest ever in the ravine. All surface water was frozen for three days, but blue jays, northern flickers, and brown thrashers traded jobs chipping the ice into tiny bits that they and several other animals ate.

That incident was a special lesson in reciprocity, a kind of altruism that certainly involves non-relatives and possible kin. Watchful birds and mammals are intelligent enough to learn it in many circumstances, some of which are rare, like the need to chip ice, and others ordinary, such as mobbing predators and flocking with knowledgeable residents. The point is survival of the larger company of actors. Indeed, altruism might be learned from wild elders as well as other humans and help us reconnect with nature.

25th. Twigs of mistletoe with white berries are an ancient symbol of peace and, therefore, a Christmas tradition. Birds eat the berries and drop the gummy seeds on tree branches where they stick, germinate, penetrate bark, absorb sap, and grow into this flowering plant that produces oxygen, bird food, and Christmas decorations. Because we like mistletoe but abhor its spread in our sunlit, fertilized, and watered trees, we have a love/hate relationship with it. Natural parasites such as mistletoe usually don't kill their hosts or they will die too, but lawns can unbalance nature's give and take in favor of the take.

26th. Before the great freeze of Christmas week, 1983 (seven consecutive days below twenty degrees), a dozen Inca doves lived at my house. We stood alone in Owl Hollow, a little bit of culture surrounded by reforestation and attractive to Incas, who prefer suburbia's open edges if not farmsteads. But after the freeze, no more Incas. No more doleful "mo-hope" songs in the greening of spring, or "no-hope" in the heat of summer. Incas never reestablished themselves, because their open ground was soon transformed into brick and asphalt. Their absence was confirmed by my dooryard screech owls who never again ate them for supper.

The great freeze killed wildlife in untold numbers, broke my house's water lines, and turned our reservoir into a car skating rink. There was no open water. At least two screech owls died after losing a third of their body weight. Five Inca doves roosted on rafters above our horses in a shed protected from the north wind, yet all died one night. Horse body heat and the bird's altruistic habit of piling to conserve heat was not enough. In cold weather, roosting Incas stay in body contact, some on top of others, and the pile reshuffles every so often, allowing outsiders inside. But Incas are tropical birds near their northern range limit and simply couldn't stand that much cold.

27th. Every winter I enjoy a new carpet. Only a few feet from my door are the deciduous trees and shrubs that craft an intricate pattern of round, oval, and lance-point shapes, long-narrow or short-fat and sharp, blunt-lobed or heart-shaped figures, some saw-toothed, others deeply incised, some rough, others smooth, thick and flat or thin and curled, an inch long or a foot. The weave is as fascinating as any oriental rug and the color relaxing and young enough that fading reds, golds, and even the green-fall of possumhaw and gum bumelia are present. This is the finest of floorings, protecting the forest with an estimated ton of leaves per acre, and its threads recycle into years of future carpets.

28th. There are very few days that I choose not to walk in the ravine, but this is one. Instead, I stack firewood, courtesy of the forest's fallen. I store two cords but will burn about one this winter, my profligate throwback to ancestral days—instinctive satisfaction, but unneeded now for safety, warmth, and cooking. I leave most downed branches and logs, because the forest must be anchored with heavy nutrients. In the afternoon I sit by the fireplace reading and listening to favorite composers. The controlled fire symbolizes my separation from nature yet feeds upon the reminder that I am here only because of nature's creativity.

29th. Long shadows dance the tall dance, as this year's favorite Christmas card says. They declare the start of winter. Blue tree shadows draw ghostly fencelines that trail me, for the sun is only two fists above the ravine's rim. A roosting screech owl is discovered by chance. Or is it chance? It sits concealed in the shadows of dead oak leaves, unknown except to us. How and why did I find it? Is it experience in looking? But I wasn't really looking. Or is intuition at work? I cannot separate years of learning, translated into subconscious awareness, from the fact that I am sometimes drawn to a messenger for no apparent reason.

30th. My generation is least concerned that environment is a critical issue, because we had no environmental education and were taught that we could do anything we wanted to after being released from restrictions of the 1930s depression and 1940s world war. Even by 1996, with mounting evidence of environmental damage, a survey showed that only thirty-nine percent of us believed we were doing too little to safeguard the environment. Conversely, sixty-six percent of those too young to know rationing and loss thought that too little was being done. My generation is about to turn its leadership over to those younger, better informed folks, and I hope they won't forget.

31st. On this, the last day of calendar time in the twentieth century —an early winter day in universal time—I find that my society has sustained the longest period of economic growth in its history by increasing its fossil fuel use and, thereby, its atmospheric carbon emissions, ozone depletion, population growth, urbanization, cancer rate, and loss of wildland, to name only a few effects on the whole-Earth community. Yet this is the end of a century in which we have learned more about who we are, where we came from, and where we could be headed than in any other period of history. Clearly, we have major choices to make. Will we listen to the wisdom of wild elders?

They are other nations, caught with ourselves in the net of life and time, fellow prisoners of the splendor and travail of the earth. *Henry Beston*

CHAPTER 6

THE PLAY OF LIFE

Biodiversity is a buzzword that describes any array of species, including humans. More importantly, it means the interdependence of all lives in natural food webs that cycle nutrient resources as they pass energy along, store carbon, supply water, provide food, housing, and medicine, and reduce storm damage among many life-giving goods and services. This play of life functions best in wildlands like the ravine, where the greatest arrays of native species send all the messages we need to hear.

Separation

The messages say that we are increasingly estranged from the natural world that gave us birth and to which we are forever tied. Despite our believed independence, we dance to the Biosphere's cyclic tunes. Earth's stages warp and crack with the consequences of our manipulations, but the rules for life do not change. Recurring seasonal events try to teach us that. Droughts, floods, and diseases harmful to culture or personal health add strong emphasis. Technological fixes such as dams, pesticides, and pills are only stop-gap, and the messages keep on coming.

Our separation arises from a big brain that allows us to use fossil fuels to invent an unnatural history that deceives us into thinking we can avoid or replace nature. Thus, many of us don't deal with nature directly anymore or do so only minimally. Increasingly isolated from our birthplace, we lose the survival knowledge of natural processes and products. Our prehistoric ancestors had that information, not in scientific detail or written record, but in tribal lore. That's why they

revered the sun, life's main source of energy, and prayed to, while prey-
ing on, other animals.

Because we are the strongest of all beings mentally, we've devised
clever ways of distancing ourselves from nature, such as using tools
that remove us from responsibility. Even prehistorically, we used fire
to secure food and clothing by driving bison herds off of cliffs. Thus
separated from physical contact with prey and hence reprisal, we
learned to kill indiscriminately and excessively. We lost the restraints
dictated by natural predation and now extinguish species without
forethought, or even knowledge of their existence, using ever more
powerful, indirect weaponry such as biocides and bulldozers.

Some say our invention of agriculture was the point of separation,
but fossils disagree. By using novel techniques to kill at a distance and
cooperative hunting enhanced by elaborate communication, evidence
suggests that our Stone Age ancestors contributed to extinctions as
no other animals did. Agriculture increased our separation, surely, as
did industrialization, even more abruptly and with greater interactive
consequences — for example when irrigation pumps powered by non-
renewable fossil fuel in wells drilled by fossil fuel deplete nonrenew-
able fossil water and change the weather with exhaust gases.

Thornbush-encircled camps that eventually became walled cities,
originally for protection from wild and human enemies, have meta-
morphosed into suburban fences for believed isolation from natural
and cultural neighbors. They continue our separatist tradition — our
false sense of security and self-sufficiency — and contribute to our disregard. Behind the barriers, we invent an urban culture in which increasingly complex tools and specialization in making and using them
require less and less personal contact with nature. As urbanization
grows exponentially, individual knowledge of and concern for its nature disappears apace.

While technical devices and commercial services contribute to the
isolation, a few of us have used the time saved and equipment invented
to relearn and reaffirm that our existence is irrevocably bound up with
nature's. But we have a new problem in personally acquiring and using that information, because we don't live anywhere long enough. We
are as temporary as seasonal cycles, but, unlike the seasons, we do not

return to repeat what works. We have little sense of place—of home—which, despite Realtor parlance, is not just a house but an interactive community of natural and unnatural history.

Our farming ancestors were bound by resources in their surroundings. The young dispersed, but not their parents, who stayed or moved cyclically with the seasons of renewal—or wrecked the environment and destroyed their culture. Today's suburbanites move linearly and often, using fossil fuels from a time and place they've never known. Some feel they don't have the time or need to know, closeted as they are in constant-temperature chambers behind unopened tinted windows in front of television and computer screens. Ours is the age of missing information.

Ignorance because of novelty and isolation often translates into fear. Wild beings are killed without learning who they are, what they do, and how interesting, helpful, or harmful they might be. When isolation breeds arrogance, natives are killed because they conflict with personal tastes. The humans versus animals dichotomy of verbal expression reflects our presumed dominion and consequent separation from nature. How can we recognize that we rebellious adolescent animals must fit into millennia-old cycles of resource give-and-take? The Biosphere is finely tuned to all life, and we newcomers can't change the rules no matter how powerful we think we are.

The Biosphere's goods and services are unrecognized because they are largely the work of unseen life, mostly bacteria, in seemingly abundant and thus easily disregarded soil, water, and air. Yet their energetic relations to familiar beings are visible and easily appreciated among garden flowers and fed songbirds. These can teach us that energy is the universal currency of life. Because money is our cultural measure of energy—for instance the cost of fertilizer, birdfeed, and the cars and gasoline it takes to get them—action to conserve the irreplaceable value of the Biosphere's goods and services must be to make them monetary costs to all human enterprises.

Essential goods and services are summarized in ten general messages sent each day by the ravine community or any wild landscape. They serve all life all the time, not just humanity. Once we grasp the enormity of the operation, the worldwide connections of multiple millions of species and physical factors, we must realize that they are impossible, or prohibitively expensive, to replace technologically. If we listen to messages from the wild and, if receptive, we learn that the more natural the landscape, the more biodiverse and thus dependable it is in providing:

Gas Production and Regulation—oxygen-carbon dioxide cycle, greenhouse and ozone shields

Climate Regulation—moderated radiation, wind, temperature, precipitation

Reduced Physical Damage—protection from storms, floods, droughts, erosion

Water Cycling and Storage—provision by watersheds, aquifers, plants

Soil Formation and Retention—weathering, decomposition, fertilization

Nutrient Production, Storage, Cycling—organic compounds made, transported, redeposited

Waste (pollution) Control—removal, detoxification, transformation

Pollination and Seed Dispersal—plant reproduction facilitated by animals

Pest and Weed Control—predators and grazers reduce pests and weeds

Food and Materials Production—wildlife, plants, lumber, minerals, medicines, etc.

Other natural provisions are unrecognized because they are spiritual and disguised by our cultural materialism. These include resistance to disease and recovery from physical trauma and the psychic stress induced by an increasingly complex, technical culture that challenges our biological capacity to cope. Now, however, some health workers send patients home from hospitals or into natural surroundings as soon as possible, because recovery and daily well-being are promoted by familiarity and greenery—in effect by acknowledged kinship with all life.

There are additional recreational and aesthetic benefits to people who immerse themselves in nature. Nature hobbies, for example, are relaxing and instructional if not subverted by distancing mechanisms like greed and control. Focus on possession and competition causes messages to be missed. Instead of taking natural goods as trophies—of ignoring process for product—people who take nature's cyclic time will benefit most from its offerings, for they will be nurtured by its reacquaintances. Said Ralph Waldo Emerson, "Nature never became a toy to a wise spirit."

Reconnection

Billing the Biosphere's provisions to human enterprises is easier said than done, because they are unrecognized or taken for granted. That some, like oxygen and clean water, are considered free and thus abused or overused is the greatest tragedy of the commons. Because culture evolves faster than nature, humans depend on learned behavior, and education is the key to change. A new effort is necessary in every community, aimed at assembling environmental advisors and preserving wildland to include outdoor learning centers that employ educational curricula for commercial licensing as well as for school children. We can change this age of missing information.

Each city council appoints an environmental planning and monitoring board to complement its city planning, zoning, and school boards. Big cities employ ecologists, who suburbs may not be able to afford, but suburbs need the same information and usually have naturalist residents who could volunteer. Some folks, especially academics, aren't used to providing opinions, only facts, but the time is past for ivory-tower withdrawal from decision-making. All must enter the public arena, for there is simply too much missing information. Participation—inclusion—is necessary, as the Biosphere instructs (and democracy requires).

Mostly we've missed understanding our role in the play of life, because our schools focus on memorizing facts instead of learning how to use them to understand processes. Moreover, business must know culture's laws but not nature's, and the media convey news about "natural" catastrophe with little or no word about its cultural connections. We learn about storm damage, for example, but not that it is worsened by clearing and burning forests, or that the Earth's increasingly erratic and severe weather is tied to climatic warming and ultimately to our abuse of the atmospheric commons as a waste dump.

Guided by its environmental and school boards, a suburb begins educational reform, protects wildlands, and develops an outdoor learning center. Five wild acres per resident is the unofficial yardstick in my suburb, although communities vary according to their climates and should begin the appropriate calculations. Lacking wildland, public or purchased land can be restored to semi-naturalness, and private developers may be required by law or induced through tax rebates to reserve wildland, which will increase property values when the missing information is found.

Suburbs may swap private debt for public good by foregoing or lowering taxes on private lands that are natural enough for saving and useful for learning about natural history. The land must be sufficiently large for regulated public use and guarded against abuse. Owners would agree to maintain natural values, perhaps even helped in this regard by volunteer management, and be legally protected from liability. If unwilling to allow public access, owners might be persuaded to preserve the land's natural services through tax relief equivalent to the wildland's calculated benefit to the community.

Ideally, nature preserves are blocks, not ribbons like the ravine, because natural history is maximized by an interior area that is large relative to its edge. The larger and more diverse, the more messages a wildland can provide. Connections to other fragments of similar lands are important to allow exchanges by organisms that move daily and seasonally. Wildlands must be chosen wisely, since the variety of interacting native species, natural goods and services, and consequent educational opportunities are positively proportional to area size, landscape diversity, edge-to-interior ratio, and number of connections.

Wildland preserves require management because culture constantly impacts nature with biological and physical punishment. But adverse influences from exotic organisms and unbuffered weather can be minimized, some removed entirely, and human presence can be controlled. Special dangers include invasive yard and garden plants that outcompete natives, loose pets and introduced animals that over-kill, and the exaggerated force of water and wind because of focused runoff, erosive trails, and lack of vegetational screens. Moreover, management practices are very effective teaching tools.

As nature centers emerge, they, in connection with community schools, develop field-trip curricula for linking the outdoors to indoor classrooms. Curricula connect all subject areas in the arts, humanities, and sciences at all grade and adult levels to reinforce learning and develop an appreciation of home according to different developmental skills and personal interests. Curricula are interactive and employ modern communicative techniques, such as computer links among classes within and among cities, in order to understand that the Biosphere is planetary despite local differences in natural and unnatural history.

Particular study projects are continued, year-to-year, with increasing degrees of difficulty, skills, and individual responsibility appropriate to age and grade. They include night classes for working adults and leaves of absence for those people to remain current. Information, stressing connections, is stored, reexamined, and integrated with new findings to produce new ideas for testing and a baseline for measuring the progressive tuning of culture with nature. One approach involves a native species confronted by natural and unnatural influences over time (grade levels) and space (different natural and unnatural communities).

The eastern screech owl says that it will mentor humans who wish to join it and other natives as interacting neighbors. This species and the equally obliging western screech owl comprise a team that is available for instruction in wooded suburbia across North America. Both readily accept nest boxes, making communication easy. Natural factors such as home sites, competitors, predators, and food, investigated together with cultural features such as biocide use, vehicle traffic, and human and pet density, permit the comparison of natural and unnatural history.

Suburban screech owls are especially important messengers, because they live in culturally simplified landscapes that contain easily understood linkages. Their lives mirror the lives of food, shelter, and predator species that share energy flow and nutrient cycles and, in doing so, reflect environmental quality. The owls monitor what humans do to themselves and other life by managing natural and cultural resources wisely, or not. In my suburb, for instance, screech owls mention that they nest earlier each year, as we promote climatic warming, and hatch fewer eggs, as we use more biocides.

Another educational approach asks us to consider ourselves as natives and compare our roles in natural food webs with webs broken by humans. Can we describe the living links and self-adjusting processes in a tuned natural versus out-of-tune cultural food web? Can we name the ways our industrial tinkering reverberates in the Biosphere? Do we understand how reducing biodiversity by monocultural farming and increasing it by genetic engineering without permits from natural selection alters the Biosphere and hence our ability to continue doing unnatural history?

As a leaf, for example, I use water and carbon dioxide produced by plants and animals that ate plants that also made the oxygen I use with solar energy to recycle carbon dioxide and water for everyone. Then I die, fall, and am eaten by decomposer organisms who return my nutrients to groundwater absorbed by plants, eaten by animals who live, die, and feed the life that feeds the continuous green relay of food energy, gas exchange, water recycling, and other services. But if I die, fall, am raked, bagged in plastic, and buried in a landfill, I cannot act in the play of life—at least not for a very long time.

Regardless of the teacher, messages from the wild always concern such opposing natural and unnatural history. Nature tells us what has worked or not over the long history of life—how our natural heritage still operates or doesn't. The messengers do not hoard resources unnecessarily, because the costs exceed benefits, but interact in ways that allow reciprocity, because that's the only directive for survival. Their messages imply that the longer we wait for reconciliation and reconnection with the natural world, the fewer options we'll have, because we will have cut too many lines from the script and eliminated too many actors.

The Age of Information

My dream of the play on that blue moon of January 1999 continues today as it has since I began hearing messages from the wild. Today's scene includes continued dialogue with a pair of screech-owl actors. They are as different as any two animals in appearance and personality. One is smaller, lighter in color, and suspicious; the other is larger, darker, mild-mannered, and confiding. Like humans and other wildlings, the owls reflect unique inheritances and life experiences. They and all beings are members of the same cast in life's only theater called Earth.

Unlike humans, however, the owls live within their needs. Extra food isn't stored unless there is a surplus and seasonal demand. Breeding is limited if individuals are many and foregone if food is scarce. Mates are sharing partners. Home is only large enough to meet basic needs and is guarded by advertisement, not by fences or violence; although offspring are defended physically if necessary, because they carry one's acting ability and training for successful future runs of the play. Residency is permanent; or, in some cousins, seasonally cyclic; and hence the owls are in regular contact with the cast, whose roles they learn to respect.

Since their particular debut perhaps twenty-five million years ago, screech owls and other cast members have used different resources, or the same ones in different ways, as the dialogue demands. A role readjusts or disappears or new actors arrive only when the stage changes in millennial time. The newest large animals are humans, only about a hundred thousand years old. They are the owls' understudies but have taken center stage in every twentieth century scene. Seasoned actors would tutor these newcomers, who ignore cues and damage or destroy scenes that had rave reviews over time spans far exceeding humanity's brief run.

Diverse props and larger stages support older, larger, and more diverse casts with enough differences among lifestyles and sufficient backup to sustain the plot if a disturbance occurs. Those scenes are long, compared to others on sets with simple props and a few short-lived actors—the scenes created by natural and unnatural damage. Energy relays and nutrient cycles are unified themes of life's plot, regardless of changes, but work best in diverse communities of many long-lived actors. Complex stages and scenes with casts of thousands evolve and may be injured but are reassembled as only the play's directors permit.

New scenes like suburbia lack most of the original cast, because their sets are simplified by humans who substitute foreign actors that don't know the dialogue and upstage remaining originals. Although screech owls continue to fill the role of small, feathered, flying, nocturnal, insect-eating, tree-cavity resident, neighbor, and teacher, they have disappeared from many casts in just the last billionth of a second of their long careers. That's the time in which humanity has used fossil fuels to value benefits to itself above injurious costs to the four-billion-year-old play.

Because natural damage is usually local and temporary, the play has the capacity to recover and run with supporting roles by multiple millions of actors. But cultural impact is global and continuing. Humanity stresses the cast's abilities to act everywhere in the theater. Late in the twentieth century, all stages built before humans arrived have been altered or replaced by unnatural ones, causing the largest-ever mass extinction of actors. At that time, much of the dialogue between nature and culture sounded like:

Act	Nature	Culture
COMPETITION	Moderated by dividing resources, times, and places among individuals and species	Increased, often purposely, resulting in increased waste of resources and extinctions
PREDATION	Vulnerable, abundant, and/or large individuals are selected; benefits equal or exceed costs	Overkill occurs despite prey status or predator need; costs are subsidized to exceed benefits

Act	Nature	Culture
POPULATION	Limited by resources, hence dynamically stable; birth and death rates balance cyclically	Grows as death rates decline faster than birth rates, resulting in resource abuse and overuse
RESOURCE USE	Energy is stored and nutrients are recycled; benefits are maximized relative to costs with tradeoffs among items	Nonrenewables like fossil fuels and metals are depleted, while renewables like water, forests, and wildlife are extinguished
LANDSCAPE DYNAMICS	Trends toward complexity and stability with more stored resources and less restricted transitions	Nature is simplified and destabilized or replaced by culture with abrupt and privatized borders

Gradually, however, discord wanes during the twenty-first century, as new human generations awaken with information that had been missing for a long time. Equipped with an environmental conscientiousness, people realize what the English poet, Francis Thompson, meant by writing that one cannot pluck a flower without troubling a star. In affirming their global and cosmic communities, the informed generations acknowledge their need for continuous tutoring from the wild, for they are powerful but inexperienced actors.

Stirred by their previous ransacking of the Earth—an estimated forty billion U.S. dollars' worth per year—people begin to balance cost:benefit ratios with the entire Biosphere in mind. Their new system, in which quality replaces quantity, charges all enterprises for using the commons and regulates economic activity according to the theater's ability to support its life-giving system. Natural areas are reserved and degraded ones restored, especially in and near cities, so the play continues to provide unmatched resources and teach about theater operation and management.

People have learned to appreciate the wild cast for its functional and instructional roles as well as for its material benefits—its processes as well as products. Human reproduction and use of resources become sustainable—dynamically stable—and violence to nature and culture subsides as kinship replaces kingship. Wild actors dialogue with humans who no longer separate themselves by illusory dominion and self-absorbed materialism but give acclaimed performances of reconciliation and reconnection. People return home in a new scene called the age of information.

Imagine a world in which carpenter knows beaver, lawyer knows eagle, and philosopher knows the silence of the deep night. *Stephen Aizenstat*

The Calendar

These are the common messengers and their seasonal messages in the ravine (31° 30′ N, 97° 12′ W). Here too are selected cycles and apparent linear trends in graphic form. I list mostly first, peak, and last appearances such as date of the first flower or song and last freeze or departed bird, plus a few cultural events. Entries are chronological based on average annual date.

I began recording biological events by comparing census methods in December 1963–November 1964. The most efficient and subsequently used was an alternate day, half-mile, half-hour trail walk, varying mornings, afternoons, and evenings in the main ravine and Butterfly Hollow (November 1964–March 1980) or main ravine and Owl Hollow (April 1980–December 1999).

Some events were not noted personally every year, because I was away, and some did not occur every year. To include a biotic record, someone had to census at least two weeks before and after its current average date after three years. That span encompassed less than a ten percent chance of error with ten years of record.

Information is range of dates, average date plus and minus one standard deviation in days, and sample size (years) in parentheses.[1] A few exceptional dates are in parentheses at the appropriate end of the range. Most events, represented by less than ten years, are given only as range of dates and sample size and grouped with related events.

I know of only one other compilation (Leopold and Jones 1947) similar to this in North America, although such study is basic information. It allows time and space comparisons (Bradley et al. 1999) that can advise us about changes ranging from local biodiversity and species temporal roles to world climate and the Biosphere's future.

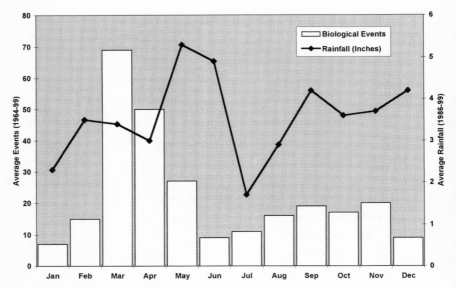

Biological events of all kinds peak in the spring, preceding peak rainfall, but coincide with seasonal rain in autumn.

January

Eastern red and Ashe junipers (*Juniperus virginiana, J. ashei*): pollen peak—Dec. 21–Jan. 20, avg. Jan. 7 ± 7 (22).

Dawn bird chorus (three or more coincidental species): Jan. 5–22, avg. Jan. 13 ± 5 (20).

Southern plains trout lily (*Erythronium mesochoreum*): blooming (white)—Jan. 12–29, avg. Jan. 22 ± 5 (19).

Ground snow-covered: (Nov. 12) Dec. 16–Feb. 22, avg. Jan. 23 ± 22 (16).

American robin (*Turdus migratorius*): arrival—Jan. 5–Feb. 19, avg. Jan. 24 ± 12 (32).

American elm (*Ulmus americana*): blooming (green)—Jan. 20–Feb. 7, avg. Jan. 28 ± 5 (21); seeds falling—Feb. 25–Mar. 3 (8).

Eastern screech owl (*Otus asio*): singing—Jan. 14–Feb. 10, avg. Jan. 30 ± 8 (11).

February

Elbowbush (downy privet, *Forestiera pubescens*): blooming (yellow) —Jan. 19–Feb. 10, avg. Feb. 2 ± 5 (15).

Henbit (*Lamium amplexicaule*): blooming (purple)—(Jan. 5) Jan. 15–Feb. 21, avg. Feb. 4 ± 15 (14).

Coralberry (*Symphoricarpos orbiculatus*): leaves—Jan. 15–Feb. 25, avg. Feb. 12 ± 13 (16).

Southern plains trout lily (*Erythronium mesochoreum*): blooming peak—Feb. 3–20, avg. Feb. 13 ± 6 (16).

Windflower (ten-petaled anemone, *Anemone berlandieri*): blooming (white, pink, blue)—Jan. 26–Feb. 27, avg. Feb. 13 ± 11 (11).

Missouri violet (*Viola missouriensis*): blooming (blue, white), hillside —(Jan. 8) Jan. 27–Mar. 1, avg. Feb. 15 ± 10; ravine bottom in same years—avg. Feb. 21 ± 8 (29).

Mourning cloak (*Nymphalis antiopa*): winter appearance—Jan. 26– Mar. 2, avg. Feb. 15 ± 11 (12).

Ohio buckeye (Texas buckeye, *Aesculus glabra arguta*): leaves— Jan. 26–Feb. 28, avg. Feb. 17 ± 7 (25); seedlings—Dec. 23–Jan. 15 (5).

Fox squirrel (*Sciurus niger*): newborns: Jan. 27–Mar. 20, avg. Feb. 19 ± 12 (15).

Purple martin (*Progne subis*): arrival—(Jan. 27) Feb. 15–Feb. 28, avg. Feb. 21 ± 4 (19).

Mexican plum (*Prunus mexicana*): blooming (white)—Feb. 7– Mar. 2, avg. Feb. 21 ± 6 (21).

Furnace turned off: Feb. 4–Mar. 17, avg. Feb. 21 ± 11 (19).

Plateau live oak (*Quercus virginiana fusiformis*): leaf fall—Feb. 5– Mar. 8, avg. Feb. 22 ± 9 (19).

Redbud (*Cercis canadensis texensis*): blooming (pink, magenta)—
Feb. 1–Mar. 6, avg. Feb. 24 ± 7 (26).

Eastern cottonwood (*Populus deltoides*): blooming (yellow)—Feb. 10–
Mar. 12, avg. Feb. 26 ± 7 (15).

March

Snow goose (*Chen caerulescens*): migrants—Feb. 15–Mar. 21, avg.
Mar. 1 ± 12 (11).

Windflower (ten-petaled anemone, *Anemone berlandieri*): blooming
peak—Feb. 18–Mar. 16, avg. Mar. 1 ± 10 (21).

Plateau spiderlily (spiderwort, *Tradescantia edwardsiana*): blooming
(blue, pink), hillside—Feb. 12–Mar. 17, avg. Mar. 2 ± 12; ravine
bottom in same years—avg. Mar. 7 ± 9 (30).

Spring ambience ("greening" rain, tiny lime-green leaves, warm
sun): Jan. 31–Mar. 27, avg. Mar. 3 ± 16 (12)

Sandhill crane (*Grus canadensis*): migrants—Feb. 15–Mar. 21, avg.
Mar. 3 ± 9 (32).

Shumard oak (Buckley oak, Texas oak, *Quercus shumardii texana*):
blooming (red, yellow)—Feb. 18–Mar. 12, avg. Mar. 3 ± 6 (23).

White ash (Texas ash, *Fraxinus americana texensis*): blooming
(reddish)—Feb. 25–Mar. 13, avg. Mar. 3 ± 4 (19).

Green dragon (*Arisaema dracontium*): leaves—Feb. 18–Mar. 17,
avg. Mar. 3 ± 9 (16).

Scalybark oak (Durand, shin, white oak, *Quercus sinuata breviloba*):
blooming (yellow)—Feb. 23–Mar. 16, avg. Mar. 4 ± 6 (19).

Eastern phoebe (*Sayornis phoebe*): arrival when not overwintered—
Feb. 26–Mar. 15, avg. Mar. 4 ± 6 (13).

False garlic (crow poison, *Nothoscordum bivalve*): blooming (white)
—Feb. 13–Mar. 28, avg. Mar. 4 ± 11 (15).

Mexican plum (*Prunus mexicana*): blooming peak—Feb. 26–Mar. 25, avg. Mar. 5 ± 6 (20).

Tufted titmouse (*Parus [Baeolophus] bicolor*): nest building—Feb. 26–Mar. 18, avg. Mar. 6 ± 7 (19).

Carolina wren (*Thryothorus ludovicianus*): nest building—(Jan. 24) Feb. 25–Mar. 31, avg. Mar. 7 ± 12 (15).

Common grackle (*Quiscalus quiscula*): arrival—(Feb. 11), Feb. 20–Mar. 30, avg. Mar. 9 ± 13 (14).

American crow (*Corvus brachyrhynchos*): nest building—(Feb. 9) Feb. 23–Mar. 24, avg. Mar. 10 ± 10 (12).

Blue jay (*Cyanocitta cristata*): nest building—Feb. 25–Mar. 28, avg. Mar. 10 ± 9 (10).

Pipevine swallowtail (*Battus philenor*): emergence—Feb. 23–Mar. 27, avg. Mar. 10 ± 10 (17).

Last freeze: Feb. 8–Apr. 13, avg. Mar. 11 ± 18 (15).

Eastern tailed blue (*Everes comyntas*): emergence—Mar. 1–23, avg. Mar. 11 ± 8 (10).

Black swallowtail (*Papilio polyxenes*): emergence—Feb. 27–Mar. 26, avg. Mar. 11 ± 10 (10).

Eastern tiger swallowtail (*Papilio glaucus*): emergence—Feb. 23–Mar. 30, avg. Mar. 12 ± 9 (29).

Gray hairstreak (*Strymon melinus*): emergence—Mar. 2–26, avg. Mar. 12 ± 8 (13).

Ohio buckeye (Texas Buckeye, *Aesculus glabra arguta*): blooming (white)—Feb. 26–Mar. 26, avg. Mar. 13 ± 7 (23).

Painted lady (*Vanessa cardui*): arrival—Feb. 27–Mar. 26, avg. Mar. 13 ± 9 (9).

Tufted titmouse (*Parus [Baeolophus] bicolor*): eggs—Mar. 5–Apr. 4, avg. Mar. 13 ± 9 (13).

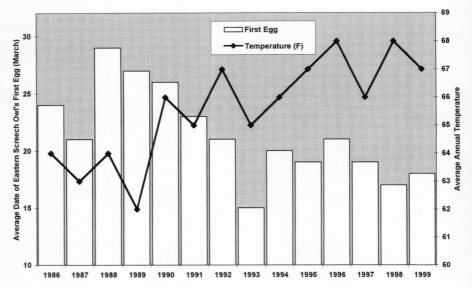

Eastern screech owls lay eggs increasingly earlier as annual temperatures become warmer (also as preceding winters become warmer).

Eastern screech owl (*Otus asio*): eggs—Mar. 4–Apr. 8, avg. Mar. 14 ± 6 (29); in 1970s, Mar. 17 ± 6 (9); 1980s, Mar. 15 ± 6 (10); 1990s, Mar. 11 ± 7 (10).

Spring coralroot (*Corallorrhiza wisteriana*): blooming (white, pink) —Feb. 12–Apr. 11, avg. Mar. 14 ± 21 (9).

Redbud (*Cercus canadensis texensis*): blooming peak—Mar. 1–28, avg. Mar. 14 ± 7 (28).

Plateau live oak (*Quercus virginiana fusiformis*): blooming (yellow) —Mar. 1–31, avg. Mar. 15 ± 9 (10).

Black vulture (*Coragyps atratus*): eggs—Feb. 10–Apr. 1, avg. Mar. 16 ± 13 (14).

Pearl crescent (*Phyciodes tharos*): emergence—Feb. 20–Mar. 29, avg. Mar. 16 ± 9 (16).

Fragrant sumac (skunkbush, *Rhus aromatica trilobata*): blooming (reddish yellow)—Mar. 3–26, avg. Mar. 16 ± 6 (13).

Deciduous tree-canopy leaves: appearance, on hillside—Mar. 6–26, avg. Mar. 16 ± 7; ravine bottom in same years—Mar. 11–31, avg. Mar. 22 ± 8 (18).

Southern plains trout lily (*Erythronium mesochorium*): leaves dying —Feb. 20–Apr. 10, Mar. 17 ± 18 (13).

Juniper hairstreak (olive hairstreak, *Mitoura grynea*): emergence— Mar. 9–30, avg. Mar. 17 ± 6 (12).

Six-spotted tiger beetle (*Cicindela sexguttata*): emergence—Feb. 27– Apr. 2 (Apr. 15), avg. Mar. 17 ± 14 (17); disappearance—Jun. 14– Jul. 10 (7).

Blue-gray gnatcatcher (*Polioptila caerulea*): arrival—(Feb. 27) Mar. 6–Mar. 29, avg. Mar. 17 ± 6 (31).

Chipping sparrow (*Spizella passerina*): migrants when not overwintered—Mar. 10–26, avg. Mar. 17 ± 5 (12).

Black and white warbler (*Mniotilta varia*): migrants—Mar. 6–31, avg. Mar. 18 ± 7 (30).

Southern dewberry (*Rubus trivialis*): blooming (white)—Feb. 28– Apr. 4, avg. Mar. 18 ± 9 (20).

Nuttall's death camus (*Zigadenus nuttallii*): blooming (white)— Feb. 27–Apr. 3, avg. Mar. 18 ± 10 (22).

White-eyed vireo (*Vireo griseus*): arrival—Mar. 9–31, avg. Mar. 19 ± 6 (28).

June bug (June, May beetle, *Phyllophaga* sp.): first species emergence—Mar. 1–Apr. 4, avg. Mar. 19 ± 9 (19).

Carolina wren (*Thryothorus ludovicianus*): eggs—Mar. 5–Apr. 8, avg. Mar. 20 ± 12 (13).

Hedge parsley (*Torilis arvensis*): blooming (white)—Mar. 1–Apr. 6, avg. Mar. 20 ± 9 (13).

Redroot (*Ceanothus herbaceus*): blooming (white)—Mar. 7–Apr. 4, avg. Mar. 20 ± 7 (13).

Mexican buckeye (*Ungnadia speciosa*): blooming (pink)—Mar. 7–31, avg. Mar. 20 ± 6 (31).

Green defoliator caterpillars (*Noctuidae, Geometridae*): descend from trees—Mar. 8–31, avg. Mar. 21 ± 6 (16).

Yellow morel mushroom (*Morchella esculenta*): peak—Mar. 13–Apr. 7, avg. Mar. 22 ± 7 (14).

Monarch butterfly (*Danaus plexippus*): arrival—Mar. 6–Apr. 4, avg. Mar. 22 ± 8 (26).

Purple finch (*Carpodacus purpureus*), pine siskin (*Carduelis pinus*), dark-eyed junco (*Junco hyemalis*): departure—Mar. 1–Apr. 25; avg. Mar. 22 ± 14 (26).

Baby blue eyes (*Nemophila phacelioides*): blooming (blue)—(Feb. 28) Mar. 12–Apr. 4, avg. Mar. 23 ± 7 (17).

Black-chinned hummingbird (*Archilochus alexandri*): arrival—Mar. 16–28, avg. Mar. 23 ± 3 (23).

Fiery searcher (*Calosoma scrutator*): emergence—Mar. 8–Apr. 7, avg. Mar. 24 ± 8 (20).

Giant swallowtail (*Papilio cresphontes*): emergence—(Feb. 14), Feb. 28–Apr. 10, avg. Mar. 24 ± 12 (24).

Narrowleaf puccoon (*Lithospermum incisum*): blooming (yellow)—Mar. 16–Apr. 9, avg. Mar. 25 ± 8 (11).

Rusty blackhaw (*Viburnum rufidulum*): blooming (white)—Mar. 12–Apr. 7, avg. Mar. 25 ± 6 (23).

Red mulberry (*Morus rubra*): blooming (yellowish)—Mar. 18–Apr. 11, avg. Mar. 26 ± 8 (20).

White-lined sphinx (*Hyles lineata*): emergence—(Feb. 26) Mar. 5–Apr. 10 (Apr. 18), avg. Mar. 27 ± 10 (16).

Silvery checkerspot (*Chlosyne nycteis*): emergence—Mar. 12–Apr. 11, avg. Mar. 28 ± 9 (11).

Black-throated green warbler (*Dendroica virens*): migrants—
Mar. 20–Apr. 8, avg. Mar. 28 ± 5 (25).

Northern cardinal (*Cardinalis cardinalis*): nest building—Mar. 18–
Apr. 12, avg. Mar. 28 ± 9 (16); eggs—Mar. 28–Apr. 23 (7).

Polyphemus moth (*Antheraea polyphemus*): emergence—Mar. 8–
Apr. 7, avg. Mar. 29 ± 9 (10); second brood—Jun. 5–15 (4).

Broad-winged hawk (*Buteo platypterus*): arrival—Mar. 9–Apr. 8,
avg. Mar. 30 ± 9 (18); passage migrants—Apr. 8–21 (5).

Plateau spiderlily (spiderwort, *Tradescantia edwardsiana*): blooming
peak—Mar. 13–Apr. 15, avg. Mar. 31 ± 8 (20).

Hill country dayflower (false dayflower, *Tinantia anomala*):
blooming (blue)—Mar. 14–Apr. 18, avg. Mar. 31 ± 9 (21).

Little wood satyr (*Megisto cymela*): emergence—Mar. 17–Apr. 14,
avg. Mar. 31 ± 9 (22).

April

Ruby-throated hummingbird (*Archilochus colubris*): arrival—
Mar. 23–Apr. 11, avg. Apr. 1 ± 6 (17); first courtship—Apr. 4–10 (5).

Possumhaw (deciduous holly, *Ilex decidua*): blooming (white)—
Mar. 12–Apr. 15, avg. Apr. 1 ± 9 (15); berries ripe (red)—Oct. 11–
Nov. 14 (8).

Whip-poor-will (*Caprimulgus vociferus*): migrants—Mar. 19–Apr. 13,
avg. Apr. 2 ± 6 (27); sing—8:12 P.M. ± 6 min. (27).

Chimney swift (*Chaetura pelagica*): arrival—Mar. 30–Apr. 7, avg.
Apr. 2 ± 2 (25).

Black vulture (*Coragyps atratus*): downy nestlings—Mar. 13–May 8,
avg. Apr. 3 ± 17 (15); courtship flying—Jan. 14–Feb. 15 (8).

Monarch butterfly (*Danaus plexippus*): migration peak—Mar. 24–
Apr. 15, avg. Apr. 4 ± 5 (11).

Green defoliator caterpillars (*Noctuidae, Geometridae*): peak descent from trees—Mar. 26–Apr. 16, avg. Apr. 4 ± 6 (22).

Nashville warbler (*Vermivora ruficapilla*): migrants—Mar. 28–Apr. 13, avg. Apr. 4 ± 4 (31).

Green hawthorn (*Crataegus viridis*): blooming (white)—Mar. 27–Apr. 16, avg. Apr. 5 ± 6 (12); berries ripe (red)—Sept. 10–Oct. 15 (4).

Black willow (*Salix nigra*): blooming (yellow)—Mar. 24–Apr. 20, avg. Apr. 6 ± 8 (15).

Green dragon (*Arisaema dracontium*): blooming (yellow)—Mar. 21–Apr. 16, avg. Apr. 7 ± 8 (16); berries ripe (red)—Aug. 14–Sept. 20 (6).

Baby blue eyes (*Nemophila phacelioides*): blooming peak—Mar. 24–Apr. 29, avg. Apr. 8 ± 9 (19).

Chinaberry (*Melia azedarach*): blooming (blue)—Mar. 27–Apr. 15, avg. Apr. 8 ± 6 (17).

Chuck-wills-widow (*Caprimulgus carolinensis*): arrival—Mar. 28–Apr. 15, avg. Apr. 8 ± 5 (23); sing avg. 8:16 P.M. ± 9 min. (23); territorial song in Apr. avg. 8:25 P.M. ± 4 min. (9), in May avg. 8:35 P.M. ± 12 min. (12).

Eve's necklace (*Sophora affinis*): blooming (pink, white)—Mar. 26–Apr. 18, avg. Apr. 8 ± 6 (18).

Yellow-crowned night heron (*Nycticorax violaceus*): nest building—Mar. 23–Apr. 17, avg. Apr. 9 ± 5 (12); incubating—Apr. 9–May 27 (5); nestlings/branchers—May 27–Jun. 28 (5).

Great-crested flycatcher (*Myiarchus crinitus*): arrival—Mar. 21–Apr. 21, avg. Apr. 10 ± 8 (32).

Franklin's gull (*Larus pipixcan*): migrants—Mar. 19–Apr. 29, avg. Apr. 11 ± 12 (18); autumn migrants—Oct. 20–Nov. 1 (8).

Early prairie-pasture wildflower display, especially Texas bluebonnet (*Lupinus texensis*), Indian paintbrush (*Castilleja indivisa, C. purpurea*), Texas star (*Lindheimera texana*): peak—Mar. 25–Apr. 20, avg. Apr. 11 ± 8 (12).

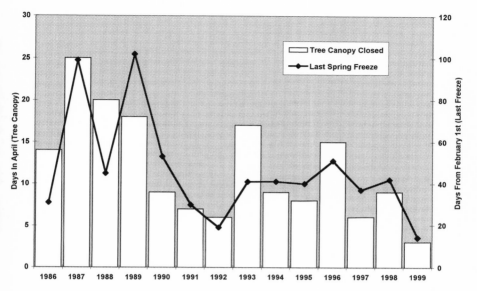

Deciduous tree-canopy closure and date of the last spring freeze
are increasingly earlier.

Broad-winged hawk (*Buteo platypterus*): nest building—Apr. 7–24,
avg. Apr. 12 ± 5 (12); incubation—Apr. 9–May 17 (7); hatchlings
—May 15–26 (4); fledglings—Jun. 23–Jul. 16 (5).

Deciduous tree canopy ninety percent closed: hillside—Apr. 3–26,
avg. Apr. 12 ± 7 (15); ravine bottom in same years—avg. Apr. 18 ± 10.

House wren (*Troglodytes aedon*): migrants—Apr. 1–27, avg. Apr. 13
± 5 (22).

Pecan (*Carya illinoiensis*): leaves and blooms (yellow)—Apr. 5–28,
avg. Apr. 14 ± 7 (10); pecans falling—Oct. 27–Nov. 14 (6).

Hoptree (*Ptelea trifoliata*): blooming (yellow)—Apr. 5–24, avg.
Apr. 15 ± 6 (16).

Clay-colored sparrow (*Spizella pallida*): migrants when not
overwintered—Apr. 2–22, avg. Apr. 16 ± 6 (12).

Tufted titmouse (*Parus* [*Baeolophus*] *bicolor*); fledglings—Apr. 13–
27, avg. Apr. 16 ± 4 (14).

June bug (June, May beetle, *Phyllophaga*): second species emergence —Apr. 10–29, avg. Apr. 18 ± 7 (9); third species—May 24–Jun. 5 (3); fourth species—Jun. 28–Jul. 9 (3).

Carolina chickadee (*Parus [Poecile] carolinensis*): fledglings—Apr. 16–30, avg. Apr. 18 ± 7 (12); excavating nest cavity—Feb. 22–Mar. 10 (9).

Summer tanager (*Piranga rubra*): arrival—Mar. 30–Apr. 26, avg. Apr. 18 ± 8 (17).

Swainson's thrush (*Catharus ustulatus*): migrants—(Mar. 19) Apr. 1–25, avg. Apr. 19 ± 6 (21).

Hackberry butterfly (*Asterocampa celtis*): emergence—Apr. 6–30, avg. Apr. 20 ± 6 (18).

Western kingbird (*Tyrannus verticalis*): arrival—Apr. 9–28, avg. Apr. 21 ± 5 (20).

Texas marbleseed (false gromwell, *Onosmodium bejariense*): blooming (white)—Apr. 11–May 1, avg. Apr. 22 ± 6 (23).

Carolina wren (*Thryothorus ludovicianus*): fledglings—Apr. 3–May 8, avg. Apr. 22 ± 10 (14); second nest eggs—Apr. 19–Jun. 7 (8); hatchlings—Apr. 24–Jun. 14 (6); fledglings—May 13–Jun. 7 (5); third nest eggs—Jun. 16–24 (4); fledglings—Jun. 17–Jul. 4 (3); fourth nest eggs—Jul. 8–24 (3); fledglings—Jul. 17, 29; fifth nest eggs—Aug. 23 (Sept. 13).

Indigo bunting (*Passerina cyanea*): migrants—Apr. 15–May 2, avg. Apr. 22 ± 5 (12).

White avens (*Geum canadense*): blooming (white)—Apr. 10–May 1, avg. Apr. 22 ± 5 (19).

Chinaberry (*Melia azedarach*): blooming peak—Apr. 9–May 2, avg. Apr. 23 ± 8 (15).

White-throated sparrow (*Zonotrichia leucophrys*): departure—Apr. 15–May 5, avg. Apr. 24 ± 5 (16).

Gulf coast toad (*Bufo valliceps*): breeding—Apr. 12–May 4, avg. Apr. 25 ± 7 (24); metamorphosis—May 31–21 (5); second breeding —Jul. 14–Aug. 29 (7); metamorphosis—Sept. 23.

Tawny emperor (*Asterocampa clyton*): emergence—Apr. 20–May 1, avg. Apr. 25 ± 4 (14).

Northern cardinal (*Cardinalis cardinalis*): fledglings—Apr. 6–May 7, avg. Apr. 25 ± 9 (12).

Hoptree (*Ptelea trifoliata*): blooming peak—Apr. 12–May 1, avg. Apr. 25 ± 5 (12).

Plains pincushion cactus (nipple cactus, *Escobaria missouriensis*): blooming (yellow)—Apr. 10–May 12, avg. Apr. 26 ± 10 (10).

Spring butterflies: second broods of twelve March-emerging species[2]—Apr. 14–May 8, avg. Apr. 27 ± 6 (31).

Painted bunting (*Passerina ciris*): arrival—Apr. 20–May 3, avg. Apr. 27 ± 3 (22).

Common nighthawk (*Chordeiles minor*): arrival—Apr. 19–May 5, avg. Apr. 28 ± 4 (23).

Roughleaf dogwood (*Cornus drummondii*): blooming (white)—Apr. 14–May 9, avg. Apr. 29 ± 7 (28).

Yellow-billed cuckoo (*Coccyzus americanus*): arrival—Apr. 18–May 8, avg. Apr. 29 ± 6 (23).

Blue jay (*Cyanocitta cristata*): fledglings—Apr. 18–May 15, avg. Apr. 30 ± 8 (19).

Firefly (lightning bug, *Photinus pyralis*): emergence—Apr. 14–May 12, avg. Apr. 30 ± 7 (30).

Mississippi kite (*Ictinia mississippiensis*): migrants—Apr. 13–May 11, avg. Apr. 30 ± 8 (22).

May

Eastern cottonwood (*Populus deltoides*): dispersing seeds ("cotton")—Apr. 20–May 12, avg. May 2 ± 7 (13).

Low petunia (*Ruellia humilis*): blooming (blue, white)—Apr. 20–May 16, avg. May 2 ± 8 (21).

Strawberry bush (purple wahoo, *Evonymus atropurpureus*): blooming (magenta)—Apr. 21–May 15, avg. May 2 ± 8 (16).

Red mulberry (*Morus rubra*): berries ripe (purple, black)—Apr. 22–May 18, avg. May 5 ± 8 (11).

Indian cherry (*Frangula [Rhamnus] caroliniana*): blooming (white)—Apr. 20–May 17, avg. May 6 ± 6 (22).

Mourning cloak (*Nymphalis antiopa*): spring brood—Apr. 24–May 21, avg. May 6 ± 9 (13).

Widow's tears (*Commelina erecta*): blooming (blue)—Apr. 24–May 18, avg. May 6 ± 8 (14).

Monarch butterfly (*Danaus plexippus*): emergence—Apr. 22–May 22, avg. May 7 ± 8 (12); eggs hatch—Apr. 20.

Southern dewberry (*Rubus trivialis*): berries ripe (black)—Apr. 28–May 20, avg. May 9 ± 6 (17).

Eastern screech owl (*Otus asio*): fledglings—May 1–19, avg. May 10 ± 5 (25).

Great-crested flycatcher (*Myiarchus crinitus*): nest building—May 6–19, avg. May 10 ± 7 (10).

Northern cardinal (*Cardinalis cardinalis*): second clutch—May 3–22 (Jun. 12), avg. May 10 ± 7 (10), brood—Jun. 8–24 (3); third nest—Jul. 13–27 (6), brood—Jul. 14–Aug. 24 (7); late fledglings—Sept. 28.

Lindheimer prickly pear (*Opuntia engelmannii lindheimeri*): blooming (yellow, orange)—May 1–22, avg. May 11 ± 7 (12).

Western soapberry (*Sapindus saponaria*): blooming (yellow)—Apr. 28–May 26, avg. May 11 ± 8 (17).

Narrowleaf snake herb (*Dyschoriste linearis*): blooming (blue)—Apr. 28–May 26, avg. May 13 ± 8 (12).

Twistleaf yucca (*Yucca rupicola*): blooming (white)—Apr. 29–May 28, avg. May 13 ± 9 (21).

Second prairie-pasture flower display, especially firewheel (*Gaillardia pulchella*) and Mexican hat (*Ratibida columnifera*): blooming peak—May 4–21, avg. May 14 ± 5 (13).

Standing cypress (*Ipomopsis rubra*): blooming (red)—May 5–28, avg. May 14 ± 6 (15).

Purple clematis (leather flower, *Clematis pitcheri*): blooming (purple) —Apr. 29–Jun. 5, avg. May 16 ± 11 (14).

Smooth sumac (*Rhus glabra*): blooming (white)—May 4–31, avg. May 16 ± 8 (14).

Black vulture (*Coragyps atratus*): feathered nestlings/fledglings— Apr. 22–Jun. 10, avg. May 19 ± 20 (15).

Roughstem sunflower (rosinweed, *Silphium radula*): blooming (yellow)—May 9–Jun. 1, avg. May 20 ± 8 (18).

Beloved underwing moth (*Catocala ilia*): emergence—May 8– Jun. 4, avg. May 24 ± 8 (10).

Eggleaf skullcap (*Scutellaria ovata*): blooming (blue)—May 15– Jun. 10, avg. May 26 ± 7 (15).

Eastern tiger swallowtail (*Papilio glaucus*): third brood—May 9– Jun. 7, avg. May 27 ± 9 (10).

Green cicada (*Tibicen* sp.): emergence—May 20–Jun. 5, avg. May 30 ± 4 (24).

Spring butterflies: third broods of twelve March-emerging species[2] —May 17–Jun. 14, avg. May 30 ± 8 (16); fourth broods—Jun. 23– Jul. 19 (7); fifth broods—Jul. 23–Sept. 14 (Oct. 10) (8).

June

Hairy sunflower (*Helianthus hirsutus*): bloom (yellow)—May 14– Jun. 10, avg. Jun. 1 ± 9 (14).

Gulf fritillary (*Agraulis vanillae*): first brood—May 22–Jun. 15, avg. Jun. 1 ± 8 (9); second brood—Jun. 21–Jul. 15, avg. Jul. 2 ± 8 (8); emergence or northward migration—Feb. 14–Apr. 28 (6).

Cicada killer wasp (*Sphecius speciosus*): emergence: May 30–Jun. 10, avg. Jun. 3 ± 4 (16).

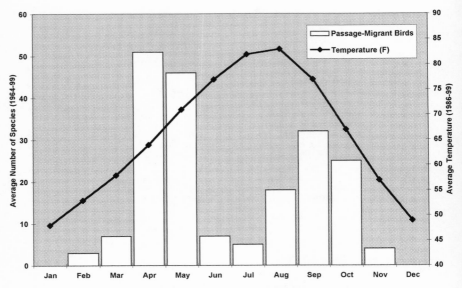

Abrupt spring and more gradual fall bird migrations
are unrelated to seasonal temperatures.

Round-winged katydid (*Amblycorpha rotundifolia*): emergence—
May 26–Jun. 15, avg. Jun. 6 ± 5 (23).

American beautyberry (*Callicarpa americana*): blooming (pink)—
May 27–Jun. 18, avg. Jun. 7 ± 6 (16).

Spotted goldbug (grapevine beetle, *Pelidnota punctata*):
emergence—May 26–Jun. 21, avg. Jun. 7 ± 10 (13).

Air conditioner turned on: May 27–Jun. 28, avg. Jun. 12 ± 9 (16).

Turk's cap (*Malvaviscus arboreus drummondii*): blooming (red)—
May 29–Jul. 2, avg. Jun. 20 ± 10 (16).

Eastern red and Ashe junipers (*Juniperus virginiana, J. ashei*): needle
fall—May 21–Jul. 25, avg. Jun. 21 ± 23 (10).

Western ironweed (*Vernonia baldwinii*): blooming (purple)—
Jun. 21–Jul. 6, avg. Jun. 29 ± 5 (15).

July

Little brown skink (ground skink, *Scincella lateralis*): first hatchlings —Jun. 21–Jul. 20, avg. Jul. 4 ± 9 (13); first clutches—Apr. 28– May 23 (4).

Ohio buckeye (Texas buckeye, *Aesculus glabra arguta*): leaves yellowing—Jun. 27–Jul. 19, avg. Jul. 6 ± 6 (14).

Purple martin (*Progne subis*): departure—Jul. 1–31, avg. Jul. 15 ± 8 (17).

Round-winged katydid (*Amblycorpha rotundifolia*): disappearance— Jul. 11–31, avg. Jul. 20 ± 7 (12).

Smooth sumac (*Rhus glabra*): berries ripe (reddish)—Jul. 2–Aug. 20, avg. Jul. 21 ± 17 (11).

First 100° day: Jun. 30–Aug. 10, avg. Jul. 22 ± 11 (10).

Flameleaf sumac (*Rhus lanceolata*): blooming (yellow-white)— Jul. 2–Aug. 8, avg. Jul. 24 ± 11 (17).

Green anole (*Anolis carolinensis*): third brood—Jul. 12–Aug. 7, avg. Jul. 25 ± 9 (15); fourth brood—Sept. 14–Oct. 2 (5).

Blue-gray gnatcatcher (*Polioptila caerulea*): migration—Jul. 9– Aug. 6, avg. Jul. 25 ± 8 (11).

Mixed-species flock of migrant birds: Jul. 15–Aug. 10, avg. Jul. 30 ± 7 (17).

Zebra butterfly (*Heliconius charitonius*): arrival—Jul. 8–Sept. 28, avg. Jul. 31 ± 17 (8).

Eastern screech owl (*Otus asio*): fledgling dispersal—Jul. 12–Aug. 30, avg. Jul. 31 ± 19 (13).

August

Green June beetle (*Cotinus nitida*)—emergence, Jul. 15–Aug. 23, avg. Aug. 7 ± 12 (13).

Green cicada (*Tibicen* sp.): disappearance—Jul. 20–Aug. 25, avg. Aug. 9 ± 10 (22).

Broad-winged hawk (*Buteo platypterus*): departure—Jul. 29–Aug. 26, avg. Aug. 12 ± 10 (10).

Eastern tiger swallowtail (*Papilio glaucus*): fifth brood—Jul. 25–Sept. 13 (Oct. 7), avg. Aug. 12 ± 16 (11).

Roughleaf dogwood (*Cornus drummondii*): berries ripe (white)—Jul. 27–Aug. 26, avg. Aug. 16 ± 8 (12).

Polyphemus moth (*Antheraea polyphemus*): emergence—Jul. 20–Sept. 8, avg. Aug. 18 ± 12 (10).

Black witch moth (*Ascalapha odorata*): arrival—Jul. 11–Sept. 25 (Nov. 22), avg. Aug. 18 ± 30 (11).

American beautyberry (*Callicarpa americana*): berries ripe (purple)—Aug. 8–Sept. 1, avg. Aug. 24 ± 7 (19).

Firefly (lightning bug, *Photurus pyralis*): second brood—(Jul. 9) Jul. 25–Sept. 14, avg. Aug. 24 ± 14 (15).

Cedar elm (*Ulmus crassifolia*): pollen—Aug. 10–Sept. 12, avg. Aug. 25 ± 12 (11).

Autumn ambience (cool front, low sun): Jul. 26–Sept. 15, avg. Aug. 25 ± 17 (13).

Prairie goldenrod (*Solidago nemoralis*): blooming (yellow)—Aug. 10–Sept. 8, avg. Aug. 26 ± 8 (20).

Frostweed (*Verbesina virginica*): blooming (white)—Aug. 11–Sept. 8, avg. Aug. 27 ± 8 (22).

Last prairie-pasture wildflower display, especially purple thistle (*Eryngium leavenworthii*) and snow-on-the-mountain (*Euphorbia marginata*): peak—Aug. 15–Sept. 9, avg. Aug. 28 ± 9 (11).

Copper lily (yellow rain lily, *Habranthus tubispathus*): blooming (yellow, orange)—Jun. 6–Oct. 14, avg. Aug. 29 ± 24 (12).

Drummond rain lily (white rain lily, *Cooperia drummondii*): blooming (white)—(Jun. 8) Jul. 3–Oct. 10, avg. Aug. 31 ± 18 (24).

September

Mississippi kite (*Ictinia mississippiensis*): migrants—Aug. 19–Sept. 10, avg. Sept. 1 ± 6 (15).

Texas aster (*Aster drummondii texanus*): blooming (white, lavender)— Aug. 21–Sept. 16, avg. Sept. 1 ± 8 (11); rarely also Apr. 10–May 18 (5).

Little brown skink (ground skink, *Scincella lateralis*): second or third brood—Aug. 8–Sept. 29 (Oct. 8), avg. Sept. 3 ± 20 (11).

Western ragweed (*Ambrosia psilostachya*): blooming ("hayfever")— Aug. 23–Sept. 19, avg. Sept. 7 ± 7 (16).

Black field cricket (*Gryllus* spp.): swarming at lights—(Jul. 12) Aug. 15–Sept. 25, avg. Sept. 9 ± 10 (16).

Shumard oak (Buckley oak, Texas oak, *Quercus shumardii texana*): falling acorns—(Aug. 19) Sept. 1–21, avg. Sept. 9 ± 6 (14).

Flameleaf sumac (*Rhus lanceolata*): fruit ripe (red)—Aug. 30– Sept. 26, avg. Sept. 10 ± 14 (10).

Broad-winged hawk (*Buteo platypterus*): migrants—Aug. 13–Oct. 24, avg. Sept. 14 ± 20 (24).

Mexican plum (*Prunus mexicana*): plums ripe (blue)—(Jul. 22) Aug. 21–Oct. 10, avg. Sept. 15 ± 16 (12).

Air conditioner turned off: Sept. 1–30, avg. Sept. 16 ± 9 (22).

Rio Grande leopard frog (*Rana berlandieri*): breeding—Aug. 25– Oct. 3, avg. Sept. 16 ± 15 (9).

Lindheimer four-o-clock (*Mirabilis jalapa lindheimeri*): blooming (pink)—Sept. 8–29, avg. Sept. 18 ± 7 (12); rarely also May 1–18 (3).

Hill country dayflower (false dayflower, *Tinantia anomala*): leaves—(Aug. 9) Aug. 20–Oct. 15, avg. Sept. 19 ± 15 (14).

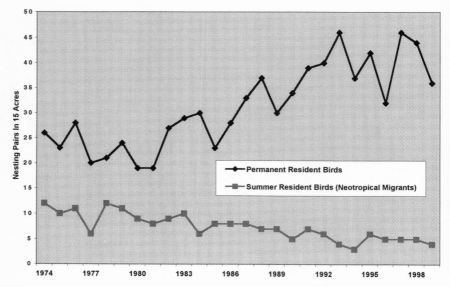

Permanent resident birds increased over two decades and stabilized
in the 1990s, while summer residents steadily declined.

Notable cold front (below 60° to below 80° F): Sept. 17–Oct. 12,
avg. Sept. 24 ± 6 (18).

Goldeneye (*Viguiera dentata*): blooming (yellow)—(July 3) Sept. 11–
Oct. 3, avg. Sept. 24 ± 6 (19).

Northern flicker (*Colaptes auratus*): arrival—Aug. 28–Oct. 7, avg.
Sept. 25 ± 11 (30).

White-eyed vireo (*Vireo griseus*): departure—Sept. 16–Oct. 10, avg.
Sept. 26 ± 5 (13).

Brown thrasher (*Toxostoma rufum*): arrival—Sept. 6–Oct. 20, avg.
Sept. 29 ± 13 (20).

Western ragweed (*Ambrosia psilostachya*): pollen peak—Sept. 16–
Oct. 15, avg. Sept. 29 ± 9 (17).

Ohio buckeye (*Aesculus glabra arguta*): seeds fall—Sept. 14–Oct. 15,
avg. Sept. 30 ± 11 (11).

False garlic (*Nothoscordum bivalve*): autumn bloom (white)—
Sept. 10–Oct. 22, avg. Sept. 30 ± 12 (10).

October

Plateau spiderlily (spiderwort, *Tradescantia edwardsiana*): leaves—
Sept. 5–Oct. 30, avg. Oct. 2 ± 18 (16).

Red admiral (*Vanessa atalanta*): overwinter brood—Sept. 14–Oct. 26,
avg. Oct. 5 ± 10 (12).

Great-horned owl (*Bubo virginianus*): hooting—Sept. 14–Oct. 17,
avg. Oct. 5 ± 9 (17); hatching Jan. 12–Mar. 12 (3).

Ruby-throated hummingbird (*Archilochus colubris*): departure—
Sept. 26–Oct. 22, avg. Oct. 7 ± 8 (30).

Sharp-shinned and/or Cooper's hawk (*Accipiter striatus, A. cooperii*):
arrival—Sept. 24–Oct. 30, avg. Oct. 8 ± 10 (17).

Chimney swift (*Chaetura pelagica*): departure—Sept. 26–Oct. 25,
avg. Oct. 8 ± 5 (30).

Monarch butterfly (*Danaus plexippus*): migrants—Aug. 22–Nov. 24,
avg. Oct. 10 ± 5 (32).

Snow goose (*Chen caerulescens*): migrants—Sept. 14–Oct. 20, avg.
Oct. 10 ± 8 (19).

Common nighthawk (*Chordeiles minor*): departure—Sept. 30–
Oct. 28, avg. Oct. 11 ± 9 (11).

Ruby-crowned kinglet (*Regulus calendula*): arrival—Sept. 7–Oct. 31,
avg. Oct. 12 ± 13 (31).

Goldeneye (*Viguiera dentata*): blooming peak—Oct. 5–22, avg.
Oct. 12 ± 5 (13).

Sandhill crane (*Grus canadensis*): migrants—Sept. 30–Oct. 31, avg.
Oct. 15 ± 9 (16).

Lincoln's sparrow (*Melospiza lincolnii*): arrival—Oct. 3–29, avg.
Oct. 16 ± 8 (12).

Orange-crowned warbler (*Vermivora celata*): arrival—Oct. 2–Nov. 9, avg. Oct. 17 ± 13 (18).

Smooth sumac (*Rhus glabra*): autumn color—Oct. 3–Nov. 1, avg. Oct. 18 ± 10 (17).

Eastern and/or spotted towhee (*Pipilo erythrophthalmus, P. maculatus*): arrival—(Sept. 7) Sept. 27–Nov. 9, avg. Oct. 21 ± 14 (13).

Autumn color in hillside trees and shrubs (yellow to orange): Oct. 15–31, avg. Oct. 24 ± 5 (26).

White-throated sparrow (*Zonotrichia albicollis*): arrival—Oct. 12–Nov. 11, avg. Oct. 27 ± 8 (29).

Indian cherry (*Frangula* [*Rhamnus*] *caroliniana*): berries ripe (black) —Oct. 10–Nov. 20, avg. Oct. 30 ± 13 (10).

November

Yellow-rumped warbler (*Dendroica coronata*): arrival—Oct. 17–Nov. 20, avg. Nov. 5 ± 10 (28).

Yellow-bellied sapsucker (*Sphyrapicus varius*): arrival—Oct. 16–Nov. 28, avg. Nov. 5 ± 11 (15).

Blue-headed vireo (solitary vireo, *Vireo solitarius*): arrival—Oct. 18–Nov. 22 (Dec. 11), avg. Nov. 6 ± 12 (10).

Polyphemus moth (*Antheraea polyphemus*): pupation (cocoons)—Oct. 22–Nov. 18, avg. Nov. 6 ± 12 (8).

Dark-eyed junco (*Junco hyemalis*): arrival—Oct. 23–Nov. 23, avg. Nov. 8 ± 10 (31).

Hermit thrush (*Catharus guttatus*): arrival—(Oct. 15) Oct. 25–Nov. 28, avg. Nov. 9 ± 11 (16).

Winter wren (*Troglodytes troglodytes*): arrival—(Oct. 7) Oct. 23–Dec. 1, avg. Nov. 9 ± 15 (10).

First frost: Oct. 17–Dec. 12, avg. Nov. 10 ± 14 days (16).

American robin (*Turdus migratorius*): departure—Oct. 17–Dec. 1 (Dec. 21), avg. Nov. 11 ± 15 (16).

American woodcock (*Scolopax minor*): arrival—Oct. 18–Nov. 27 (Dec. 11), avg. Nov. 12 ± 13 (10).

Autumn color peak—Nov. 3–25, avg. Nov. 13 ± 6 (24).

Brown creeper (*Certhia familiaris*): arrival—Oct. 16–Dec. 1 (Dec. 16), avg. Nov. 14 ± 20 (16).

Cloudless sulphur (*Phoebis sennae*): overwinter brood—(Oct. 15) Nov. 1–Dec. 1, avg. Nov. 15 ± 12 (12).

Coralberry (*Symphoricarpos orbiculatus*): berries ripe (rose pink)— Oct. 17–Dec. 1, avg. Nov. 15 ± 14 (10).

Scalybark oak (Durand, shin, white oak, *Quercus sinuata breviloba*): autumn color (gold)—Nov. 8–30, avg. Nov. 16 ± 6 (14); acorn fall—Sept. 9–Oct. 10 (5).

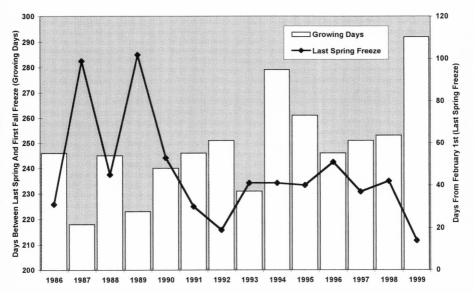

Growing days increase as date of the last spring freeze becomes progressively earlier.

Harris sparrow (*Zonotrichia querula*): arrival—Nov. 3–30 (Dec. 17), avg. Nov. 18 ± 9 (14).

First freeze: Oct. 21–Dec. 22, avg. Nov. 20 ± 16 (17).

Smallmouth salamander (*Ambystoma texanum*): breeding migration —Oct. 14–Dec. 21, avg. Nov. 21 ± 25 (13).

Shumard oak (Buckley oak, Texas oak, *Quercus shumardii texana*): autumn color (red)—Nov. 3–Dec. 10, avg. Nov. 21 ± 9 (31).

Furnace on: Nov. 6–Dec. 9, avg. Nov. 24 ± 11 (18).

American goldfinch (*Carduelis tristis*): arrival—Nov. 11–Dec. 16, avg. Nov. 27 ± 12 (12).

Deciduous tree canopy ninety percent bare: hillside—Nov. 19– Dec. 12, avg. Nov. 28 ± 7 (22).

December

Strawberry bush (purple wahoo, *Evonymus atropurpureus*): autumn color (red)—Nov. 24–Dec. 9, avg. Dec. 2 ± 4 (14); fruit ripe (red) —Oct. 12–Dec. 14 (7).

Indian cherry (*Frangula* [*Rhamnus*] *caroliniana*): autumn color (red, orange, yellow)—Nov. 22–Dec. 15, avg. Dec. 3 ± 6 (18).

Cedar waxwing (*Bombycilla cedrorum*): arrival—Nov. 23–Dec. 12 (Dec. 21), avg. Dec. 4 ± 6 (23).

Strecker's chorus frog (*Pseudacris streckeri*): breeding chorus— Nov. 3–Dec. 21, avg. Dec. 5 ± 18 (11).

Frostweed (*Verbesina virginica*): "frost" (extruded sap frozen on dry stem)—Nov. 24–Dec. 23 (Jan. 28), avg. Dec. 10 ± 10 (27).

Purple finch (*Carpodacus purpureus*): arrival—Nov. 25–Dec. 30, avg. Dec. 11 ± 12 (11).

Eastern red and Ashe junipers (*Juniperus virginiana, J. ashei*): pollen —(Nov. 8) Nov. 25–Dec. 28, avg. Dec. 14 ± 7 (27).

Common dandelion (*Taraxacum officinale*): blooming (yellow)—
Nov. 29–Dec. 29, avg. Dec. 15 ± 9 (12); seed head—Dec. 6–Jan. 21
(7).

Fox squirrel (*Sciurus niger*): mating chase—Dec. 5–Jan. 15, avg.
Dec. 26 ± 12 (12).

The voice of the earth is my voice;
it is beautiful indeed.

Dene (Navajo)

Notes

1. Standard deviation is a measure of variation in data and may be used with
the average to make predictions. Two standard deviations subtracted from the
average and two added to it bracket ninety-five percent of likely data. Relative to
the average peak of juniper pollen (January 6), for example, twice the standard
deviation (7), or fourteen days, gives December 23–January 20 as the period in
which one expects pollen to peak with only a five percent chance of human error
or perhaps environmental change. Thus, juniper pollen is predicted to peak during December 23–January 20 in ninety-five years of the twenty-first century.

2. Butterflies with approximately coincidental broods are spring azure (*Cela-
strina argiolus*), red-spotted purple (*Limenitis astyanax*), variegated fritillary (*Eup-
toieta claudia*), and, as already listed in March, eastern tailed blue, pipevine swallowtail, gray hairstreak, black swallowtail, eastern tiger swallowtail, pearl crescent,
juniper hairstreak, giant swallowtail, and silvery checkerspot.

REFERENCES

These books and journal articles are a personal cross-section of the wealth of popular (marked by an asterisk) and scientific publications about the messages I've received. I include mostly recent works with a sample of historically important ones. All reveal the breadth of thinking about Biosphere function and the interplay of natural and unnatural history. The sources are so varied that I've added a brief personal comment and/or quotation about each.

Ayres, Ed. *God's Last Offer: Negotiating for a Sustainable Future.* New York: Four Walls Eight Windows, 1999.
> Why we are inured to the rise of biospheric toxins, extinctions, human population, and materialism.*

Barney, G. O., ed. *Entering the 21st Century.* The global 2000 report to the president, vols. 1–3. U.S. Council on Environmental Quality and Department of State, 1981.
> Strictly a quantitative summary; from the introduction: "Problems of preserving the carrying capacity of the earth . . . are enormous and close upon us."

Baskin, Y. *The Work of Nature: How the Diversity of Life Sustains Us.* Washington, D.C.: Island Press, 1997.
> Introduction to nature's necessary provision of goods and services.*

Bedichek, R. *Adventures with a Texas Naturalist.* Austin: University of Texas Press, 1947 (revised 1961).
> The classic of Texas natural history writing, renowned for its folklore.*

Beebe, W. *The Log of the Sun.* New York: Henry Holt & Co., 1906.
> An historic almanac of natural history in a northeastern U.S. year.*

Borland, Hal. *Hal Borland's Twelve Moons of the Year.* New York: A. A. Knopf, 1979.
> My favorite natural history almanac, also about the northeastern U.S.*

Bormann, F. H., D. Balmori, and G. Geballe. *Redesigning the American Lawn: A Search for Environmental Harmony.* New Haven: Yale University Press, 1993.
> About our suburban lawn addiction and getting over it.*

Bradley, N. L., A. C. Leopold, J. Ross, and W. Huffaker. "Phenological changes reflect climate change in Wisconsin." *Proceedings of the National Academy of Sciences* U.S.A. 96 (1999): 9701–9704.

Data showing that spring is now earlier than recorded by Leopold and Jones (1947) and used for comparison in my Chapter One.

Brown, L. R., C. Flavin, H. French, and L. Starke, eds. *State of the World 1999.* W. W. Norton Co., New York, 1999.
  World Watch Institute's annual review of the human predicament, an important continuing series.*

Brown, L. R., M. Renner, B. Halweil, and L. Starke, eds. *Vital Signs 1999.* W. W. Norton Co., New York, 1999.
  World Watch's series complementary to *State of the World.**

Callenbach, Ernest. *Ecology: A Pocket Guide.* Berkeley: University of California Press, 1998.
  An easy introduction to natural essentials and unnatural history.*

Carson, Rachel. *Silent Spring.* Boston: Houghton Mifflin, 1962.
  The classic work that reinvigorated environmentalism.*

Comstock, Anna B. *Handbook of Nature Study.* Ithaca: Cornell University Press, 1911 (revised edition reprinted 1986).
  From the publisher's foreword of this pioneering book: ". . . an aesthetic experience as well as a discipline."*

Costanza, R., et al. "The Value of the World's Ecosystem Services and Natural Capital," *Nature* 387 (1997): 253–260.
  Newest attempt to assign monetary value to life-sustaining features; my list in Chapter Six is modified from this study and Daily (1997).

Daily, Gretchen C., ed. *Nature's Services: Societal Dependence on Natural Ecosystems.* Washington, D.C.: Island Press, 1997.
  Explanations, economic evaluations, and case studies.*

Ehrlich, Paul R. *Human Natures: Genes, Cultures, and the Human Prospect.* Washington, D.C.: Island Press, 2000.
  Treatise on humanity's biological and cultural evolution (see also Eiseley, 1978, and Shepard, 1998).*

Eiseley, L. *The Star Thrower.* New York: Times Press, 1978.
  Selections from the whole-brained writings of this quintessential mid-twentieth century naturalist.*

Emerson, R. W., and H. D. Thoreau. *Nature walking.* Boston: Beacon Press, 1991.
  Republication of early Emerson (1836) and late Thoreau (1862), who recognize our belonging to nature before modern scientific evidence.*

Evans, B., and C. Chipman-Evans. *How to Create and Nurture a Nature Center in Your Community.* Austin: University of Texas Press, 1998.
  Extensive instructions, largely from successful experience in central Texas.*

Gehlbach, F. R. "Investigation, Evaluation, and Priority Ranking of Natural Areas," *Biological Conservation* (1975) 8:79–88.
  About weighing natural condition, biodiversity, educational suitability, and human impact in selecting preserves.

————. "Forests and woodlands of the northeastern Balcones Escarpment," in *Edwards Plateau Vegetation: Plant Ecological Studies in Central Texas.* B. B. Amos and F. R. Gehlbach, eds. Waco: Baylor University Press, 1988. Structure and dynamics of the ravine's vegetation.

————. "The East-West Transition Zone of Terrestrial Vertebrates in Central Texas: A Biogeographical Analysis," *Texas Journal of Science* 43 (1991): 415–427.
Living landscape patterns and their prehistoric changes in central Texas.

————. *The Eastern Screech Owl: Life History, Ecology, and Behavior in the Suburbs and Countryside.* College Station: Texas A&M University Press, 1994. My special mentor's teachings.

Giono, Jean. *The Man Who Planted Trees.* White River Jct., Vt.: Chelsea Green Publishing Co., 1985.
My favorite story of environmental conscientiousness.*

Hairston, N. G. Jr., and N. G. Hairston, Sr. "Cause-Effect Relationships in Energy Flow, Trophic Structure, and Interspecific Interactions," *American Naturalist* 142 (1993): 379–411.
A recent review of natural community essentials.

Hardin, G. "The Tragedy of the Commons," *Science* 162 (1968): 1243–1248.
The classic concept explained.*

Holland, W. J. *The Butterfly Book.* New York: Doubleday, Page & Co., 1898.
Example of a pioneer naturalist's whole-brained love of subject.*

Kaufmann, R. K., and D. I. Stern. "Evidence for Human Influence on Climate from Hemispheric Temperature Relations," *Nature* 388 (1997): 39–44.
We've met climatic warming and it is partly us!

Knapp, C. E. *In Accord With Nature: Helping Students Form an Environmental Ethic Using Outdoor Experience and Reflection.* Clearinghouse on Rural Education and Small Schools, Charleston, West Virginia, 1999.
A unique teaching guide.*

Landsberg, Helmut E. *The Urban Climate.* New York: Academic Press, 1981.
A review of this important but often overlooked environmental feature.

Leopold, A. *A Sand County Almanac and Sketches Here and There.* Oxford: Oxford University Press, 1949.
Naturalist philosophy and ethics that undergird modern environmentalism; a classic.*

Leopold, A., and S. E. Jones. "A Phenological Record for Sauk and Dane Counties, Wisconsin, 1935–1945," *Ecological Monographs* 17 (1947): 81–122.
The multi-species calendar used for comparison in Bradley, et al. (1999).

Lewington, Richard, and David Streeter. *The Natural History of the Oak Tree.* London: Dorling Kindersley Ltd., 1993.
A beautifully illustrated, unique review of the diverse cast of actors in the English oak's seasonal scenes.*

Lovelock, James E. *Gaia: A New Look at Life on Earth.* Oxford: Oxford University Press, 1979.
How life's biogeochemistry keeps Earth habitable with the view that human dominion is doomed to failure (Gaia is Greek for Mother Earth).

Lundelius, E. L., Jr. "Late Pleistocene and Holocene Faunal History of Central Texas." in *Pleistocene Extinctions: The Search for a Cause,* edited by P. S. Martin and H. E. Wright, Jr. New Haven: Yale University Press, 1967.
Prehistoric central Texas' changing beasts and environments.

Margalef, R. *Perspectives In Ecological Theory.* Chicago: University of Chicago Press, 1968.
Important ecological concepts, also summarized by the author in *American Naturalist* 97 (1963): 357–374.

Marra, P. P., K. A. Hobson, and R. T. Holmes. "Linking Winter and Summer Events In a Migratory Bird by Using Stable-Carbon Isotopes," *Science* 282 (1998): 1884–1886.
An example of important space-time connections.

Marsh, G. P. *Man and Nature.* New York: Charles Scribner and Sons, 1864 (reprinted 1965).
The pioneering study of adverse industrial impact on nature.*

Martin, P. S. "Prehistoric Overkill: The Global Model." In *Quaternary Extinctions: A Prehistoric Revolution,* edited by P. S. Martin and R. G. Klein. Tucson: University of Arizona Press, 1967.
Extinction-causing predation by stone-age humans world-wide.

Marzluff, J. M., F. R. Gehlbach, and D. A. Manuwal. "Urban Environments: Influences on Avifauna and Challenges for the Avian Conservationist." In *Avian Conservation,* edited by J. M. Marzluff and R. Sallabanks. Washington, D.C.: Island Press, 1998.
What we know and need to know about the urbanization of native species.

McHarg, Ian L. *Design With Nature.* Garden City: Natural History Press, 1969.
Recognizing nature as essential to human communities and including it in landscape architecture and regional planning; another classic.*

McKenzie, R., R. Connor, and G. Bodeker. "Increased Summertime U.V. Radiation in New Zealand in Response to Ozone Loss," *Science* 285 (1999): 1709–1711.
Links among atmospheric contamination, ozone loss, increased ultraviolet radiation, and increased human skin cancer.

McKibben, Bill. *The Age of Missing Information.* New York: Random House, 1992.
About information gained from nature versus television and my source of the missing information epithet.*

McLaren, B. E., and Peterson, R. O. "Wolves, Moose, and Tree Rings on Isle Royale," *Science* 266 (1994): 1555–1558.
An example of energy flow tying life together in a simple community and the regulatory role of a top predator.

Nash, R. *Wilderness and the American Mind.* New Haven: Yale University Press, 1967.
A history of human use, fear, and domination of nature.*
———. *The Rights of Nature: A History of Environmental Ethics.* Madison: University of Wisconsin Press, 1989.
Our evolving concern broadened by increasing ecological knowledge.*
Odum, E. P. "The Strategy of Ecosystem Development," *Science* 164 (1969): 262–270.
A review of natural communities in process and product.
———. *Ecology: A Bridge Between Science and Society.* Sunderland: Sinauer Associates, 1997.
Paraphrasing from the preface: a beginning textbook and citizen's guide to principles relating to planetary threats.*
Odum, E. P., and H. T. Odum. "Natural Areas as Necessary Components of Man's Total Environment," *Transactions of the North American Wildlife and Natural Resources Conference* 37 (1972): 178–189.
A prescription for the ratio of wild:cultural land mentioned in Chapters Three and Six.
Ostrum, E., et al. "Revisiting the Commons: Local Lessons, Global Challenges," *Science* 284 (1999): 278–282.
Management is necessary at the level of Biosphere.
Redman, C. L. *Human impact on ancient environments.* Tucson: University of Arizona Press, 1999.
Archaeological evidence of environmental and consequent human population and cultural destruction.*
Robinson, S. K., et al. "Regional Forest Fragmentation and the Nesting Success of Migratory Birds," *Science* 280 (1995): 1987–1990.
Lessons for determining preserve size and site.
Rockefeller, S. C., and J. C. Elder, eds. *Spirit and Nature: Why the Environment is a Religious Issue.* Boston: Beacon Press, 1992.
Many faiths converge on the kinship of all life and necessity for human stewardship.*
Roszak, T., M. E. Gomes, and A. D. Kanner, eds. *Ecopsychology.* San Francisco: Sierra Club Books, 1995.
Explanations for humanity's distance from nature and nature's importance in safeguarding the human psyche.*
Sagan, C. *Billions and Billions: Thoughts on Life and Death at the Brink of the Millennium.* New York: Ballantine Books, 1997.
Messages from our universal community by the coauthor and narrator of *Cosmos,* the classic educational television series (in my view, the twentieth century's finest).*
Sauer, P., ed. *Finding Home: Writing on Nature and Culture From Orion Magazine.* Boston: Beacon Press, 1992.

From the introduction: ". . . the effort each of us must make to reforge our bonds to nature."*

Shafer, C. L. *Nature Reserves: Island Theory and Conservation Practice.* Washington, D.C.: Smithsonian Institution Press, 1990.
A review of concepts and a practicum for conservation biology.

Shepard, P. H. *Coming Home to the Pleistocene.* Washington, D.C.: Island Press, 1998.
A personal view of human nature as a genetic and environmental product of its prehistory.*

Soule, M., et al. "Reconstructed Dynamics of Rapid Extinctions of Chaparral-Requiring Birds in Urban Habitat Islands," *Conservation Biology* 2 (1988): 75–92.
Case study of the negative effects of habitat shrink, isolation, and loss of large predators.

Stein, B. A., L. S. Kitner, and J. S. Adams, eds. *Precious Heritage: The Status of Biodiversity in the United States.* Oxford: Oxford University Press, 2000.
A comprehensive geography of diversity, endangerment, and protection.*

Terborgh, J. *Where Have All the Birds Gone? Essays on the Biology and Conservation of Birds That Migrate to the American Tropics.* Princeton: Princeton University Press, 1989.
Avian declines related to habitat use, abuse, and loss, including in suburbia.*

Thoreau, H. D. *Walden.* New York: Viking Press, 1854 (reprinted 1947).
The classic original messages from the wild.*

Turner, B. L. (ed.) *The Earth as Transformed by Human Action: Global and Regional Changes in the Biosphere Over the Past 300 Years.* Cambridge: Cambridge University Press, 1990.
A sequel to Marsh (1864).*

Ulrich, R. S. "View Through a Window May Influence Recovery from Surgery," *Science* 224 (1984): 420–421.
Medical evidence of nature's healing power.

Vernadsky, V. I. *The Biosphere.* New York: Nevraumont-Copernicus, Springer-Verlag, 1926 (reprinted 1998).
The inclusive concept introduced and enhanced by modern editorial comments.

Vitousek, P. M., et al. "Human Domination of Earth's Ecosystems," *Science* 277 (1997): 494–499.
Large-scale negative results of humanity's separation from nature.

Ward, Barbara, and R. Dubos. *Only One Earth: The Care and Maintenance of a Small Planet.* New York: W. W. Norton Co., 1972.
Collaboration with 152 world citizens, who recognize their unity in the Biosphere.*

Wauer, Roland H. *Heralds of Spring in Texas.* College Station: Texas A&M University Press, 1999.

Messengers as viewed by many amateur and professional Texas naturalists.*

Weniger, D. *The Explorer's Texas*. Vol. 1, *The Lands and Waters*. Austin: Eakin Press, 1984.

From the dedication: ". . . to all Texans to let them know how great their estate originally was."*

———. *The Explorer's Texas*. Vol. 2, *The Animals They Found*. Austin: Eakin Press, 1997.

Extension of the preceding book.*

White, G. *The Natural History of Selborne*. London: Penguin Books, 1788 (reprinted 1987).

An historic natural history of home in southern England; another classic.*

White, L., Jr. "The Historical Roots of our Ecological Crisis," *Science* 155 (1967): 1203–1207.

Judeo-Christian religion's controversial role in humanity's misconceived dominance over nature.*

Wilcove, D. S., et al. "Quantifying Threats to Imperiled Species in the United States," *Bioscience* 48 (1998): 607–615.

How and how much we destroy.*

Wilson, E. O. *Sociobiology, The New Synthesis*. Cambridge: Harvard University Press, 1975.

Behavior of other animals and its continuity in humans.*

———. *The Diversity of Life*. New York: W. W. Norton & Co., 1992.

An overview of biodiversity and the modern extinction problem.*

⚡

How indispensable to a correct study of nature is a perception of her true meaning . . . Mere accumulators of facts . . . are like those plants growing in dark forests which put forth only leaves instead of blossoms.

Henry David Thoreau

INDEX

Acorn. *See* Fruit and nut; Oak

Agalinis, prairie (*Agalinis heterophylla*), 150

Agriculture, 24, 57, 149, 164, 200; fossil-fuel powered, 200; genetic engineering, 206; monoculture, 107, 138, 206; overgrazing, 41, 102; prehistoric, 200–201

Alder (*Alnus* sp.), 22

American, first (Indian, Native American), 19, 22, 68, 103, 107, 116, 131, 138–139, 150, 151, 181. *See also* Human

Ammonite (Cephalopoda), 1, 61, 133–134

Anemone. *See* Windflower

Anhinga (*Anhinga anhinga*), 127

Anole, green (*Anolis carolinensis*), 23, 30–31, 33, 63, 70, 102–103, 110, 114, 141, 169, 227

Ant, 26, 80, 95, 126; acrobat (*Crematogaster lineolata*), 94–95; carpenter (*Camponotus* sp.), 17, 80; fire (*Solenopsis invicta*), 49, 65, 82, 89, 103; harvester (*Pogonomyrmex* sp.), 109–110

Aphid (Aphididae), 124, 133

Arboretum, 104

Armadillo, nine-banded (*Dasypus novemcinctus*), 7, 15, 26, 43, 86–87, 111, 119, 123, 128, 148, 160, 181, 185

Ash, 43, 55, 121; prickly (*Zanthoxylum clava-herculis*), 54, 107; white (*Fraxinus americana*), 2, 41–42, 62, 173, 174, 214

Aster, Texas (*Aster drummondii*), 41, 172, 180, 229

Asteroid, 61

Audubon, John James, 73–74

Avens, white (*Geum canadense*), 9, 35, 72, 222

Bacteria, 18, 55, 182, 201; as Biosphere providers and translators, 18, 40, 47, 151, 193

Balcones Escarpment, 1, 24, 42, 70, 175. *See also* Limestone

Basswood (*Tilia americana*), 22

Bat (Chiroptera), 80

Bear: black (*Ursus americanus*), 22, 35, 146; grizzly (*U. arctos*), 113, 147

Beautyberry, American (*Callicarpa americana*), 49, 97–98, 111, 137, 150, 157, 172, 188, 226, 228

Bee, 78, 80, 136, 141; bumble (*Bombus* sp.), 77, 181; honey (*Apis mellifera*), 20, 42, 77, 126, 181

Beetle, 170, 193; ground (Carabidae), 17; ironclad (*Zopherus nodulosus*), 126, 128; leaf miner (Chrysomelidae), 133; longhorn (*Prionus* sp.), 86; ox (*Xyloryctes* sp.), 86; six-spotted tiger (*Cicindela sexguttata*), 51, 59, 217; water scavenger (*Hydrophilus* sp.), 9. *See also* Bug; Elator; Fiery searcher; Firefly; Weevil

Behavior: aggregative, 69; altruistic, 196, 197; cooperative, 185; courtship/mating, 9, 19, 52, 59; death-feigning, 147, 166; defensive/aggressive, 21, 79, 132, 142, 166; dispersal, 11, 13, 41, 167; dominance, 21, 56, 86; escape, 31, 86, 100; false eyes, 79, 86; foraging (hunting), 8, 9, 103, 105, 193; habituation, 19, 48; inexperience (juvenile), 117–118; innovative, 186;

Food web. *See* Energy flow

Forest: color, 4, 168, 172, 181, 232, 233; development (succession), x, 2, 5, 16, 41, 49–50, 74–75, 85, 112, 115, 121–122, 132, 134–135, 169, 176; fire, 82, 137, 194, 204; human damage to, 178, 204; leaf seasons, 3–5, 55, 66, 179, 217; mott, 2, 68, 70, 100–101; movement, 151–152; prehistoric, 24; as protection, 5, 32, 122; structure, 68–69, 115. *See also* Habitat; Leaf; Trail; Tree; Weather

Four-o'clock, Lindheimer (*Mirabilis jalapa*), 150–151, 229

Fox, gray (*Urocyon cinereoargenteus*), 72, 77, 86, 111, 165

Frass, 62–63. *See also* Leaf litter

Frog, 118; Rio Grande leopard (*Rana berlandieri*), 27, 39–41, 140, 155, 166, 229; southern leopard (*R. sphenocephala*), 27, 40; Strecker's chorus (*Pseudacris streckeri*), 27, 185, 195–196, 234

Frostweed (*Verbesina virginica*), 125, 136, 150, 161, 180, 183, 185, 188, 228, 234

Fruit and nut: attractive features of, 45, 85, 120, 150; dispersal, 19, 45, 75, 85, 101, 120, 151–152, 183

Fuel, fossil, xi, 5, 74, 89, 103, 129, 151, 194, 198, 199, 200–201, 208

Fungus, 55; decomposer, 41, 47, 193; micotrophic, 47; pathogenic, 22, 24, 170; tree cavity, 80, 170, 180

Gecko, Mediterranean (*Hemidactylus turcicus*), 60, 72, 127, 136, 153, 170–171

Germany, 97, 143

Gnatcatcher, blue-gray (*Polioptila caerulea*), 49–50, 122, 143–144, 157, 217, 227

Goldeneye (*Viguiera dentata*), 61, 71, 172, 180, 230, 231

Goldenrod, 125, 150, 161, 180; prairie

(*Solidago nemoralis*), 136–137, 228; tall (S. *canadensis*), 136–137

Goldfinch, American (*Carduelis tristis*), 8, 14, 53–54, 84, 158, 160, 234

Goose, 42, 157; Canada (*Branta canadensis*), 172; snow (*Chen caerulescens*), 172, 214, 231

Gourd, balsam (*Ibervillia lindheimeri*), 120

Government. *See* Suburb

Grackle, 53, 164; common (*Quiscalus quiscula*), 43, 186, 215; great-tailed (*Q. mexicanus*), 186

Grape, mustang (*Vitis mustangensis*), 85, 120

Grass: fire, 42, 82, 101; little bluestem (*Schizachryrium scoparium*), 100; San Augustine (*Stenotaphrum secundatum*), 2, 107, 122; sideoats grama (*Bouteloua curtipendula*), 100; tall dropseed (*Sporobolus compositus*), 100; Texas needle (*Nassella leucotricha*), 100. *See also* Biome; Forest

Grasshopper (Orthoptera), 136

Great Plains, 24

Greenbriar (*Smilax bona-nox, S. tamnoides*), 29, 45, 71, 75, 85

Green dragon (*Arisaema dracontium*), 45, 111, 120, 214, 220

Greenhouse (CO_2) layer, 14, 73, 192, 139, 141

Grosbeak, rose-breasted (*Pheucticus ludovicianus*), 77

Grouse, willow (*Lagopus lagopus*), 129

Gulf of Mexico, 7, 100, 157, 159, 172

Gull, 100, 157; Franklin's (*Larus pipixcan*), 68, 220

Habitat: change, 22, 57, 84, 127; damage/destruction, 84; fragmentation, 50; reduction, 24, 50. *See also* Edge; Forest; Preserve

Hackberry, netleaf (*Celtis reticulata*), 71. *See also* Sugarberry

Hairstreak: dusky blue (*Calycopis iso-*